UB Law and Political Science Quarterly

University of Buea

UB Law and Political Science Quarterly

Vol. 1, N° 1, October 2020

L'Harmattan
Cameroun

5-7, rue de l'Ecole-Polytechnique, 75005 Paris

http://www.editions-harmattan.fr

ISBN : 978-2-343-23509-7
EAN : 9782343235097

CONTENTS

The right to participate in elections in the context of democratic governance in Africa: A tale of disenfranchisement*

By

Atangcho N. Akonumbo

Professor of Laws and Dean,
Faculty of Laws & Political Science,
University of Buea, Cameroon
Email: atanjiak@gmail.com

Abstract

Democracy is a well-established and accepted system of political governance based on majority rule in a pluralistic context. It has, however, been copied and sometimes contextualised or literally reinvented in different political settings, notably Africa, largely depriving it of its conventional or essential qualities. Without actually engaging an idealistic dissection of the very wavy concept of democracy, this paper explores democracy in the African context, hinging on the African Union's framework on democracy. It examines the factors militating against the effective participation of citizens in electoral processes, showing how this pays disservice to the concept of democracy. The paper argues that in the Africa, democracy (in its delegative form which projects the participation of citizens in electoral processes) has been adulterated or reinvented by politicians to serve their selfish ends. It also argues that the context of poverty in Africa has greatly facilitated this thwarting of the system, pushing citizens to contribute in their own disenfranchisement. The paper proposes the empowerment of citizens and all other political stakeholders through education and sensitization on democratic principles and values, processes, their respective rights and duties, as well as the transparency and accountability of electoral processes. It further stresses the need for respect of the rule of law, and an effectual system of separation of powers characterised by a strong and independent judiciary with competent courts capable of exercising their power of judicial review of political decisions and unconstitutional processes, to enhance citizens' participation in electoral processes.

Key words: Elections, democratic governance, Africa, disenfranchisement

---

* This paper is a revised version of a presentation by the author at a round table conference organised by the Cameroonian section of the Inter-Parliamentary Union (IPU) on the occasion of the 6th International Day of Democracy on the theme: '*Strengthening Voices for Democracy*'. Yaoundé, National Assembly, 15 September 2013.

Introduction

Over the last three decades, the spread of democratic political institutions has been one of the most remarkable trends in world politics. However, the manner and extent of incorporation, implementation and preservation of democracy is a matter of time, place and circumstance, particularly in the African context. The spread and sustainability of democracy is, consequently, presented primarily as a matter of national interest. This possibly explains the questionability of democratic credentials in several African countries to the extent that democratic governance on the continent, as a whole, remains a serious challenge. In fact, Africa has been the stage of various political ramifications characterised by warped democratic values under more or less oppressive models of governance. While some African countries such as Ghana, Senegal, Nigeria, and Namibia are registering commendable sustainable democratic achievements, others like Zimbabwe, Uganda, Congo Brazzaville, and Burundi are undergoing the destruction of years of flawed democracy in the wake of socio-political unrest and violence perpetrated by disenchanted citizens or radical groups, sometimes in the name of religion. Still, others are experiencing a new move towards restrictive legislation, which raises concerns about the devolution and constitutional change of power, respect for the rule of law, human rights, freedom of expression and the space of the civil society.

Statistics in 2015 polled in 28 African countries show that 52 percent Africans were of the opinion that their countries are democratic.[1] 46 percent were satisfied with their national democracies, down from 50 percent in 2013/2014.[2] It is surprising that despite a general atmosphere of disillusionment on democratic practices in Africa, up to 70% of Africans believe that elections were free and fair in their countries.[3] This is telling that perceptions about democracy are complex and inconsistent, and cannot be safely explained on the basis of theoretical assumptions. One could also argue that the recent ouster of long serving leaders in

[1] Data from the research firm Afrobarometer, released on September 15, 2015 from a survey conducted in 28 African nation. See Mohamed, O. (2015). 'More than half of Africans believe they live in democracies, but fewer are happy with them'. *Quartz Africa*. Online at: http://qz.com/503098/more-than-half-of-africans-believe-they-live-in-democracies-but-fewer-are-happy-with-them/ (accessed 20 October 2015)

[2] See Mohammed *supra.*

[3] *Ibid.*

countries such as Burkina Faso, Zimbabwe, Algeria and Sudan point to the general dissatisfaction with the pace of democracy on the continent.[4]

Democracy is a most challenging form of ***government*** for both politicians and the ***people***. It has always been a means to an end rather than an end in itself – good governance. Today, it has been defined as 'a government based on majority rule and the consent of the governed, the existence of free and fair elections, the protection of minorities, respect for basic human rights…[presupposing] equality before the law, due process, and political pluralism[5] However, sometimes innocent or deliberate misconstructions of the ideals of democracy have emptied the concept of its substance and, to some, it is a meaningless tale or cliché often used to justify unconventional (unconstitutional) means of grabbing, retaining or sanctifying autocratic power. This is the case, where voters are disenfranchised, elections rigged, electoral disputes thwarted by law courts and electoral laws tailored to suit particular candidates, political parties or *electoral constituencies*. Sometimes, electoral constituencies are redefined to secure more votes for a ruling party or group, or an incumbent candidate, a technique known as *gerrymandering*.[6] Meanwhile, democracy could be perceived as a system and a tool depending on the context in which it is used. As a system, it is a genre of political governance by freely *chosen* representatives. This calls for a participatory approach whereby citizens

---

[4] Felter, C. (2019). 'Africa's Leaders for Life' *Council on Foreign Relations*, 29 April 2009.

[5] Kekic, L. (2007). *The World in 2007*. The Economist Intelligence Unit's Index of Democracy, p. 1. On line at: https://www.economist.com/media/pdf/DEMOCRACY_INDEX_2007_v3.pdf (accessed September 5 2018). Marc Plattner defines democracy as 'a regime based on majority rule, tempered by the separation of powers, the rule of law and constitutional protections for individual liberties.' Plattner, M. (1999). 'From Liberalism to Liberal Democracy', *Journal of Democracy*, Vol. 10, N° 3, 121-134.

[6] In political contexts ***gerrymandering*** is manipulating the boundaries of electoral districts to give an advantage to a particular party or class. The term was coined when Elbridge Gerry, governor of Massachusetts in 1812, created a new voting district that appeared to favour his party. This has been seen in Cameroon where the CPDM ruling party has pushed the redefinition of the Fako decision in the South West Region to avoid losing the district to the opposition, into four districts: Fako North, Fako South, Fako East and Fako West. By creating four districts instead of one, it is easier to inflate 'registered voters' and hence votes, in those constituencies that the ruling party has support and decrease the voters where it would likely lose thus ensuring an overall majority votes in the whole Division. Similarly, 'special constituencies' have been created in opposition strongholds to ensure that the ruling party in Cameroon, Cameroon Peoples Democratic Movement (CPDM) gets a parliamentary seat. The cases of the Balikumbat and Jakiri special constituencies in the Northwest region are illustrative.

choose their representatives through regular, free and fair elections in a pluralistic setting, and, where necessary, are involved in decision making processes. As a system, therefore, citizens are at the centre, making use of their right to choose their representatives who shall be accountable to them. As a (political) tool, it is the effective use of the system to achieve citizens' participation (inclusiveness) in the edifice of democratic nation building. Intrinsically, therefore the *tool* operationalises or materialises the *system.*

However, democracy is not just about elections and citizens' participation therein. Elections certainly stand out as a distinguishing feature, but other standards are equally called into play. At its very core, democracy is a system of good political governance by a consented majority emanating from free and fair elections in a pluralistic setting. Good democratic political governance is guided by the principles of impartiality, dialogue, respect for the rule of law, respect for human rights and freedoms, protection of minority rights as well as the observance of equality, non-discrimination, transparency and accountability, amongst others. In a democracy, citizens choose their leaders/representatives to guarantee these ideals through political actions and decisions in order that their (citizens) aspirations could be met. Democracy can therefore be projected as a value-based system of political governance whereby citizens partake in the construction and consolidation of the democratic edifice through free and fair elections and other decision making processes.

But then, in the typical African context characterised by sheer disregard for democratic values, what is the contextual (democratic) framework for citizens' participation? How can such participation bolster democracy? What are the challenges encountered and how can they be obviated? In the context of Africa, democracy, especially in its participatory form (which should normally enable citizens' participation through free and fair elections and the holding elected officials to account), has literally been caricaturised, whereas such participation is not only a right and a duty, but it is also, a precursor of the very culture of democracy. Besides, effective citizens' participation is a first step in good democratic governance, which instils a sense of social justice, establishes an atmosphere of confidence between the ruling class and the governed, reduces socio-political tensions, ends conflict and ensures stability. Only that, in the African context where the sense of democratic values has been lost, effective participation is hard to achieve as a result of a good number of endemic factors, which may be blamed on both citizens and their leaders/representatives. Yet, there are quite a good number of effective tools that can guarantee and galvanise citizens' participation rights towards the consolidation of good political democracy in Africa.

This is an opportunity for restating the need for the effective participation of citizens in electoral and decision making processes not only as a right, but also, as a way of fostering good democratic governance in Africa. As a matter of fact, citizens' participation in electoral processes is a unique opportunity for them to have their voices heard, and by ricochet, a medium for consolidating the culture of good democracy as a distinctive system and tool of good political governance.

This paper starts by drawing a conceptual framework of democracy to situate the participation of citizens as an essential component of principle of good democracy. It contextualises democracy in Africa, showing how its thwarted form hardly guarantees the right of citizens to participate at elections (since the essence or effect of thwarting democratic principles by the ruling class, amongst other things, is to disenfranchise the electorate variously). The paper then sets the legal basis of the right to participate in elections and identifies some major factors that impinge on this right. Some avenues which could guarantee citizens' effective participation in elections and other decision making processes as ways of strengthening the culture of democratic governance in Africa are advanced as concluding recommendations.

It should be noted that the scope of *participation* in this paper has been limited to participation of citizens at elections through voting and does not include participation in other political decision making and implementation processes.

1. Conceptualisation of democracy

'Democracy' is a very wide and slippery concept with overlapping halves not capable of any precise definition nor is there consensus on the definite types. Kekic rightly remarks that '[t]here is no consensus on how to measure democracy, definitions of democracy are contested...'[7]

In its most simplistic conception, democracy is government by the people in which supreme power is vested in the people and exercised directly by them or by their elected representatives in free, fair, transparent and regular elections.[8] The mere existence of democratic institutions, such as parliaments, does not make a system democratic, and such institutions

[7] Kekic, *op. cit.*, p. 1

[8] Garner, B [Ed] (1999) Black's Law Dictionary, 7th Ed, p. 444.

do also exist in a 'democratic monarchy'. Examples here are the constitutional monarchies of Britain, Canada, and Sweden generally considered as democracies in practice.[9] Here the monarch is a figure head as s/he reigns but does not govern and therefore merely symbolizes and ensures the continuity of the monarchy. In any case, the key qualities of democratic practice include: citizens' participation through regular, free and fair elections in choosing their leaders/representatives. In the context of this paper, free and fair competitive elections is considered a cut-across factor; it marks political freedom in a true democracy, particularly of the liberal type, although most, if not all African 'democracies', are electoral and not liberal. For example, freedom of expression, assembly and holding politicians to account is hardly practised in African electoral democracies.

1.1. Forms of democracy

Democracy may be explained in *thin* and *thick* forms for in a democracy, 'you must first enable the government to control the governed; and in the next place oblige it to control itself'[10]. In its thin form it describes the process by which government derives its authority or mandate from the people; that is, how they are chosen through elections – electoral democracy. This is also known as the *who*. But it also has to do with the management of the mandate proper and the consequences – thick democracy – also known as the *how*. The latter invariably involves issues such as governance, rule of law and the protection of fundamental freedoms - liberal democracy. Thus, while electoral democracy is the process by which leaders gain public office, liberal democracy results when clear limits are placed on what they can do when they get there since citizens are often guaranteed protection of their civil liberties (freedoms) from infringement by government or other citizens. Both these facets of democracy constitute the basis of good democracy[11] and the degree of their coexistence

[9] *'Democracy,'* The American Heritage New Dictionary of Cultural Literacy, 3rd ed, Houghton Mifflin Company, 2005. Online at:: http://dictionary.reference.com/browse/democracy (accessed 16 October 2015).

[10] Madison, J. *Federalist Papers,* N° 51. Online at: http://www.founding fathers.info/federalistpapers/fed51, (accessed 16 May,2015).

[11] Morlino considers a quality or good democracy as one 'presenting a stable institutional structure that realizes the liberty and equality of citizens through the legitimate and correct functioning of its institutions and mechanisms. A good democracy is thus first and foremost a broadly legitimated regime that completely satisfies citizens (quality in terms of result). When institutions have the full backing of civil society, they can pursue the values of the democratic regime. If, in contrast, the institutions must postpone their objectives and expend energy and resources on consolidating and maintaining their legitimacy, crossing over even the minimum threshold for democracy becomes a

determines its quality and durability in any given situation. Thomas Jefferson said that without liberal democracy, electoral democracy is 'nothing more than mob rule where 51% of the people may take away the rights of the other 49.'[12]

The thin and thick combination of democracy as a system of political governance is best understood when directly opposed to pure autocratic systems. Here leaders accede to power or authority through heredity, conquest, coup, or appointment and once in power, all rights and responsibilities are vested in the government over which they preside. Yet, it is not surprising that even in such situations (where in addition, elections are not regular, never free and fair and pluralism is inexistent), governments freely employ the term 'democracy' and often refer to democratic principles and standards in policy statements and political propaganda. However, even when the expression 'democracy' is so employed abusively, the alert political observer will not tarry to qualify it with pejorative adjectives such as *restrictive* democracy, *defective* democracy,[13] *tutelary* democracy, or *delegative* democracy[14]. Meanwhile, *electoral*

remarkable feat. Second, a good democracy is one in which the citizens, associations, and communities of which it is composed enjoy at least a moderate level of liberty and equality (quality in terms of content). Third, in a good democracy it is the citizens themselves who have the power to check and evaluate whether the government pursues the objectives of liberty and equality according to the rule of law. They monitor the efficiency of the application of the laws in force, the efficacy of the decisions made by government, and the political responsibility and accountability of elected political officials in relation to the demands expressed by civil society (quality in terms of procedure)'. Morlino, L (2002), 'What is a "Good" Democracy? Theory and Empirical Analysis', University of Florence (Italy) & Institute for International Studies, Stanford University, p. 4.

12 Cited in 'What is a Good Democracy?' *supra.*

13 This category includes 'exclusive' democracies, which offer only limited guaranties for political rights; 'dominated' democracies, in which powerful groups use their influence to condition and limit the autonomy of elected leaders; and 'illiberal' democracies, which offer only partial guarantees on civil rights. Morlino *infra*, p. 2

14 O'Donnell, G. (1994). *'Delegative Democracy'*, Journal of Democracy, 5 (1): 55-69. Delegative democracy is very close to the pure kind of democracy only that the accountability feature disappears as voters have no control over elected political officials and state mechanisms which are supposed to play the watchdog function equally fail to do their job. Also referred to as *populist democracies*, delegative democracies are often based on a majority system. They host "clean elections", 'parties, parliament, and the press are usually free to express their criticisms', and 'the courts block unconstitutional policies'. In practice, however, citizens in these democracies 'delegate other to make decisions on their behalf' at the moment that they vote, but then they no longer have the opportunity to check and evaluate the performance of their officials once they are elected. Other organs of government, even those meant for this purpose,

democracies are hybrids which fail to meet human rights demands and so fall short of democratic standards.[15] The use of *electoral* is a dangerous half-truth here. This again tells us that although 'election' is a central feature in a democracy, it is not exclusive of other factors. *Autocratic* democracies are good examples of electoral democracies where (trumped) 'elections' may be held but all other democratic ideals are shunned and swept aside. For the purposes of this paper, delegative democracy has been retained as good democracy. It is the purest of all forms of democracy since it brings together the essential qualities of democracy although the accountability arm is missing.[16] Besides, delegative democracy contains the element of citizens' participation as a means of enhancing the practice of the culture which is the focus of this paper. It thus comprises both *participatory* democracy and *representative* democracy. The idea here is that those who are governed, participate in the democratic process by choosing those who govern them.

The foregoing extrapolations clearly show that the study of democratic governance is complex especially in the African context where it has been implemented in many diluted and unsustainable ways. This is the result of democratisation and de-democratisation as institutions, values, and attitudes change in the face of internal factors. Such factors include demographic, geopolitical, economic and social pressures, structure strength and transparency of government institutions, the economy, press freedom and civil society organisations (CSOs). External factors such as the promotion of democracy by other nations,[17] regional and international organisations, and the influence of non-democratic nations are also important.

---

also neglect or fail to carry out their watchdog function and, consequently, the so-called rule of law is only partially or minimally respected. See generally, O'Donnell *supra.*

[15] Freedom House has outlined a four prong criteria for an electoral democracy: a competitive, multiparty political system; universal adult suffrage; regularly contested elections conducted on the basis of secret ballots, reasonable ballot security and the absence of massive voter fraud; and significant public access of major political parties to the electorate through the media and through generally open campaigning. See Kekic, *op. cit.,* p. 1 *supra.*

[16] See footnote 5 *supra* for the full meaning of delegative democracy.

[17] The promotion of democracy by other countries is important here. This is known as *snowballing* or *demonstration effects.* The idea is that as one country after another successfully and peacefully democratized, they set examples for others. 'Democracy Around the World in 2008', Issue 3, August 2008. Online at: http://worldsavvy.org/monitor/index.php?option=com_content&id=183&Itemid=297 (accessed 10 September 2013).

It should be noted that beyond internal pressures for improved democracy in Africa, the culture of good democracy[18] has also been pressured by international institutions, organisations and partners. It would recalled that a recurrent principle in the African Union (AU) framework on democracy beginning with the Constitutive Act, is the respect for democratic principles, human rights, popular participation and the rule of law.[19] Democracy has in recent years moved from the pure political space and discourses into conditionality in development assistance between nations and regional economic blocs. For example, the revised Lomé IV Convention (Cotonou Agreement 2002 – between Europe and Africa and the ACP countries) and the African Growth and Opportunity Act (AGOA) on preferential trade measures between the US and Sub Saharan African countries, both place democracy and the respect for human rights and the rule of law at the centre of any continued partnership. This means that democracy is a vector of economic development and why not development in all its facets. This is not to say that non-democratic states do not receive development aid. Egypt for instance, which cannot qualify as a democracy is the biggest recipient of US aid in Africa and the second globally, after Israel.[20]

1.2. 'Good democracy' in democracy

It has been submitted that good democracies are characterised by participation of 'people' in its practice, economic development, processes and outcomes (which advance the rule of law and human rights), electoral and liberal factors (which generate functioning, stable and prosperous and peaceful conditions), and the absence of war.[21] Questions like who are 'people' and what percentage of the latter have to be enfranchised to validate their participation in a political system as 'people' remain and then clear the system as 'democratic'. It follows therefore that not all 'democracies' are *democracies* i.e. good or real democracies.

This however, runs contrary to the preceding note that some democracies are better even with just some of the factors. In any case, the

---

18 Good democracy is that which, amongst other things, requires peace, respect for the rule of law, fundamental rights and accountability.

19 Article 4(m) AU Constitutive Act; 4 (1) AU Charter on Democracy, Elections and Governance; Article 3(1) AU Convention on Preventing and Combatting Corruption.

20 The Borgen Project (2018) "Top 10 Recipients of US Foreign Aid in 2018". Online at: https://borgenproject.org/top-10-recipients-of-u-s-foreign-aid/ (accessed 11 September 2019).

21 "Democracy Around the World"… *op. cit.*

electoral and peace/absence of war factors need elucidation for purposes of understanding the concept of good democracy. As mentioned earlier, it is not wholly true that holding elections is the unique overarching standard of democracy, it being understood that even under authoritarian regimes characterised by the absence of pluralism, there may be elections. For example, The 'constitutional change of power' in the sense of the African Union Charter on Democracy, Elections and Governance (AU Charter on Democracy)[22] following so called 'democratic elections' is not a necessary trait of good democracy simply because the process was constitutional i.e. held pursuant to 'a constitution'. The question is, which constitution (that is, what is the quality of this constitution?) The argument here is simple. Recent experiences around Africa show that incumbent presidents resort to constitutional reforms towards the end of their mandates to either prolong their stay in power or to bring in their political dauphins or biological sons to succeed them through tailored elections.[23] This means that where such attempts succeed, the (tailored) elections resulting in the re-election of the incumbent or his political dauphin are 'constitutional'. This may be (and has often been) a source of discontent and conflict leading to putsches against the 'democratically' elected government dubbed 'unconstitutional change of government'.[24] In fact, the toppled 'democratically elected' regime' would not have met at least the qualities of 'respect for the rule of law' and 'peace' in a good democracy. The question in such circumstances is, would the chapter 8 sanctions under the AU Charter on Democracy against a putsch-led unconstitutional government if implemented be justified - it being understood that it is the overthrown government is actually the cause of the unstable condition, characterised by popular discontent which eventually led to the putsch?

The AU framework on democracy promotes best practices in the management of elections for purposes of peace, political stability and good governance.[25] It defines what constitutes unconstitutional changes of government and responses to thereto.[26] In as much the framework recalls the common values and principles of democratic governance with strong

---

[22] Adopted in Addis Ababa, Ethiopia, on 30 January 2007 and entered into force on 15 February 2012, Article 5.

[23] See for instance in Cameroon by Paul Biya, Uganda by Yoweri Museveni and in Gabon by the Bongo dynasty.

[24] See articles 3(10) and 23(1), Charter on Democracy.

[25] Article 2 (13), Charter on Democracy.

[26] See the AU Declaration on Unconstitutional Changes of Government adopted in Lome, Togo in July 2000.

emphasises on the adoption of a democratic constitutions (in terms of preparation, content and method of revision in conformity with generally accepted democratic principles), it does not address responses to undemocratic constitutions which are often the cause of the so called unconstitutional changes. This leaves the impression that so long as an undemocratic constitution has gone operational (even amid widespread national dissent and discontent), it is legitimate and democratic together with all its institutions, including the government formed under it. Hence, a military coup which topples a government based on that constitution, constitutes an unconstitutional change of government. In other words, for purposes of running reprisals against an 'undemocratic' and unconstitutional change government, the coup as much as the entry into force of the constitution, whitewashes retrospectively, the undemocratic constitution and its institutions. This contention is comforted by the then OAU while expressing grave concern over the resurgence of *coups d'états* in Africa.[27] The Organisation considered coups as a 'threat to peace and security and a setback to the democratisation strides on the continent', but failed to address unconstitutional or undemocratic practices within states which fomented favourable conditions for instability and coups. This is the case, for example, where a government carries out constitutional reform without national consensus through a referendum, contrary to the Charter on Democracy.[28] The OAU failed to be preventive and proactive and was rather reactive.

The AU Declaration on the Principles Governing Democratic Elections in Africa[29] states that holding of regular elections is an important dimension of conflict prevention, management and resolution[30] and that democratic elections should be conducted under democratic constitutions and supportive legal instruments.[31] Again, this instrument fails to address the question of elections conducted under undemocratic constitutions which may provoke conflict and instability. Whereas, the AU Charter on Democracy, enjoins states parties to develop legal and policy frameworks to establish and strengthen a culture of democracy and peace.[32] The Charter therefore obligates states parties to promote peace, security and stability in their respective countries and regions as well as on the

[27] *Ibid*, Preamble.
[28] Article 10(2).
[29] Adopted in Durban, South Africa, July 2002.
[30] Article 3.
[31] Article 4(b).
[32] Article 11.

continent as a whole by fostering 'participatory political systems'.[33] It further promotes best practices in the management of elections 'for purposes of political stability and good governance.'[34]

The foregoing analyses explain the fact that the concept of 'good democracy' may be accepted or rejected on ideological basis. It can be seen as representing capitalism, free market and trade. But then, it is thought that these are the very conditions that enable participatory democracy contribute to prosperity and the improvement of peoples' lives.[35] Good democracies are at least more peaceful than non-democracies. This is a tenet in liberal international theory; a thesis that can be traced way back in the writings of Immanuel Kant.[36]

1.3. Pluralism and legitimacy in democracy

Beyond regular, free and fair elections as core elements of democracy, there are two other complementing pillars which give sense to participation. The first is *pluralism.* Under the AU Declaration on Unconstitutional Changes of Government, African leaders agreed on the principle of promoting political pluralism or any other form of participatory democracy. Political pluralism ordinarily denotes a situation of multiple political parties or candidates that vie for political space and governing power and between whom citizens have to choose by casting votes at elections. It is therefore a democratic trait which ordains the participatory approach and translates the *raison d'être* of elections.

The second is the *status and legitimacy of political parties and the press* in a democratic setting. In the African context, the status and legitimacy of political parties is often problematic. Opposition parties are often under the shadow of the imposing and influential ruling parties. The *status*

---

33 Article 38(1).

34 Article 2 (13), Charter on Democracy.

35 See also Shimko, K. (1998). *International Relations: Perspectives and Controversies.* Boston/New York: Houghton Mifflin Company, p. 103.

36 Kant was the first philosopher to propose that democratic or republican states would be less likely to wage war against each other. He argued the emergence and spread of liberal democratic or republican institution would be accomplice by the emergence of a zone of peace. Kant was not saying that democracies do not go to war or that they cannot start a war (democratic wars) but that the likelihood was very slim because going to war 'would mean calling down on themselves all the miseries of war'. They can go to war to defend themselves but can hardly wage war amongst themselves and so the more democracies there are, the rarer the possibility of war and therefore a larger zone of peace. Kant, I *Perpetual Peace* quoted in Doyle, Michael (1997) *The Ways of War and Peace.* New York: WW Norton, p. 280. See also Shimko *op. cit.*, pp. 104/5.

parameter is a simple issue to determine. It refers to the stature of the party from the standpoint of its leaders, followership (numbers and quality of members), financial power and therefore prowess/possibility to win at elections. *Legitimacy* is rather complex. It turns on the why the electorate chooses a party in question; the perspective from which they see or consider it as really being capable of representing them and their interests and, hence, winning elections, whether on the basis of the party's status or not and/or its proposed political agenda. In most African countries, ruling parties tend to secure both status and legitimacy whether truly or not but essentially because they have the means and machinery to win elections. This is common in the party-state kind of political 'democratic' monism or pluralism where there is hardly any or no distinction at all between the state and the ruling party. In the party-state *scenario*, the ruling party is usually made up of the majority of civil servants, private sector operators, civil society stakeholders and the press which have lost their sense of vocation, and all those who matter in their communities including intellectuals. The reason for such adherence is essentially to gain prestige and other indirect benefits (appointment to government positions, possibility of swindling public funds once appointed, ease in the preferential award of public contracts, etc.) Consequently, the ruling party remains the reference, in terms of status and legitimacy – the sure winner who takes it all at 'democratic' elections. This explains why and how ruling political parties in most African countries can invariably win almost all elections because of their followership, financial and institutional power. But this is a forged status and legitimacy.

In a democratic set up, pluralism is not only expressed in the existence of multiple political parties, but also a plurality of the press. There are government-run media and privately owned media. However, while the former often enjoys free expression within government canons and propaganda, the latter enjoys little tolerance, sometimes as a result of lack of professionalism. The question of a pluralistic press in a pluralistic democratic setting is how and what is their contribution to the advancement of democracy? Here again similar considerations on status and legitimacy discussed above about political parties arise. The explanations are close but other issues arise such as: which press, how does the press operate, who uses the press, whom does the press represent, who is the audience of the press, who finances the press? These help to define the substance of the press, how it can contribute to shape votes, and to determine the degree of dissidence it can tolerate during elections, (especially as between government media and the private, opposition-prone media). Broadly speaking only a competent and responsible press can receive credence here. In fact, the AU Charter on Democracy instructs states parties to promote freedom of expression particularly, freedom of press and a professional media.[37] In most African countries, government owned media is often too well better equipped in every respect than the private press which prides in mediocrity and amateurism as a result of lack of financial, infrastructural and human resources. In such circumstances the private press cannot sufficiently contribute in influencing vote casting at elections but in deepening the disenfranchisement of voters (already initiated by government's rigging machinery) by proffering lessons on why and how they should not participate in elections.

In most African countries, the concept political pluralism has been destroyed, not just misconstrued. In fact, it has been deliberately given a different outfit and significance altogether. Pluralism in this sense refers to multiple political parties, candidates and media which are aligned with and serve the purpose of the ruling party-regime. This is a failed democracy and is noT different from a one-party-state with a state owned and run media. Besides, democracy has been whitewashed by the respect of electoral calendars and the existence of multipartism.

2. Democracy in the context of Africa

The practice of democracy in most of African countries is a mockery of the system as shall be seen later under relevant sections of this paper. As the Australian based society, Friends of Democracy note on their blog '...in modern times the concept of democracy has become little more than an excuse for those politicians in power to justify their actions by the mere fact that they won the last election rather than by manifesting the true beliefs and values of the ... people.'[38] Yet, the existence of regular elections and multiparty politics is not synonymous to free and fair elections, and least, democracy.

The Economist democracy index points to the existence of five factors, which include aspects of the minimum quality of functioning of government, as standards of true democracy (irrespective of the type): political culture, free and fair competitive elections, civil liberties, and

[37] Article 27(8).

[38] 'Compulsory Voting, Not'. Online at: http://compulsoryvoting.org/aboutus_.html (accessed 27 September 2015).

participation.[39] The second factor is a driver of participation and is important to this discourse.

Free, fair and competitive elections are considered a cut-across factor and a hallmark of political freedom. A healthy democracy requires the active, freely chosen participation of citizens in public life (not to take part in the political processes), but who are at the same time, free to express their dissatisfaction by not participating.[40] In the 2007 Economist Index, all Central African Countries for example, including the Democratic Republic of Congo, ranked very low as they occupied the bottom positions out of 167 countries worldwide. They were in addition, all rated amongst authoritarian regimes, which represent 38.2 percent of world population, as opposed to 38.3 percent for flawed democracies (Table 1). Ten years later, in 2017, very little progress was registered amongst some of these same countries, as there was a general global decline.[41] Only Cameroon, Central African Republic (CAR) and Gabon made an improvement. Gabon was best moving 20 positions up. Cameroon and CAR gained 4 and 2 positions respectively, while Chad stagnated and Equatorial Guinea and Congo Brazzaville lost 5 and 1 positions respectively. The Democratic Republic of Congo (DRC) was the worst performer as it declined by 19 positions. The recent peaceful transfer of power in the DRC did not improve its ranking on the Index despite initial enthusiasm.[42]

Table 1: Democracy ranking of Central African Countries on the global ranking

Country	Rank out of 167 (2007)	Rank out of 167 (2017)	Rank out of 167 (2019)
Cameroon	130	126	141
Chad	165	165	163
Congo Brazzaville	131	132	134
Equatorial Guinea	156	161	161
CAR	166	164	165
Gabon	146	126	121
DRC	144	163	166

Source: *The Economist Intelligence Unit (EIU)*, 2018, pp. 8/9

[39] Kekic, *op. cit.*, p. 2.

[40] *Ibid.*

[41] Table 1.

[42] France24 (2019) "DR Congo's historic transfer of power after chaotic election" (accessed 11 September 2019).

Table 2: Central African countries on the African and global ranking (2019)

Country	World rank	Rank in Africa out of 50
Cameroon	141	40
Chad	163	48
Congo Brazzaville	134	38
Equatorial Guinea	161	47
CAR	165	49
Gabon	121	29
DRC	166	50

Source: *2019 ranking of democracies in Africa according to the EIU 2020*

An examination of the 2017 Mo Ibrahim index on democratic performances across African countries for the year 2016 on the single head, *Participation and on the dual head for 2017, Participation and Human Rights* (Table 3), shows respectively a decline in participation by citizens, confirming the Index of the Economist and fluctuation in terms progress and decline in 2017 amongst 21 African countries. In fact only 12 out of 21 selected African countries experienced slight progress. On a hundred percent score, all Central African countries fell below the average line compared to the other sub-regions, with Equatorial Guinea scoring lowest almost at the last position. Countries which have clearly shown proof of enhancing citizens' participation in the democratic practice of free and fair elections and public affairs, in recent years, scored very high on the ratings, thereby occupying prime positions in the ranking. Table 2 above shows that only Gabon and Chad had made some minimal progress by 2019. Elections were held in Gabon but the progress cannot be explained by elections alone and/or power change since DRC, for example, which experienced elections and power transition rather retrogressed. This is evidence of the fact that democratic virtues cannot be limited to 'elections' and 'change in power'. The manner in which these happen and other governance factors including participation constitute the full democratic package.

Table 3: Participation and human rights ratings in select African countries

Country	Score (2016)	Rank out of 54 (2016)	Score (2017)	Rank out of 54 (2017)
Cameroon	31.1	41	39.0	39
Chad	22.5	48	31.2	45
Congo Brazzaville	29.1	42	36.4	42
Equatorial Guinea	16.4	51	22.0	51
CAR	35.2	35	41.2	36
Gabon	37.9	33	46.3	32
DRC	23.5	45	31.1	45
Botwsana	83.3	4	63.3	13
Namibia	83.3	4	74.9	3
Zambia	58.8	23	57.5	19
Uganda	47.2	29	54.6	23
Kenya	61.0	20	55.6	22
Tanzania	57.4	24	62.1	16
South Africa	80.1	8	74.4	4
Benin	82.1	6	71.5	6
Ghana	81.2	7	73.0	5
Senegal	76.9	9	67.8	8
Sierra Leone	65.9	14	62.2	15
Nigeria	62.7	17	53.2	24
Togo	44.2	31	51.5	27
Cote d'Ivoire	62.2	19	55.8	21

Source: *2017 & 2018 Ibrahim Index Reports of African Governance*

The present instituted practice of attempting to or actually amending national constitutions by incumbent presidents across Africa to prolong their mandates, sometimes causing social and political tension, is good proof of the caricaturisation. In Nigeria, Senegal, DRC and Burkina Faso, for example, these attempts failed. In the Burkina Faso, it led former President Blaise Compaoré's political demise as he was removed from power through a 'civil coup' on October 30, 2014 orchestrated by the populace. Burkina Faso has now become ground zero for democratisation efforts in West Africa.[43] In Nigeria, Olusegun Obasanjo's attempt to amend the constitution and provide for a third term was defeated in

[43] Penney, J. (9 January 2015). 'Burkina Faso: After the revolution', *New African*. Online at: http://newafricanmagazine.com/burkina-faso-30-october/ (accessed 07 October 2015).

parliament, while in Senegal, former President Wade attempted but when discontent started flaring, he sensed danger and was wise enough to end the ambition. Joseph Kabila's attempts to amend the constitution and run for another mandate faced stiff opposition and he finally relinquished power in January 2019 to opposition candidate Felix Tshisekedi after his party's candidate lost the December 2018 poll. Other attempts were successful such as in Cameroon where President Biya has succeeded to extend the presidential term of office twice: 1996 and 2008 through constitutional amendments. President Denis Sassou Nguesso of the Republic of Congo, one of Africa's longest serving presidents (35 years), has followed suit by successfully conducting a referendum on 25 October 2015 and obtaining a 92 percent 'yes' to enable him amend the constitution and take on a third mandate, which he finally obtained. In Uganda, Yoweri Museveni has succeeded in amending the constitution to remove an age limit of 75 years for presidential candidates. This means that Museveni, who is now 74, will be eligible to run in the 2021.[44] These aside, there is a new brand of democracy which may be called 'hereditary democracy'. Generally, Francophone Africa has long-term rulers who could follow in Compaoré's footsteps (Cameroon's Paul Biya has been in power for 37 years; Denis Sassou-Nguesso has ruled for a total of 35 years over two stretches; Idriss Deby has led Chad for 29 years). However, sometimes such long term rulers also adopt the monarchical or chieftaincy system of power through direct or indirect inheritance schemes. Such hereditary systems have been seen in Togo where Fuare Gnassingbé Eyedema succeeded his father who died; Gabon where Ali Bongo succeeded his father who died; and the DRC where Joseph Kabila took over from his father who was assassinated. This inheritance technique failed in Senegal when Abdoulaye Wade tried to position his son, Karim Wade, to succeed him.

Only few countries like South Africa, Nigeria and Senegal have come very close to an ideal democratic standard. South Africa was able to smoothly move out of apartheid and ensured democratic governance and changes without turmoil. Although Senegal staggered, it quickly regained its democratic gaits. On its part, Nigeria, like South Africa, has learned the lessons of its chequered past characterised by several coups and military juntas that caused the country to lose its position as a giant on the continent for several decades. Since 29 May 1999, when Nigeria returned

---

[44] Antihuman, H. (2018). 'Uganda Court Ruling allows President Museveni to rule for life', VOA. Online at: https://www.voanews.com/africa/uganda-court-ruling-allows-president-museveni-rule-life (accessed 11 September 2019).

to civilian democratic rule, it has experienced four democratic power transitions through elections.[45] However, Benin like Nigeria and Mali presents a case where former presidents (Some military or civilian dictators) have been re-elected to office.[46]

Leaders with autocratic tendencies have become savvy at constructing democratic facades, since democracy has become a universal ideal for civilised nations. Examples of what have become known as *adjective democracies* have been mentioned earlier. Democracy has been used often as a smokescreen for different forms of tyranny– a tool of oppression, arbitrary rule and exclusion. A possible reason why democracy has been given this face could be traced right back to the era of colonial rule in Africa.

It has been submitted that colonial masters spent much money on social control and oppression of indigenous peoples than on social services - policing, armed forces and prison services.[47] Colonial policies favoured stratification and discrimination thereby bedevilling ethnic frameworks resulting in socioeconomic disparities between ethnic groups. Any moves or claims during the colonial era by the indigenous populations, which stand today as democratic ideals, such as participation, liberalisation, human rights and freedoms, rule of law, accountability,

---

45 1999 (Olesegun Obasanjo: 1999- 2007), 2007 (Umarou Mousa Yar'Adua: 2007-2010), 2010 (Goodluck Jonathan: 2010-2015) and 2015 (Muhamamadu Buhari: 2015-re-elected in February 2019).

46 In Benin the Marxist-Leninist leader Mathieu Kérékou who came to power in a 1972 coup, enjoyed almost two decades (1972-1991) of fragile but unprecedented stability. In December 1989 Kérékou himself abandoned the Marxist-Leninist ideology that he had promulgated in the mid-1970s. In December 1990 a new constitution was approved, guaranteeing human rights, freedom to organize political parties, the right to private property, and universal franchise. He was defeated in the 1991 presidential election, elected 1996 and re-elected in 2001 on a last mandate which lasted until 2006. At his death in 2015, Beninese venerated him as the father of the country's democracy. In Nigeria, General Olesegun Obasanjo succeeded General Murtala Mohammed who was assassinated in January 1976 but resigned in October 1979. He was democratically elected in May 1999–2007. Mohammadu Buhari first acceded to power through a military coup in December 1983 but was deposed in August 1985. He was democratically elected in May 2015. In Mali, Amadou Touamani Tuouré seized power in March 1991 and led a transition until March 1993. In June 2002 he was elected to power until March 2012 when he was forced to resign in a subtle through a more or less military coup by Amadou Sanogo.

47 Pierre de Vos. (2004). 'A New Beginning ?: The Enforcement of Social, Economic and Cultural Rights Under the African Charter on Human and Peoples' Rights', *Law, Democracy & Development,* Vol. 8 (1), p. 4.

openness and the like, were met with resounding repression, since they were often tied to struggles for liberation and self-determination.

These evils die hard and have lived on as blue prints for post-colonial African leaders who have made very little use of democratic values, if not of thwarting them each time to secure their power like their colonial predecessors. No doubt, therefore, that when the pressure for increased democratic measures came from the former colonial masters, African leaders pretended to be preoccupied 'with their own sovereignty and saw this as justification for a strict enforcement of the principle of non-interference' in their internal affairs. In fact, after six decades of post-colonial rule, many African states are barely struggling to hold together their developing and fragile foundations.[48] Some African states have been less moved by the calls, the pressure and, sometimes, actual threats from former colonial masters for increased democratic practices; the same practices they (former colonial masters) once ignored. Even when African leaders cede to democratic pressure, they often use democracy as a mere *façade* to consolidate their authoritarian rule.

African leaders have largely made a mockery of democracy; from dismal democratic progress to shunting and to shear retreat. In fact, most hybrid or adjective forms of democracies are found in Africa. Table 3 below clearly shows that until 2007, Africa was largely lagging behind on the world democracy index; occupying the last but one position. There is no subsequent evidence that this state of affairs had changed since then except that it has worsened as evidenced in Table 2 above and Table 3 below. The message is therefore clear; *democracy* is a misnomer in most of Africa, despite the existence of *regular* elections and *multiparty* politics.

[48] *Ibid.*

Table 3: Summary of the State democracy across regions of the world (2007)

	Democracy index average	Number of countries	Full democracies	Flawed democracies	Hybrid regimes	Authoritarian regimes
North America	8.64	2	2	0	0	0
Western Europe	8.60	21	18	2	1	0
Eastern Europe	5.76	28	2	14	6	6
Latin America & the Caribbean	6.37	24	2	17	4	1
Asia & Australasia	5.44	28	3	12	4	9
Middle East & N Africa	3.53	20	0	2	2	16
Sub Saharan Africa	4.24	44	1	7	13	23
TOTAL	**5.52**	**167**	**28**	**54**	**30**	**55**

Source: *The Economist Intelligence Unit's index of democracy 2007(Kekic, p. 6)*

3. Paying Service to Democracy Through Citizens' Participation

It has been mentioned earlier that democracy is a form of political governance based on a set of variables including objective standards in accessing power based on citizens' free choice. In a good democracy, the power and strength of government come from the people. This is exhibited when they choose their leaders/representatives at regular intervals through free and fair elections, how they are involved in decision making processes and hold the leaders/representatives accountable for their actions. In the United States of America, the oldest constitutional democracy, this rule works as the President cannot take major decisions without having the fiat of Congress, the peoples' representative. Quite recently (September 2013), although the Obama Administration was resolved on intervening militarily in the Syrian crisis, the President recalled that he needed to consult with the people first (Congress) to get their approval. The participation of citizens in this wise enables the assessment of the threshold of the ideals of democracy as an instrument of good governance in the interest of both the governors and the governed for social cohesion, justice, peace and development.

3.1. Consecration of the right to participate in elections

In most societies (social, political or religious), leaders and managers of institutions are chosen by members through democratic processes – elections. Elections translate the inalienable right to vote and are considered the most outstanding feature of (participatory) democracy. Voting is a fundamental right and civic duty of citizens; the hallmark of a citizen's participation in the political life of his/her nation or community. The AU Charter on Democracy obligates states to implement measures that guarantee the principle of *effective participation of citizens in democratic processes and to recognise popular participation though universal suffrage as the inalienable right of the people.*[49]

3.1.1. Scope of the right to participate

'Rights' are legal entitlements (power, privilege, claim, immunity) which are provided for by law and enforceable thereunder. The African Charter on Human and Peoples' Rights (ACHPR) prescribes the right of every citizen to participate in the government of his country directly or indirectly through freely chosen representatives in accordance with the law.[50] In democratic societies, representatives of the people are freely chosen through elections. Citizens are therefore at the centre of the democratic process. This calls into play the participatory and deliberative prongs of democracy. However, it also entails political will and engagement at both ends of the governors and the governed, and more so on the part of the former to bring about this.

Voting rights bring together two competing legitimate interests: the unfettered fundamental right of citizens to vote; and the prerogative of the state under constitutional law to substantially regulate elections as a practical matter to ensure fairness. In relation to the former interest, Souter and Ginsburg JJ of the US Supreme Court dissenting[51], affirmed the fundamental nature of the right to vote, citing the case of *Burdick v Takushi*,[52] which was itself citing another case[53] where the court had held that "[I]t is beyond the cavil that 'voting is of the most fundamental significance under our constitutional structure' ". The balancing of both

---

49 See article 4(2).

50 Article 13. See also The AU Declaration on the Principles Governing Democratic Elections in Africa, adopted in Durban, South Africa, July 2002.

51 *William Crawford Et Al v. Marion County E. election board et al; and Indiana Democratic Party Et Al v. Todd Rokita, Indiana Secretary of State, Et Al* (2008) 533 US 76-21 & 7-25.

52 (1992) 504 US 428 at 433.

53 *Illinois Bd. Of Elections v. Socialist WorkersParty* (1979), 440 US 173 at 184.

interests is difficult as the state must use its prerogative to qualify the citizens' through substantial regulation. However, in *Reynolds v. Sims*[54] the court warned that the judiciary has a skeptical eye on the exercise of that right. Any alleged infringement by the state in the process or in the name of regulation must be 'meticulously scrutinized' since the right to exercise a franchise should be exercised in a 'free and unimpaired manner, which is preservative of other basic civil and political rights'.

Democracy is not too parochial to be seen as a one-sided issue. Just as citizens have a cluster of rights which bestow obligations on the state through those holding delegated power or authority, citizens also have duties which reinforce and give meaning to those obligations to promote, protect, respect and fulfil the rights. One of such duties is the civic duty to vote. This is important because the very essence of (delegative) democracy is to confer authority or power to chosen leaders/representatives through elections to govern in view of their (citizens') interests. If citizens wish to have their interests met, they have to vote for the leaders/representatives whom they consider can meet this goal. Generally, voting is a civil and political right[55], which is effected through the duty to vote. But it has been doubted whether the existence of the right to impose a corresponding duty to vote as it obtains in Australia and some Western European, South East Asian and South American countries, where it is considered only as a duty.

While a legal right is an entitlement under the law, a 'legal duty' is an obligation under the law to have something done and for which liability accrues for failed or partial fulfillment.[56] Although these are opposing concepts that hardly coexist in the same situation, in the case of voting, they have been formulated to do so sometimes. Australia is historically, a leading country in the world in electoral reform, but is one of the few democracies that maintains the questionable practice of compulsory voting. In trying to identify a common argument for compulsory voting

---

[54] (1964) 377 US 533, at 561-562.

[55] This right is consecrated under Article 25 of the International Covenant on Cavil and Political Right consecrates as follows: "Every citizen shall have the right and the opportunity, without any of the distinctions mentioned in article 2 and without unreasonable restrictions:

(a) To take part in the conduct of public affairs, directly or through freely chosen representatives;

(b) To vote and to be elected at genuine periodic elections which shall be by universal and equal suffrage and shall be held by secret ballot, guaranteeing the free expression of the will of the electors;..."

[56] Garner, *op. cit.*, pp. 1322 and 521 respectively.

in Australia, the Joint Standing Committee on Electoral Matters stated that 'obligations may be imposed on an individual for the benefit of the society generally'.[57] This same Committee has also stated that 'Voting is a civic duty'.[58]

Sheridan is quoted as saying that, 'It is a central conservative insight that democracy confers both rights and responsibilities. Attending a polling booth on election day is the mildest possible responsibility.'[59] Where this is so, mandatory voting is sometimes seen as a corrective to unequal or low turnouts at elections that can truncate polling results.[60] In voting Polls in 2010 in Australia, for example, 44 per cent of 18-24 years old voted, while 76 per cent of those aged over 65 turned out[61]. This was a good reason for accentuating the compulsory voting system since the first age group with lower turnout would normally have many more voters and could have affected the outcome.

In approximately a quarter of the world's democracies, including Belgium, Australia and much of South America, it is mandatory to attend the polls.[62] Not all actively enforce the legal requirement to turn out on election day, but among those that do, enforcement is usually underpinned by means of small fines.[63] In so doing, the duty to vote is stretched to a legal obligation, although seldom or never enforced.[64] In fact, some even

[57] See, '*Report of the Inquiry into the Conduct of the 2004 Federal Election and Matters Related Thereto*', Joint Standing Committee on Electoral Matters, October 2005, p. 194.

[58] '*Report of the Inquiry into the Conduct of the 2001 Federal Election and Matters Related Thereto*', Joint Standing Committee on Electoral Matters, June 2003, p. 249.

[59] Greg Sheridan, *The Australian* 10 Nov 2005 cited in 'Compulsory Voting, Not', *op. cit.*

[60] Darlington, R. (2012). 'Voting is a duty, not a right'. Online at:, http://leftfootforward.org/2012/05/voting-is-a-duty-not-a-right/ (accessed 10 October 2015) .

[61] *Ibid.*

[62] Belgium, Luxemburg, Bolivia, Argentina, Austria, Singapore, Switzerland, France (with respect to Senate), Mexico, Singapore, Gabon Peru, Italy, Philippines, Paraguay, Nauru, Thailand, Uruguay, Turkey, Honduras, Greece, Fiji, Ecuador Chile, Costa Rica, brazil, Bolivia, Dominican Republic, Egypt, Liechtenstein, Guatemala, Cyprus and Australia. Belgium has the oldest record having introduced compulsory voting in 1892 for men and 1949 for women. Venezuela and the Netherlands opted out of the practice (1933 and post 1967 respectively) but saw low voters turn out in the next polls – 20% and 30% respectively. See Frankal, E. (2005), '*Compulsory Voting Around the World.*' The Guardian. Online at: http://www.theguardian.com/politics/2005/jul/04/voterapathy.uk (accessed 04 March 2015).

[63] Darlington, *op cit.*

[64] Some examples abound. In Belgium, citizens aged 18 and more who fail to vote face a moderate fine and if they fail to vote at 4 elections, they lose the right for 10 years. Non-voters also face difficulties getting jobs in the public sector. In Greece, failure to

take a contrary and more radical view that voting is a duty than a right.[65]Yet, voting is not an intrinsic obligation and its enforcement under law is an infringement of a fundamental freedom. In Africa, only two countries currently exercise mandatory electoral participation – Egypt and Gabon.

The ACHPR is a graphical example of how citizens' rights, broadly, should necessarily be accompanied by corresponding individual extensive duties to give effect to those rights.[66] It is thought that these duties are onerous to the extent that, like claw back clauses under provisions guaranteeing the rights, they may be used by governments in relevant situations to violate these rights.[67] However, these duties in some instances should not be read as if they were absolute statutory obligations. Rather, they could, for example, be seen as discretionary powers within the ambit of fundamental freedoms.

3.1.2. Substance of participation

Etymologically, *democracy* is from the Greek compound word *demo kratos*, and literally means that the people are in power. They are impliedly in power through representatives they have chosen to act on their behalf and defend their interests. In essence, therefore, all democracies are participatory. In participatory democracy, citizens' empowerment participation is not limited to participating in voting at elections. Is also entails, opportunities created for them to make meaningful contribution to political decisions and policies affecting their lives, especially directly than through elected representatives. Broadly, though decision making processes should be read as including both electoral and other decision making processes. Participatory democracy is a process of emphasising the broad participation of constituents in the direction and operation of

vote makes it difficult to obtain a new passport or driver's licence. In Australia, non-attendees face fines and possible imprisonment for not paying as punishment for not paying and not for not voting. Frankal *op. cit.*

[65] Darlington, *op cit.*

[66] The ACHPR goes way beyond other human rights instruments like the Universal Declaration on Human rights (UDHR), International Covenant on Civil and Political Rights (ICCPR) and International Covenant on Economic Social and Cultural Rights (ICESCR) which only make mention of duties individuals owe to the society or the European Convention on Human Rights (ECHR) and the American Convention on Human Rights which do not even mention them.

[67] See De Vos *op.cit.*, p. 7 citing Ige, T. (1998). *'The African Charter on Human and Peoples' Rights'* unpublished manuscript quoted in Oloka-Onyango, J. (2000). 'Human Rights and Sustainable Development in Contemporary Africa: A New Dawn or Retreating Horizons?' *Buffalo Human Rights Law Review* 39 p. 56 note 65.

political systems. Participatory democracy is a form of democracy but its qualities underlie all democracies even in principle of those that have been thwarted.

While promoting the adherence of African states to the universal principles of democracy and the rule of law in its objectives, the AU Charter on Democracy enjoins them to implement its principles including: promoting a system of government which is representative; holding regular, transparent and free elections; strengthening political pluralism; and ensuring *effective participation of citizens in democratic and development processes and governance of public affairs.*[68] In fact, the Plan of Action Against Impunity adopted at the 19th ordinary session of the African Commission on Human and Peoples' Rights in 1996 underlines, amongst other things, the need to observe the principles of good governance, primacy of the law, human rights, democratisation and, above all else, *the popular participation by the African peoples in the process of governance.*

The participatory prong in democracy comprises issues such as information, dialogue, and involvement. These factors promote the participation of citizens in elections and their outcome to the extent that they should not be or would be hardly contested. The participatory tools referred to below as prongs can be used to strengthen democracy through Parliament as the people's representatives, and through which citizens participate in the political life of their nation. It should be noted that Parliament promotes the following forms of democracy: representative democracy (who); and participatory democracy (how).

In an electoral democracy, voters must be sure that their votes would be taken into consideration even if their political leaning does not carry the day. Of course, some voters may not be moved by political communications, agendas or propaganda of the contesting sides in an election and simply go in for a blank ballot. But the bottom-line is that they have exercised a civic duty. When voters have the feeling that electoral processes are trumped in favour of some political party or candidate(s) and therefore that the outcome is subjectively predictable, they simply shy away from registration and election processes. The reason being that voting is a waste since the elections would be rigged. However, it is also important to note that even when citizens participate in the vote and put in blank votes, they pass a message to their leaders. It is indeed a

[68] Article 2(1) (2) & (3); Article 3 (3)(4)(7) & (11).

mark of lack of confidence or the answer to failed promises following accountability or no accountability.

When political parties, candidates and voters are or feel disenfranchised at elections, there should be due legal and administrative avenues for them to vindicate their respective rights. A trait of delegative democracy is that political parties, Parliament, and the press are usually free to criticise, but the courts can also block unconstitutional laws and policies, and review political decisions to remedy violated rights.

3.1.3. Participatory Rights of vulnerable groups – the case of women

In a good democracy, there must be gender and minority rights considerations in the *who* parameter whereby vulnerable groups such as women and minorities are given the opportunity to be part of electoral processes on equal terms as their male counterparts both as candidates for political leadership positions and as voters.[69] In other words, non-discrimination in every respect (sex, race, colour, religious belief, political opinion, ethnic grouping, etc.), should be a cardinal policy in a democratic state.

With respect to gender and women, recent strives around the globe are focused on increasing their participation in politics. The Protocol to the ACHPR on the Rights of Women in Africa (Maputo Protocol)[70] requires states parties to take positive measures to promote participatory governance, including equal participation of women in politics through affirmative action, legislation and other measures. Thus, it prescribes the participation of women without discrimination in all elections, enjoyment of equal representation as their male counterparts in all electoral processes as well as increased participation and representation in all levels of decision making in the political lives of their countries.[71] Meanwhile, the Declaration on the Principles Governing Democratic Elections in Africa assigns states parties to encourage the participation of African Women in all aspects of the electoral process in accordance with the laws.[72]

---

[69] This consideration should also hold true with regards to direct nominations/appointment to leadership and managerial (non-elective) positions in public institutions.

[70] Adopted in Maputo, Mozambique on 11 July 2003 and entered into force on 23 November 2005.

[71] Article 9.

[72] III(j).

Beyond national efforts, within sub regional groupings in Africa, efforts are working towards attaining this objective. In the Sothern African Development Community (SADC), for example, community legislation requires that women should have a 50 percent representation in the SADC Parliament and all other community institutions. However, the truth is that the extent of compliance which these legal exigencies at both the national and community levels in Africa is very doubtful. Within the SADC itself, female representation is still relatively weak despite efforts to get them into community institutions. One reason is that women are not sufficiently empowered to partake in political processes. Even in situations where they need to put in no effort, as in case of appointment, they are often not considered or deemed fit to hold certain positions. Still, (and this is a point female gender activists hate to hear but which is true) women sometimes are not just interested; they shy away in the traditional shackles of servitude and throw back the ball to men on the ground that certain things including politics, management and leadership are the men's thing. Yet, in most cases where women have received positions of political authority or management, they have proven to be good or better leaders and managers, as the case may be, than their male counterparts.

Concurrent to the observance of women's rights in a democracy, is observance of the rights of political minorities. In the context of this discourse, these could be political, racial or ethnic minorities. It is true that democratic values cut tread nearly all aspects of modern society, including, to some extent, traditional societies. As such, political, civil, religious, or social institutions are governed by the majority rule. This does not however mean that the minority groups have no rights. Sometimes to achieve equity, maintain equilibrium and avoid discrimination, positive discrimination may be implemented in their favour. Thus, to encourage the participation and representation of small ethnic groups, for example, electoral districts may be specially carved giving them the possibility to have more representation than they normally would have (Gerrymandering).

3.2. Capacity to participate

Like in many other domains of exercise of legal rights, participation in democracy via elections requires that eligible citizens should fulfil the necessary condition of capacity. Generally, under the African Charter on the Rights and Welfare of the Child (ACRWC) or under received English statute law applicable in some common law jurisdictions in Africa such as in Anglophone Cameroon, capacity would normally entail the attainment of the age of majority, which is 18 years[73]. This would also include other circumstances such as soundness of mind, citizenship, and absence of any subsisting prohibitions or incompatibilities under law, as the case may be. These conditions are mutually inclusive. For the purpose of this paper, only citizenship is elucidated.

Citizenship is not the same as nationality although the line between them is too fine. Citizenship is the quality of being a citizen. A citizen is defined as a person who, by birth or naturalization, is a member of a political community, owing allegiance to the community and being entitled to enjoy all its civil rights and protections. In other words, a member of a civil state entitled to all its privileges.[74] Citizenship is a legal status within a country or region acquired by naturalisation, inheritance, descent or origin, registration with the government of a country or region under the law etc.[75] Thus, citizenship is gained by meeting the legal requirements of a region, national, state, or local government.[76] A country grants certain rights and privileges to its citizens and in return, they are expected to obey their country's laws and defend it against its enemies.[77] The value of citizenship varies from one state to another. In some countries such as in the United States and South Africa, citizenship can mean a citizen has the right to vote, the right to hold government offices, and the right to collect employment insurance payments, to name a few examples.

Nationality, on its part, refers to the relationship between a citizen of a nation and the nation, involving allegiance by the citizen and protection

---

[73] See the ACRWC, article 2. This article states that for the purposes of the Charter, anyone below the age of 18 years is a child. Family La Reform Act 1969, article 1(1).

[74] Garner, *op. cit.*, p. 237.

[75] In the European Union, for example, the easiest path to living and working in the EU is to claim EU citizenship through descent or origin should you have an ancestor born in one of the current European Union member states or non-EU countries of Iceland, Liechtenstein, Switzerland and Norway. See, *'Acquiring EU Citizenship through Ancestry or Naturalization'*. At: http://livingingreece.gr/2008/03/18/how-to-acquire-eu-citizenship-through-ancestry-or-naturalization/#ixzz3o45Ceimy (accessed 10 October 2015)

[76] Rashad, R. (2013). *The Power of Family Unity: How to use it to gain economic freedom for generation*. Xlibris Corporation, p. 75. Also available on line at: https://books.google.fr/books?id=VAPALOC9PxAC&pg=PT75&lpg=PT75&dq=Citizenship+is+gained+by+meeting+the+legal+requirements+of+a+national,+state,+or+local+government.&source. See also, Whipple, W (2015) 'What is the definition of Citizenship?' *Democracy at Work*. Online at: http://teacher.scholastic.com/activities/government/civics.htm (accessed 29 September 2015)

[77] Whipple *supra*.

by the state.[78] The general principle is that nationality is acquired by descent (*jus sanguinis* – right of blood), by birth or adoption in a country, (*jus soli* – right of the soil), or by marriage or a combination of all three means. Citizenship is a legal status that historically precedes nationality and, till date, remains on top of nationality for legal practical purposes. The criteria for citizenship are not the same for all countries and vary considerably. There are cases on citizenship without nationality and rare cases nationality without citizenship. Nationality is therefore not proof of citizenship. It is common nowadays though, in the domain of sports for athletes to hold dual nationalities with or without citizenship. Also, someone with parents of different nationalities can hold their two nationalities. Or, a child born abroad of two parents with the same nationality has the nationality of the parents and of that of the place of birth. If the parents have different nationalities, then the child has all of all three nationalities – that of the country of birth and the two of the parents. Thus, a national in one country may hold the citizenship of another country or a regional community to which s/he belongs. Citizenship confers rights and duties including the right to vote. Mere nationality does not confer such right.

The question is how does a citizen express his/her the right to participate? S/he must be an eligible citizen, that is, one capable of fully enjoying the rights accruing from the status. 'Fully' because not all citizens may enjoy all rights at all times. Some cannot enjoy certain rights (civil and political rights) by virtue of their age (minors) or circumstances (unsound mind) and others because they have been stripped of their rights under law such as non-rehabilitated offenders. In some countries, such as Cameroon or the United States, nationality alone confers full citizenship rights, save in these situations just mentioned where these rights may be stripped off. It is clear from the foregoing explanation that in strict legal terms, no individual can partake in the political life of his/her country without acquiring the status of citizen.

Besides, each eligible citizen must be identifiable under the law. This identification manifests in the acquisition of a number of the relevant identification documents, each sequentially having an incidence on the next over time. In Cameroon, for example, the identification starts at birth with the acquisition of a birth certificate, followed by a national identity card or other relevant document on attaining the age of majority and eventually, a voter's card. The voter's card cannot be issued without the

[78] Garner, *op. cit.*, p. 1047

national identity card, while the identity card itself cannot be issued without the birth certificate. Thus, citizens with no birth certificates cannot be eligible for electoral processes because they cannot have national identification cards, as much as those without national identification cards *simpliciter*.

However, whether in a social or political setting, each eligible citizen should be given the same chances to participate in electoral processes. For example, the conditions for the issuance of voter's cards should be transparent and the same for all eligible citizens. In Africa, the most common form of electoral fraud often decried by political parties of the opposition is the issuance of multiple voter cards under different identities to one person or to underage persons, disenfranchising voters by not issuing or delivering their voter's cards before the day of the election, and intentionally swapping electoral lists between polling stations. In the first *scenario* just mentioned, the implication is that such voters hold fake national identification cards established from fake birth certificates. Thus, the rigging of elections is a whole process starting there right up to voting itself and the proclamation of results.

3.3. Challenges to effective participation

The challenges that affect the participation of citizens in the construction of democracy in Africa are manifold and cannot all be examined here. The following sections attempt a discussion of some of the challenges.

3.3.1. Widespread corruption, poverty and illiteracy

Some of the greatest enemies of good democracy are corruption,[79] unemployment, poverty and illiteracy. This *quattro* is a deadly cocktail, which unfortunately, is rife in Africa and its consequences devastating to nascent and staggering democracies. The *trio* has been a serious cause of direct or indirect disenfranchisement of voters during elections especially when they are bought over out of their free will and convictions to vote for financially viable corrupt political ruffians. To put an end to this dilemma, the AU Charter on Democracy, in a solitary voice, obligates states parties to implement strategies, policies and programmes to generate

[79] AU Charter on Democracy, Article 3(8) enjoins states partied to condemn and reject acts of corruption and related offences and impunity.

productive employment, alleviate poverty and eradicate extreme poverty and illiteracy.[80]

The corruption bane is endemic in Africa and is against democratic values. Most African countries are within the lowest arm of the global corruption perception index marks i.e. between 0 - 40,[81] and this is not good news for democratic strives on the continent. In recent years, the interests of citizens have been marginally taken into account by delegated leaders because the latter have imbibed corrupt practices. In most African countries, state property has been capitalised as shares of companies quoted in the Stock Market– *commodification or corporatisation of the state* (better expressed in French as "*patrimonialisation de l'Etat*" or *capitalisation de l'Etat*). In short, the state is being used as a profit making institution by and for those in power. At worst, it is being manipulated as an inheritance fund for the ruling clan. In such situations, the state loses legitimate authority and citizens no longer have any respect for it and its institutions since elected officials seem to believe that they owe no duty to render services to the state if not for looting it with impunity.

Corruption is disservice to citizens, the state and democracy. It undermines accountability and transparency and fosters impunity. When the state is impoverished by this practice, government cannot certainly meet its traditional duties including most especially, realising socio-economic rights of its citizens and other electoral promises. This explains the need for accountability in a democratic setting.

Participation is not just about choosing representatives; it is also about choosing the right (competent) persons. Coerced choices as a result of direct or indirect and psychological compulsion, and the deliberate misdirection of citizens' choices by politicians because of poverty, (buying over votes with food or money *–money and food for votes*), trumps democratic choices. The question is to what extent can democratic values be held in a context of poverty and how can citizens make their voices heard through free and fair elections?

Sometimes, voting rights are violated by voters themselves when they make mistaken or misguided choices as a result of poverty, lack of political education and awareness. Failed choices engender leadership quality problems as elected officials would hardly meet the expectations of their

---

80 Article 40.

81 Transparency International. (2012). 'Governments must prioritise the fight against corruption'. Corruption Perceptions Index 2012 Online at: http://www.transparency.org/cpi2012/results (accessed 05 September 2013).

electorate. The result is socio-political discontent, which in some fragile and unstable conditions may lead to violent conflicts, civil unrest and insecurity. Mistaken choices of representatives may result when initially supposed competent representatives fail to meet campaign promises or political agendas once elected; either because their personal motives/interests override the interests of their electorate, or because the circumstances on the ground do not permit them. In 'dominated democracies' for instance, elected political officials find it difficult to deliver because powerful groups use their influence to condition and limit their autonomy, rendering them incapable of meeting electoral promises.

3.3.2. Fleeting freedom of speech and an incompetent press

Fundamental freedoms in democracy include freedom of expression by citizens, political parties, parliament and the press amongst others. Freedom of expression is a participatory tool for these individuals and institutions, which can be effectively used to enhance citizens' participation at elections as well as the outcome of elections. Under the AU Charter on Democracy states parties commit themselves to promote freedom of expression particularly of the press and to foster a professional media as a measure of advancing political governance.[82] States equally commit themselves to strengthen the capacity Parliaments and legally recognised political parties to perform their core functions.[83]

The press provides avenues for triggering answerability of leaders in specific constituencies and the general population, depending on the electoral context. But such freedom in a democratic set up should be within the confines of the law. Political parties should be allowed to freely express themselves when evaluating their counterparts especially in media duels between the ruling party(ies) and opposition parties. This helps in informing government action and political debates of the times and offers the possibility for the governed to judge the efficiency of their chosen leaders. Meanwhile, Parliament as the representative of the people, should be capable of debating laws, questioning government action and controlling government action. It may sometimes even play the role of the ombudsman through relevant *ad hoc* committees set up to debate and/or investigate and question government action in particular situations. This is efficient when done in all objectivity; obviating party or majority lines in the general interest of the represented populations.

82 Article 27 (8).

83 Article 27 (1).

The press is the whistle blower and an independent accountability investigator. Nevertheless, under authoritarian regimes the whistle blowing may be meaningless since the outcome can only meet with resistance or oppression. In some circumstances, freedom of press exists just for the sake of democracy but its effect in terms of informing and questioning government actions, and by rebound, influencing the re-direction of government policies and political decisions, is inefficient. The reason is that political leaders often consider freedom of expression as a viable psychiatric tool for venting the peoples' grudging and overburdened minds.

The Declaration on the Principles Governing Democratic Elections obligates states parties to ensure that the media while covering electoral processes should maintain impartiality and refrain from broadcasting and publishing abusive language, incitement of hate and other forms of provocative language that may provoke violence.[84] Sometimes, the media in Africa refuse to toe these lines and delve into subjective and sensational journalism, misrepresenting existing political facts and debates - unreliability. This raises a number of questions[85] some of which were addressed earlier on in this paper: What kind of press can enhance the participation of citizens towards the promotion of democratic ideals? What degree of freedom does the press enjoy? What status and legitimacy does the press enjoy from the standpoint of representation of popular opinion? This is not the place to address these issues although they have been addressed briefly earlier on in this paper. But the concerns they raise are important. This is so because, in most African countries, the press like political parties are incompetent to drive debate and advance democratic values as a result of generous coarse amateurism.

The requirement by the charter on democracy that states should ensure fair and equitable access by contesting parties and candidates to state controlled media during elections[86] is illusory. The fair and equitable standard is not an objective one and would thoroughly depend on the manner in which government representing the ruling party would consider 'fair and equitable'. In most cases it would be construed in a restrictive manner to isolate political parties/candidates of the opposition. The

---

[84] IV(10).

[85] These questions were raised by Professor Boyomo Assala during his presentation at the round-table discussion on the theme of the 6th edition of the International Day of Democracy on the topic: "*Faire Mieux Entendre la Voix de la Democratié*", Yaoundé, National Assembly, 15 September 2013.

[86] Article 17(3).

frustration here has led opposition parties to resort to, and catch up with the often amateurish and incompetent private media which is often caught in the spate of violating the canons of professionalism by broadcasting and publishing disparaging language, inciting hate and other forms of provocation that may provoke violence.

3.3.3. Poor political propaganda on participation by political parties and candidates

Political communication and propaganda are at the centre of politicking in a democracy. They are more effective when freedom of press is real and are strong tools which help shape voters' choices. It can be constructive when it informs political debates, options, choices and decisions. But it can also be destructive when the contrary is achieved, and the public is led into in illusionary expectations, hatred and provocation through political communication propaganda. AU Declaration on the Principles Governing Democratic Elections instructs states to make ensure that candidates and political parties respect the impartiality of the public media when airing campaign messages.[87] The Declaration further obligates states parties to ensure that political parties and individuals do not engage in violence or deprive others of constitutional rights and freedoms such as inciting hate speech defamatory allegations, abusive or provocative language.[88]

Briefly political propaganda consists of all measures including campaigns, speeches, communications activities, adverts, publicity, and so on, employed by politicians and political parties to rally popular support behind them and their political agendas. Political communications may be used to vehicle propaganda information to militants of political parties or to inform the public opinion about the activities and agendas of political parties or candidates. The problem is that, by its very nature, propaganda, like advertisement, is all about convincing not about conviction. To this extent therefore, every single available tool towards this end may be used, including falsities, unfounded, thwarted thoughts, misstated ideas, and facts, and unrealistic promises. This is especially true when politicians are canvassing for votes at political campaigns; they can ask to kiss the feet of voters, say just anything, and make wild, overzealous and unattainable promises without the faintest ability or conviction or idea on how to go about such promises. This is dangerous and here lies the death-knell of democracy because when failed promises abound, voters despair and

---

[87] IV (11).

[88] IV (8).

become reticent to participate in future electoral processes. This raises issues of vertical accountability discussed in the next section. The protracted registration process in Cameroon leading up to the September 2013 legislative and municipal elections partly explains this situation. Potential voters were visibly reticent to register because of discouragement from past experiences of failed electoral promises and other disenfranchisement concerns such as non-issuance of voter's cards.

Disenfranchisement

Disenfranchisement consists in depriving someone of their right to vote. This is a common practice across Africa. Disenfranchisement may be direct or indirect. It is direct when the act consists of explicitly prevent people from voting or having their votes counted. The following are typical techniques.

- Not issuing voter's cards to some citizens on grounds of their regional or ethnic origin, which is often considered, truly or falsely, to the driver of their political leaning;
- Refusing to deliver voter's cards even after issuance by deliberately keeping them and only making them available after election day with the pretext that the beneficiaries did not withdraw them, particularly where the voter comes from a region or ethnic group where opposition against the ruling party is rife;
- Restrictive and arbitrary registration practices. For example, issuing voter's cards only to citizens of a particular region or ethnic group and in some cases multiple cards to one individual to enable them vote severally in different polling stations for the same party. Also, not issuing national identity cards to citizens of a particular ethnic group or region. In Cameroon, this latter technique has been cured by the acceptance of the voter's card as the valid voter's card in the absence of a national identity card for voting on Election Day since voter's card is issued on the basis of a valid national identity card.
- Issuing threats against members of a particular party or ethnic group or region, for example, not to vote. In the US, an Enforcement Act of 1870, prohibited individuals from conspiring "to injure, oppress, threaten, or intimidate any citizen with intent to prevent or hinder his free exercise and enjoyment of any right or privilege granted or secured to him by the constitution or laws of the United States."

In all the scenarios above, the tag is the name which tells the voter's ethnic group, region of origin or political affiliation. This is particularly common to most African countries where there are several ethnic groups or minorities, which are the target groups of disenfranchisement.

Indirect disenfranchisement techniques essentially consist in attempts to prevent people's votes from having an impact on political outcomes such as gerrymandering, ballot box stuffing, falsifying vote counts or, swapping votes or vote counts between candidates or political parties – electoral fraud, or failure to count votes effectively cast, and stripping elected officials of their powers.

Also, the complicit nature of the national elections bodies and local administrative and judicial authorities in all these situations strengthens the disenfranchisement. Local administrators orchestrate it while the judiciary thwarts electoral disputes by striking out complaints alleging disenfranchisement and other forms of fraud on grounds of either lack of sufficient evidence, non-respect of procedures, or lack of merits.

3.3.4. Little or no accountability of political leaders/institutions

In good democracy, the principles of transparency and accountability are crucial. Transparency is the knob of accountability. The AU framework on democratic governance attaches great importance on these principles. The AU Charter on Democracy[89] and the Convention on Preventing and Combatting Corruption[90] requires states parties to strive to instil good political governance through an 'accountable, efficient and effective public administration'. Meanwhile, more specifically, in relation to elections, the AU Declaration on the Principles Governing Democratic Elections provides as one of its guiding principles that democratic elections should be conducted by impartial, 'all-inclusive competent accountable electoral institutions'.[91] Accountability, for one, is both personal (vertical) and institutional (horizontal).

The AU framework on democracy requires African governments to ensure transparency and accountability starting with the main stakeholders, political parties. Of course, since they are in the quest to conquer power, their route to power should be hitch-free and must be proof of their actions once in power. The AU Convention on Preventing and Combatting Corruption obligates states parties to incorporate transparent funding of political parties. African governments are therefore

[89] See Articles 12(1) & 32 (1).
[90] Article 3(3).
[91] II (4) (e).

expected to adopt legislative and other measures proscribing funds derived from illicit and corrupt sources to finance political parties.[92]

The effect of accountability of elected leaders in a representative democracy cannot be undermined. Accountability is a check and balance mechanism which ensures effective governance for the benefit of the electorate. According to Morlino therefore, 'accountability - a core feature in the experience of representative democracy - becomes a truly central dimension in as much as it grants citizens and civil society in general, an effective means of control over political institutions.'[93] Accountability and transparency instil confidence in the electorate and motivate them to participate in democratic processes. If there is anything which is lacking in the African kind of democracy, it is lack of transparency and accountability. This is just normal in thwarted 'democracies' around the continent which are no more than one party-sate autocracies.

Accountability can be either vertical or horizontal. Vertical accountability is an issue between the electorate and elevated political officials (representatives). It is answerability to electors by elected political officials. Electors can only re-elect a representative in light of accomplished pre electoral promises. Electors can thus punish their representatives in the next election by voting for another candidate, abstaining from the vote, or by nullifying the ballot, if they are not satisfied. Horizontal accountability is the responsibility elected officials have to answer to other institutions or collective actors who have the expertise and power to control their behaviour. These intermediary actors include: a responsible, vigilant political opposition; independent judiciary and media which is conscious of its civil function; and a well-developed network of active, informed Civil Society Organisations (CSOs) and associations which share democratic values.[94]

The judiciary has a cardinal role to play in the accountability processes not only with respect to electoral disputes. It must be capable of concretely exercising the checks provided for by law; in particular, reviewing political decisions, blocking unconstitutional processes/laws and enforcing states' obligations. Also, African governments are required under the AU Convention on Preventing and Combatting Corruption, to create an enabling environment for civil society and the media to hold governments

---

[92] Article 11.

[93] Morlino, *op. cit.*, p. 5. The AU Charter on Democracy instructs states parties to create conducive conditions for civil society organisations to exist and operate within the law.

[94] Morlino *supra*, p. 10.

to the highest levels of transparency and accountability.[95] In contrast to vertical accountability, the actors are for the most part political equals. Horizontal accountability is relatively continuous, being formally or substantially formalised by law.

In several African countries the vertical and horizontal arms of accountability are lacking and that is why there is continued impunity since elected officials ward off electoral promises and go scot free. They are sure to win because they have the machinery in place to keep them on and on. Campaigning during elections has become a mere show because with or without the electorate's vote, they are sure to win at elections. This discourages the electorate to register for elections for no one is accountable to them and their voice does not count.

3.3.5. Weak and unaccountable judiciary

The judiciary is the overseer and regulator of the effectiveness of the constitutional law theory of separation of powers among the executive, the legislative and the judiciary. In good democracy, the courts are independent and free from political control or influence of the executive, as their duty is to the constitution – ensure respect of the constitution by itself and the other arms of power. The AU Charter on Democracy directs states parties to institutionalise good political governance through an independent judiciary.[96] Meanwhile, the Declaration on the Principles Governing Democratic Elections in Africa states that democratic elections should be conducted under a system of separation of powers that ensures the independence of the judiciary.[97]

However, separation should not be understood as if each arm were to exist in its own right in a vacuum. Instead, it presupposes collaboration for effective definition, coordination and implementation of government policies. Each of them should use its prescribed competence collaboratively towards this end without pressure of influence from the other. Politicians are sometimes tempted to use judicial acts to reinforce their own positions against the opposition.[98] In other cases, when there is collusion among politicians, judges themselves, with the support of the

[95] Article 12 (2).
[96] Article 32(3).
[97] II (4)(c).
[98] Morlino, *op. cit.*, p. 21.

media, are tempted to turn to the judiciary in retaliation for certain political decisions which they consider unacceptable.[99]

The extent to which the judiciary is independent in most African countries is doubtful. They have rather been known to conspire with the executive to sanctify rigged elections and with Parliament (with fictitious majorities) to pass bad electoral laws. At the end, despite constitutional provisions on the separation of powers, the executive, judiciary and parliament cooperate to disenfranchise the electorate. Whereas, in true constitutional democracies, the duty of the courts is to the constitution in guaranteeing and enforcing all rights, duties and standards under it, without pressure, fear or favour from political authorities. In South Africa, for example, the courts enjoy this privileged position and have always ingeniously reminded the executive that their duty is to the constitution and *not* to the executive.[100] In a good democracy therefore, citizens, political parties and even government should be capable of vindicating their (electoral) rights before the law courts and benefit from fair trial. As seen earlier, in the accountability discussion, the judiciary plays an important role in enforcing accountability standards in the interest of the governed especially in situations of failed promises and abusive actions by government.

4. The Way Forward: Overcoming challenges to citizen's participation

Achieving full democracy is nearly impossible in view of its malleability and indefinite confines which have favoured deviant versions especially in the African context where current 'democratic' trends are a near ridicule. The benchmark for good democracy is regular, free and fair elections. Through elections, citizens can freely and objectively participate to make their voices heard, thereby also giving a voice to democracy. From elections, all other democratic values and standards such as rule of law, equality, human rights and freedoms, accountability, etc. take their rise to complete the full democratic package. Good democracy occurs in the electoral and liberal fronts but it can only be better perceived as a palatable system of political governance if its standards are met and constantly fine-tuned in view of changing circumstances and new exigencies, within the strict confines of its true spirit. One of the greatest blows to delegative

[99] *Ibid.*

[100] See Jacoob CJ. (2002). In *Minister of Health v Treatment Action Campaign*, (TAC) 5 SA 721 (CC).

democracy is low turnouts at elections either because, eligible citizens cannot vote as a result of non-registration for various reasons, or non-issuance of voter's cards or other reasons such as discouragement from past unfulfilled electoral promises fraudulent management of the process. It is true that democracy is increasingly being paid lip service, ending the disenfranchisement of citizens' right to vote; but it is also true that its confines can still be drawn to remove the impediments to citizens' participation. Therefore, delegative democracy is workable in Africa if the following are considered.

Firstly, creating awareness in all aspects and at all levels of democratic processes is cardinal. Political communications, campaign slogans, propaganda and meetings as well as in-house training/sensitisation workshops, should focus on this. Building the capacity of citizens on best democratic practices which would enable them know and understand their democratic rights and strive to avail themselves of these rights through all legal avenues is therefore crucial. Capacity building should also include other political stakeholders such as government, legalised political parties, electoral commissions and the media.

Secondly, a rights-based approach to participation would enable people to influence government decisions that affect their lives.[101] It promotes transparent, fair, equitable, responsive and participatory governance.[102] It

[101] A human rights-based approach is a conceptual framework for the process of human development that is normatively based on international human rights standards and operationally directed to promoting and protecting human rights. It seeks to analyse inequalities which lie at the heart of development problems and redress discriminatory practices and unjust distributions of power that impede development progress. Mere charity is not enough from a human rights perspective. Under a human rights-based approach, the plans, policies and processes of development are anchored in a system of rights and corresponding obligations established by international law. This helps to promote the sustainability of development work, empowering people themselves - especially the most marginalised – to participate in policy formulation and hold accountable those who have a duty to act. See 'Frequently Asked Questions on a Human Rights-Based Approach to Development Cooperation', United Nations Office of the High Commissioner foı Human Rights (OHCHR). Online at: www.ohchr.org/Documents/Publications/FAQen.pdf (accessed 25 April 2015). In a nutshell, the rights-based approach "means describing situations not in terms of human needs, or areas of development, but in terms of the obligation to respond to the rights of individuals. This empowers people to demand justice as a right, not as a charity." See Robinson, M. (1999). 'Introduction.' in Santos Pais, M. (1999). *A Human Rights Conceptual Framework for UNICEF*, Florence, Italy: UNICEF, p. iv.

[102] Theis, J. (2004). *Promoting Rights-Based Approaches: Experiences and Ideas from Asia and the Pacific*, Thailand: Save the Children Sweden, p. 15.

reduces opportunities for corruption, deters the diversion of justice and broadens democratic spaces at all levels of society. Ruling elites all over the world are creative in maintaining their power and in increasing their control over people and resources. At the same time, much of the pressure from below is poorly organized and unfocused, unimaginative and divisive, dissenting and sometimes paranoiac, often fomented by government.

Thirdly, early participation of citizens in social community groupings is apprenticeship in building democratic experience in choice making. It does not only build leadership qualities and skills but also qualities for choosing between competent leaders who can deliver.

Fourthly, democratic values such as free, fair, regular and timely elections; equality, including gender and minority considerations; guarantees to freedoms including a strong free and rational press; human rights; rule of law should be constantly protected by states. Here there must be a strong political will by government to end direct and indirect forms of disenfranchisement, which constitute a direct violation of citizens' right to vote. As a joinder, national bodies responsible for conducting electoral processes should be truly independent and credible.

Fifthly, transparency, accountability and anti-corruption measures must be privileged to ensure government's performance. For purposeful accountability, interested intellectuals and informed citizens who have internalised the fundamental values of democracy must remain involved in political processes to ensure quality control of democratic standards and blow the whistle when things are going wrong. But it should be noted here as well that in most situations in Africa, educated and informed citizens have become government friends who use their knowledge and intelligence to help government ingeniously thwart democratic standards including the violation of citizens' rights during electoral processes. For purposes of focused and successful accountability, sources of information like the private press, investigators and observers must exist in democracy. The presence of all these actors as whistle blowers has proven to be an efficient tool in the accountability process.

Lastly, an effectual separation of powers characterised by the independence of the courts both capable of integrating legal and political action, providing a remedial framework for judicial review of political decisions blocking unconstitutional processes/laws and enforcing states' obligation to ensure citizens' rights, makes ample sense in a good democracy. To this end, the rule of law in the sense of existence of good laws, and the existence access to enforcement mechanisms should be real. Besides, rule of law, in the sense of supremacy of law should also be real. These entail at least the state's political will and capacity to cause elected and non-elected official authorities to respect laws, and to institute laws which are non-discriminatory, universal, stable, and unambiguous.

The fate of rural women after the 1974 land tenure reforms: tenants at sufferance?

By

Irene Sama-Lang

Associate Professor of Law,
Department of Public Law and Public Administration,
University of Buea, Cameroon
Email: finds_1999@yahoo.com

Abstract

Land is the umbilical cord of a rural woman. Her very essence and power is intrinsically linked to land. The customary law gave her access to land mainly for crop cultivation purposes and only for as long as the men did not need it, thereby reducing her rights to land to merely a derivative. Her continuous stay on the land is dictated by men's competing needs or outside pressure. This fluidity in her rights became even more worrisome when by section 1(2) of Ordinance No. 74-1 of 6th July 1974 the state made itself the guardian of all land. The situation became dire with the nationalisation of all unregistered lands by virtue of sections 14 and 15 of same. The individualisation of land rights by especially section 1(1) of Decree No. 76/165 of 27 April 1976 begs the question whether with such sweeping powers of the state, compounded by patriarchy these women who have been making use of the land for decades have not been reduced to tenants at sufferance. Using Content analysis and observation in answering the above question, the paper concludes that if that were the case, the state has obligations under international law to respect, protect and fulfil the rights of rural women if only to save them from the sting of poverty.

Key words: Rural women, land tenure reforms, tenants at sufferance

Introduction

That land is a source of political power, cultural identity, and most especially a vehicle for economic empowerment[1]and development to especially customary communities cannot be over-emphasised.[2] Access to land, ownership and tenure security are not only critical to a rural woman as a vehicle for socio-economic and political empowerment but an escape route from the biting sting of poverty. This development implement which is the essence of a rural woman[3] is hinged onto her status over the land she occupies. In Cameroon, although women supply 56% of agricultural labour and 60% of food production[4], history, backward traditions and custom continue to deny majority of them land ownership and by extension power. This is so because majority of the land which they cultivate are not only unregistered[5] but are under the control of their male relatives.[6] In such a situation, their weak and unsecured rights are withdrawn immediately[7] the men feel pressure from other competing and conflicting land use. This situation becomes even more worrisome with the nationalisation of all unregistered land by the Ordinance No. 74-1 of 6th July 1974.[8] As the guardian of all land, the state has sweeping powers to withdraw lands from whomsoever and make same available for the rational use and development in tandem with its economic, socio-political

1 Fonjong, L.N., Sama-Lang, I. N.F., and Fombe, L., *Land tenure practices and women's rights to land in Anglophone Cameroon: Implications for sustainable development*, Canada, International Development Research Centre, 2013. See also Palmer, R., *Gendered Land Rights-Process, Struggle, or Lost Cause*, Oxfam Great Britain, 2002.

2 According to Robin Palmer, the importance of land rights as not only being essential to food and social security, cultural identity and a means to our livelihoods, it depicts land as very complex and difficult terrain of highly sensitive political nature and a source of potential conflicts. This age old conflict exists between the powerful (state, elites, entrepreneurs, multi-national companies) and powerless (rural woman, in-migrants), etc, R. Palmer, Working On Land For Oxfam, 1997-2007 Or Last Rites For Land Rights? Extracts from a farewell talk by Robin Palmer, Oxfam GB Global Land Adviser.

3 All class of women need land for different purposes even though it is the mainstay of the rural woman.

4 USAID Camer –Property Rights and Resource Governance Profile, 2011, p. 4.

5 Agriculture takes up about 20% of all Cameroonian land.

6 Goheen, M., *Men own the Fields, Women Own the Crops, Gender and power in Cameron Grassfield,* University of Wisconsin Press, 1996, p.4.

7 Schneider, E.A., "What sh-Lang, I. N.F., and Fombe, L., *Land tenure practices and women's rights to land in Anglophone Cameroon: Implications for sustainable development*, Canada, International Development Research Centre, 2013. See also R., Palmer., *Gendered Land Rights-Process, Struggle, or Lost Cause*, Oxfam Great Britain, 2002.

8 To establish Land Tenure laws in Cameroon

and cultural agenda. Against this background, adopting content analysis, observation and interpretational approach of qualitative research methodology, this paper investigates in order to ascertain the rights and the plight of these women who more often than not are customary users of land with only derivative rights. It assesses the combined effects of sections 1(2), 14 and 15 of Ordinance No.74-1 of 6th July and the individualisation and formalisation of land rights by section 1 of Decree No. 76/165 of April 1976 on their right to land. In so doing, it questions whether the copious powers of the state as the owner of such lands would not have taken away from the customary women the very inalienable first generation rights it seeks to protect in the constitution, thereby making them tenants at sufferance. These will be addressed from three perspectives: the context of women's land rights within the historical evolution of land law, the requirements of international law and the effect of the 1974 land laws.

1. Context of the study

The contentious issue of tenancy at sufferance which is conceived in this paper as a tenant's continuous occupation of leased property without the landlord's expressed consent after the tenancy agreement has lapsed[9] is apparently the precarious situation in which the majority of rural women are exposed. It is so conceived because of their derivative user's rights and patriarchy that continue to deny them equal access and ownership rights like their male counterparts. This was especially seen when cash crops were introduced to farmers in line with the state's policy of Operation Green Revolution which intended amongst others to convert farmers into

[9] See Black's law Dictionary 9th edition page 1605. Where it is defined as a tenant who has been in legal possession of property and wrongfully remains as a holdover after their term has expired without the landlord's assent or dissent. The difference with trespasser is that his/her initial entry into the premises was lawful. The tenancy can be determined at any time by the landlord. See also Scrutton LJ in *Remon v. City of London Real Property Co Ltd* [1921] 1 KB 49 where he explained that « tenants at sufferance seem to have been confined to persons who held over without the assent or dissent of their landlords, and not have included persons who have held over wrongfully the land in spite of the active objection of their landlord ». Elias defines it as a person who has an estate *pur autre vie*, continues to hold after the death of *cestui que trust*, or a person holds over at the end of a lease without his landlord's consent, T.O Elias, *Nigerian Land law*, London, Sweet & Maxwell, 1981, p.270. According to Judith Bray, the rights of the tenant at sufferance do not allow him to maintain an action in trespass. If the landlord refuses to tenant the right to continue inhabiting his estate, the tenant automatically becomes a trespasser. J. Bray, Unlocking *Land Law*, Hodder Education, 2011, p. 436.

bourgeoise planteurs.[10] Such a lofty programme did not of course include food crop which is the mainstay of the rural women. Such a policy implied that the pieces of land that had been handed over customarily to the women after marriage or otherwise were called back by these men who needed it for the cultivation of cash crop[11]. In so doing, these women who could not be handed land by inheritance which is the first means of ownership were compelled to either borrow, use marginal lands in urban peripheries or plantations, rent[12], buy or go further afield, while their male kins continue to enjoy superior rights simply because they are men[13].

The introduction of cattle by some indigenous cattle grazers did not help the situation as more land was syphoned from the women[14], which would not have been so if these women had equal customary land rights like their men. This position was/is compounded by the nationalisation of all customary lands by sections 14[15] and 15[16] of ordinance No. 74-1 of 5th July 1974[17] and the government making itself the guardian of same, with the right to use any land in tandem with its socio-political and economic

---

[10] See the third five years Development Plan - July 1971- June 1976 of Cameroon.

[11] As observed by P.M Kaberry, some rural communities for fear of food crop shortages had prohibited the planting of cash crops like coffee. See P.M Kaberry "Report on farmer-grazer Relations and changing pattern of agriculture", Buea Archives, File No. Ab17(10), 1959, p. 16.

[12] In a recent research carried out by Fonjong *et al.*, it was found out that these women loss livelihood when the commons and customary land is given to investors. In areas where they rented lands, the land owners dictated the type of crops to cultivate. Such companies reserve the right to call back the land at any time whenever need arises, Fonjong, l. *et al.*, *Large-Scale Land Acquisition: Implications for Women's Land Rights in Cameroon,* Canada: International development Research Centre, 2016, pp. 104-106.

[13] See Generally P.M. Sone, "The Concept of Equality and Access to land in Cameroon: The case of the Anglophone Regions of Cameroon" Published PhD thesis, Codesria, 2013, p. 45-79.

[14] C.F. Fissiy, *Power and Privileges in the Administration of Law,* Leiden, African Studies Centre, 1992, p. 241-252.

[15] Section 14 (1) National lands shall as of right comprise lands which, at the date on which the present ordinance enters into force, are not classed into the public or private property of the state and public bodies. Section 14(2) National lands shall not include lands covered by private property rights as defined in Article 2 of same.

[16] National land shall be divided into two categories :

1) Lands occupied with houses, farms and plantations and grazing lands manifesting human presence and development
2) Lands free of any effective occupation

[17] No. 74-1 of 6th July 1974 to establish rules governing land tenure.

agenda[18]. The commoditisation of land which was hitherto not possible,[19] is now the case with the introduction of the 1974 land reforms means that customary land that was owned collectively is now a subject for private ownership. Individualisation and formalisation of land ownership insists in section 1 of Decree No. 76/165 of 27th April 1976 [20] that a land certificate is the only document that attests to land ownership. Although these women are usually those on the land, most of them do not have registered titles.[21]Long use of land by these women is of no consequence as it accords no title to them[22]. Their continuous stay on the land therefore is at the mercy of their matrikin/patrikin, investors or the state, thereby reducing them to tenants at sufferance waiting only for the day that the overlords will ask them to leave the land.

It is trite law that native law knows only community of property, it does not attach itself to a title.[23] This fact is buttressed by Viscount Haldane in the *locus classicus* in *Amodu Tijani v. Secretary of Southern Nigeria*[24]that :

> "... the next fact which it is to bear in mind in order to understand the native land law is that the notion of individual ownership is quite foreign to native ideas. Land belongs to the community, the village or family never to the individual. All members of the community, village or family have an equal right to land ..."

It can be gleaned from this decision that all members of such communities (men and women) have the same rights to access land. Why then are customary (rural) women treated as legal minors with precarious

---

18 Section 1(2) Ordinance No. 74-1 of No 74-1 of 6th July 1974 to establish rules governing land tenure.

19 Like water, fire and air, land is seen as an element of nature incapable of individual ownership. See Henry, H., "The role of land law in the Rural Development in Niger, The Ivory Coast and Nigeria Under Development law Aspects", The State and the law, Vol. 28., 1983, p. 72-74.

20 To establish conditions for obtaining land certificates as modified, Decree No 2005/481 of 16th December 2005.

21 Yanou, M.A. & Patience Sone "Women and land Registration in Anglophone Cameroon: Lessons from South Africa", in Fonjong (ed) *Issues in Women's Land Rights In Cameroon,* 87-100, 2012, p. 97.

22 Schneider, E.A.," What Shall We Do without our land? Land Grabs and Resistance in Rural Cambodia", International Conference on Global Land Grabbing, University of Sussex, second edition ,2011.

23 James, R.W., *Modern Land Law of Nigeria,* Nigeria, University of IFE Press, 1973, p.21.

24 [1921] 2.A.C.399.

rights over such lands? Such a position as observed by Njeassam[25] is triple discrimination against the rural poor women on the basis of their gender as women; their economic class as majority of the rural women are poor (for that reason are unable to buy their own land) and in the case of indigenous women, their ethnicity. It was hoped that the 1974 land reforms would cater for the needs of such vulnerable but it missed the point.

2. The protection of customary women's land right under international law

The right to own property is an inalienable right inherent in all humans which must be protected by law, and has been so preserved by the preamble of Cameroon Constitution of 1996[26]. This right to ownership is quite distinct from rights of possession and access which give the possessors only rights to *usus* and not maximum rights which are allodial[27]. This ownership means the right guaranteed to all by law to use, enjoy and dispose of this property without permission from an overlord. It is therefore the radical title to land which in customary jurisprudence rests with the family/ community and not the individual[28]. No person with such

[25] Njieassam, E.E., "Gender inequality and land rights : The situation of Indigenous Women in Cameroon" PER/PELJ 2019 (22) .

[26] S. 65 of the 1996 Constitution makes preamble provisions part and parcel of the Constitution.

[27] The characteristics of the absolute or maximal interest over land include the right to disposition; commit waste (destruction- carrying out of an act which alters the nature of the land); unlimited user and possession. Such allodial rights are in contrast with inferior or determinable rights which is what these women have which are large parcels of land over which there are many inferior interests of different qualities that may be enjoyed simultaneously but whose duration is very precarious. See R.W James, *Modern Land Law of Nigeria*, *op.cit.*, p.19-20. See also C.F. Fisiy, *op.cit.*, p.5.

[28] According to the corporate personality theory, land is seen as a customary law corporation- a form of land holding which is an integral part of the economic, social and cultural organisation of a people in any early society and according to him, is sui generis. This he explained finds root in the fact that such societies and individuals belong primarily to a group. Customary communities are therefore not a collection of individuals but an aggregation of families. As explained by Viscount Haldane in Amodou Tijani v. Secretary of state of Southern Nigeria [1921] A.C. 399 "The next fact which it is important to bear in mind in order to understand the native land law is that the notion of individual ownership is quite foreign to native ideas. Land belongs to the community, the village or the family, never to the individual. All members of the community, village or family have an equal right to the land, but in every case the chief or headman of the community or village, or head of the family has charge of the land and in loose mode of speech is sometimes called the owner. He is to some extent in

maximum rights shall be deprived thereof save for public purpose and subject to payment of compensation. [29]

A plethora of international laws duly ratified by Cameroon protects women's land rights. For example, Article 17[30] of the United Nations Declaration of Human Rights 1948 guarantees the right of all to own property communally as well as alone and one should not be arbitrarily deprived of this right safe with due compensation. In addition, Article 2 (a)[31] (f),[32] 5[33] and 16(h)[34] of the Convention for the Elimination of all forms of Discrimination Against Women, (CEDAW)1979[35] enjoin state parties to protect and enforce women's rights. In the same vein, article 14 of the African Charter 1986 guarantees women's right to property as well as

---

the position of a trustee, and as such holds the land for use of the community or family. He has control of it, and any member who wants a piece of it to cultivate or build upon, goes to him for it. But the land so given remains the property of the community or family. He cannot make any important disposition of the land without consulting the elders of the community or family and their consent must in all cases be given before a grant can be made to a stranger. This is pure native custom … and wherever we find. individual owners, this is again due to the introduction of English ideas… except where land has been bought by the present owner there are very few natives who are individual owners of land." P. 404.

29 Art. 17(1) of the Universal Declaration Of Human Rights Provides that everyone has the right to own property alone as well as in association with others. See in the same light, Art 14 of the African Charter on Human and Peoples Rights 1981 and the Preamble of the Charter of the United Nations 1945.

30 This is not an absolute right as it recognizes that this right may be interfered with, for that reason, it must be done with due compensation should the need arise. Though a soft law, it can still be applied directly by virtue of the fact that it has been made hard law by the Constitution of Cameroon 1996 as revised.

31" …. To embody the principle of equality of men and women in their national constitutions or other appropriate legislation if not yet incorporated therein and to ensure, through law and other appropriate means, the practical realisation of this principle".

32" to take all appropriate measures, including legislation, to modify or abolish existing laws, regulations, customs and practices which constitute discrimination against women".

33 Places responsibility on state parties to modify their social and cultural pattern which is based on superiority of either sex or stereotyped roles for men and women.

34 Rights of ownership to women together with men to acquire with or without consideration, own, dispose of or administer property. This position has been upheld in the Supreme Court of Cameroon case of *Zamcho Florence Lum v. Chibikom Peter Fru.* Supreme court Judgment No. 14/L of 14th February 1997.The Commission on the Status of Women Resolution 42/1 that *inter alia*, urges States to design and revise laws to ensure that women are accorded full and equal rights to own land and other property, and the right to adequate housing, including through the right to inheritance.

35 Which Cameroon signed on 6th June 1983 but ratified on August 23rd 1994.

Articles 6 (j), 7(d) Articles 13(h), 20 and 21 of the Protocol to the African Charter on Human and People's Right On the Rights of Women in Africa (Maputo Protocol) 2003[36]. Article 25 of same enjoins states through their competent government agencies to redress all land rights violations suffered by these women. Article 26 on its part requires state parties as part of their triple pronged responsibility to ensure the implementation of this protocol and to give periodic reports in accordance with article 62 of the African Charter to show their level of legislative compliance and measures taken to ensure the realisation of these rights.

The situation on the ground still leaves much to be desired as one year to the target 2020 set aside for domestication of the Protocol, no concrete measure are being taken to specifically address the situations raised above, leaving these women in doldrums.

In the same vein in a bid to promote, protect and respect women's right to property, article 19(a), (b) and (c) on the Right to Sustainable Development, enjoins states parties to take all appropriate measures to introduce gender perspective in their national development planning procedures, ensure participation of women at all levels in the conceptualisation, decision-making, implementation and evaluation of development policies and programmes, take all appropriate measures to "promote women's access to and control over productive resources such as land and guarantee their right to property." This of course is not the right most customary land users (who in the main are women) possess as most are users (possessors) of native land in perpetuity without the right to singularly alienate[37]. In Cameroon, the Land Consultative Board that manages national land[38](unregistered land) whether or not intended has no statutory representation of women on the board. In this regard, the voices of especially the rural women are missing.

The Sustainable Development Goals 1,2,5, and 10 set by the United Nations General Assembly in 2015 to transform the world by 2030 all touch on women's empowerment. The customary women may not be

---

[36] Ratified by Cameroon on 13th September 2012. Although this Protocol gained force in 2005, ushering in an era of domestication and implementation of the law, with full enforcement of the law by 2015 and total domestication by 2020.

[37] See generally Viscount Haldane in the *locus classicus* case of *Amodu Tijani* v *Secretary of Southern Nigeria*, A.C. 399, 1921. See also Rayner C.J's *Report on Land Tenure in West Africa* ,1898. See generally on this Elias, T.O.: *Nigerian Land Law*, 4th Edition, London, Sweet & Maxwell, 1971; R.W. James, *Modern Land Law of Nigeria*, University of Ife Press.

[38] By virtue of section 16 of Ordinance No. 74/1/6th July 1976 and section 12 of Decree No. 76-166 of 27th April 1976.

able to meet these goals since a rural woman's mainstay is agriculture which is linked to land. There may not be any meaningful development[39] if her land rights are fluid, capricious or if they remain as tenants at sufferance. As opined by Oliver De Shutter, for these women who depend on agriculture for their livelihood, ultimate tenure security (ownership) should be understood as the right to live decently from agricultural activities that feed them which is possible only with secured and stronger land rights.

3. An evolution of women's land right before 1974 land ordinance

A critical assessment of women's land rights before 1974 is imperative to better capture the position and implications on rural (customary) women post -1974. In Cameroon, before the colonialists arrived, custom[40] held that a woman is her husband's chattel once brie price is paid and so cannot own realty in her own right. In the eyes of native laws and custom she remains a legal minor, an occupier of land, a factor of production (labour implement) for her husband's farm. For this reason, she had/has to continue to provide her labour in his farm in order to ensure continuous access to her husband's land, never as an equal. As opined by Fonjong *et*

[39] FAO, *The role of women in agriculture,* ESA Working Paper No. 11-02, Agricultural Development Economics Division of FAO, of the UN, 2011.

[40] This is the totality of rules, tradition and usage practiced over a period of time by a community which is recognized as a norm of that community. It is defined in S. 18(1)(a) Customary Courts Ordinance Cap 142 of 1948 as "the native law and custom prevailing in the jurisdiction of the court so far as it is not repugnant to natural justice, equity and good conscience, nor incompatible either directly or by natural implication with any written law for the time being". Native laws have direct application to the land laws of Anglophone Cameroon which is the two regions under study by virtue of section 27 of Southern Cameroons High Court Laws so long as it is not repugnant to natural justice, equity and good conscience. Since customary laws in Cameroon is largely unwritten in Cameroon, the party relying on the custom must prove according to S. 14 of the Evidence Act Cap 62 of Nigerian Law 1958 that the custom is notorious, it has been acted by superior courts. It will be law if local persons regard the law as binding on them- S. 14(3). In the hierarchy of sources of laws in Cameroon, native laws and customs rank lowest below case law and statutes. According to s. 16(c) of the Law No. 89/19 of 29th December 1989 on judicial organisation as amended by the 2006/ 015 of 29th December 2006 on Judicial Organisation sees customary courts as a court of original jurisdiction in customary law matters. These customs continue to linger even though proscribed. See CEDAW especially in its articles 5 and 15 which Cameroon has duly ratified.

al[41] this gender discrimination is steeped in four fallacies: i) marriage fallacy which holds that a woman is a pilgrim to her natal family, her identity is with the family she will be married to. She is just passing to be married to another family and so giving her land is tantamount to carting away her natal family's estate into that of her husband's. By this take, she becomes a stranger to her father's estate and cannot be granted tenure rights over same ; ii) family name and remarriage fallacy argue that a woman should not be given tenure rights over the land her husband gives to her as upon death or divorce, she may remarry which will amount to a transfer of that land into the property of that of her new husband ; iii) Woman as chattel fallacy, a point buttressed by Ngwafor[42], who avers that once bride price is paid, a customary wife is regarded as the property of her husband[43] and as compounded by Inglis JCA's decision in *Rose Ndollo Achu v. Richard Achu*[44],"... cannot own property". It can be gleaned from this decision that not only does patriarchy have a strong hold on the law, it has tremendously enhanced the drowning of women's land ownership right; iv) levirate marriage fallacy holds that marriage is a union between two families and so upon death of her husband it was only 'logical' that she re-marry her husband's brother in order to protect the family property. This is so because, the whole idea was for her to get continued access to her husband's land and as Elias [45]contends "it is a social insurance against neglect and hunger for the deceased's dependents." In this regard therefore, there is no need for her to have tenure rights over such land. Failure to comply in such situations led to the woman loosing access to the land she had farmed all her marital life.

Rural women have always had access to land but not tenure rights which amounts to ownership. It was hoped that the colonialist, from the Germans through to the British and French, will usher in laws that will enhance her rights but as can be gleaned from the laws passed, they instead pursued laws that reduced women's land right. The German *Kronland Act* 1896 and its Policy of *herrenloss* (empty land, vacant land, *terra*

---

[41] Fonjong, L. *et al.*, *Land tenure practices and Women's Rights to Land in Anglophone Cameroon, Implications for Sustainable Development,* Canada, International Development Centre, 2013, pp. 23-26.

[42] Ngwafor, E.N., *Family Law in Anglophone Cameroon,* University of Regina Computer Services, Regina-Saskatchewan ,1993, p. 197.

[43] The levirate or widow inheritance is still a common practice in Cameroon.

[44]North West Court of Appeal Suit No. BCA/62/86 (unreported).

[45] Elias, T.O., *Nigerian Land Law, Op. cit,* p. 195.

nullius)[46]which was passed in flagrant disrespect of the Treaty of Annexation 1884[47] appropriated native lands against insignificant or no compensation. Since most lands occupied by the natives were comparatively insignificant as compared to those which were unoccupied, native land consequently went into the hands of the German imperialists.[48] By this therefore, the Germans conveniently stepped into the shoes of the natives as the land 'owners' giving the natives rights to only 1.5 hectares per hut. With this pressure of land on the community, the women felt the brunt and the amount of available land which they could access significantly reduced. The introduction of the *grundbuch* (land register) by the Germans signalled the end of communal land ownership. It was the great leap towards commoditisation, individualisation and formalisation of land ownership in Cameroon as this became the harbinger of nationalisation of land as seen in the Land Ordinance of 1974. The consequence of this is that women's access to land rested on shifting sand. The policies pursued by the British and French did nothing more to improve on native land ownership that could redress the women's land rights[49] situation.

---

46 According to Scot, This is a misleading representation of not only available rights to land but also a false supposition that such land is available for exploitation since as per the empirical facts theory, even if such lands are not effectively occupied, it does not mean that the natives do not have rights over such lands as was held in *Mabo v. Queensland No.2*. Such lands could be communal forest reserve, virgin forest where women harvest NTFPs, village hunting ground or land under fallow. See "Land and Power The Growing Scandal Surrounding the New wave of Investments in Land", *151 Oxfam Briefing Paper*, 22 September, 2011.

47 The German rule (1884-1914) in Kamerun was ushered when Nachtigal ratified the Treaty of Annexation (Protectorate Treaty) on 12th July 1884 that was signed by King Akwa on behalf Kings and chiefs of Douala and Adolf Woerrman on behalf of two German firms. The chiefs by this Treaty agreed to abandon all theirs relating to sovereignty, legislation and administration of the territory to the Germans. In return, the Germans were to respect the customary laws of the natives.

48 The natives were carted into *reservaats* (reserves) around protestant and catholic missions and their lands converted into plantation agriculture. See generally missions Clarence-Smith, W.G., "From Plantation to Peasant Production in German Cameroun," in Geschiere, P.G., & Konings, P. (eds), *Conference on Political Economy of Cameroon. Historical Perspectives,* Leiden, African Studies Center, Research Report No. 35, 1989.

49 See Generally Fonjong L., Sama-Lang, I., Fombe, L. " An Assessment of the Evolution of Land Tenure System In Cameroon and its effects on Women's Land Rights and Food Security," *Perspective on Global Development and Technology,* Vol.9, No.1-2, 2010.

4. Are the Women Tenants at sufferance? What implications?

As opined by Njoh[50], the post-colonial land laws of Cameroon are ironically bolder and less tolerant of customary entitlements and rights to land. In a bid to provide an integrated institutional framework for land tenure which was haphazard and in order to give land its true value within the context of its socio-economic agenda, the State as per sections 14 and 15 of Ordinance No. 74-1 of 6th July 1974 accordingly nationalised all land in Cameroon whether or not under occupation except state lands[51] and freehold lands[52]. It created Land Consultative Boards (S. 16 Ord. No. 74-1/74) chaired by sub prefects or district heads[53] (S. 12 Decree No. 76-166 of 27th April 1976) to assume management of all such national lands. To ensure that the nationalisation is effective it enacted in S. 1(2) of Ord. No. 74-1/74 that: "The state shall be the guardian of all lands. It may in this capacity intervene to ensure rational use of land or in the imperative interest of defence or the economic policies of the nation." To cement the nationalisation process, section 8 (2) and (3) of same penalises any form of land alienation of such unregistered lands. The implication of this on the rural woman is that since her rights are derived, she can no longer use or occupy land as before without due authorisation otherwise as provided for in section 8(5) of same, the court will order the eviction of the occupant at his[her] expense.[54] The direct application of the Maputo Protocol and the other laws that Cameroon duly ratified would have given these rural women the desired respect and protection of land rights they need in order to enhance especially their economic power amongst others.

S. 4 of Ordinance No. 74-1 of 5th July 1974, requires all customary communities that had been in effective occupation of lands now described as national land before 5th August 1974 to register all such lands within 10 years if it is located in an urban area or 15 years if in a rural area, otherwise such rights over the unregistered land shall be forfeited. Very

---

[50] Njoh, A. M., "The Political Economy of Urban Land Reforms in a Post-Colonial State", International Journal of Urban and Regional Research. 22(3) 408-424, p. 411.

[51] Though not directly defined in the land statutes of 1974, it can be gleaned from section 14 Ord No .74-1 of 6th July 1974 and section 1 of Ord. No. 74-2 of 6th July 1974, that is all land except national land or property classed into public and private property of the state and other public bodies.

[52] These are lands with registered title deeds in private hands.

[53] Taking away the control of customary lands (unregistered lands) from the control of traditional rulers.

[54] It does not cancel the fact that she may be sued as a trespasser in tort- *Conway v. George Wimpey & Co. LtD* [1951] 2 KB 266, 273. See Jones, M.A, *Torts,* Blackstone Press Limited, 1995, pp.325-326.

few customary communities to date heeded to this call for registration. It was hoped that the 1974 tenure reforms which formalised and individualised land ownership from collective/agrarian and customary state would improve the situation of women's rights from the disadvantages they had suffered from patriarchy. Though the 'new' laws are gender blind, it created room for gender neutrality and so all could own land. It however did not take into consideration the specific discrimination that women suffered for a long time as a result of patriarchy. As a result it gave room for the status quo to linger on because though the statutory laws are gender neutral, the customary laws are gender discriminatory. In such a legally pluralistic context, the laws in force are trumped. The implication of this on women is that under customary law, women have purely derivative rights which are merely rights of *usus* without more. Nationalisation of the land implies that the women are "technically dispossessed" of the land they have been farming on as the statute failed to give opportunity for such derivative users to register their land rights even if they had been there for decades. This made nonsense therefore of their long use and by extension enforcing their status as tenants at sufferance at the whims and caprices of the state.

In addition, according to section 1 (2) of Ordinance No. 74-1 of 6th July 1974, the state assumed guardianship of all national land (unregistered land which whether or not registered) and reserved the right to use such land in tandem with its socio-economic- political agenda. The state's policy of Second Generation Agriculture as contained in the Growth and Poverty Reduction Strategy Paper: Vision 2035 needs large expands of land over which to carry out large scale mechanised agriculture. To be able to do this, some of the land which these women have been using may be withdrawn from them by the state for reallocation[55] to either rich multinationals, the state itself or local elites as investors[56]. Majority of the land which these

[55] See sections 4-11 of Decree No. 76-166 to establish terms and conditions of management of national lands.

[56] As Mope pointed out, clientelism has fuelled the syphoning of lands that are in the hands of customary communities. Mope, S., "Challenges to Chieftaincy Today: Governance issues and How Fons Strategise to overcome the Obstacles of Overarching Structures in the eastern Grassfield", in Tamanjong (ed), *Les Mutations en Afrique*, Yaounde, Presse d'CAC, pp. 159-193. As observed by Fonjong, *et al.*, "the interchange of favours and support between the government and chiefs has created a new type of chief whose pursuit of wealth and political power has relegated the respect of customs and community interest to third place" Fonjong, *et al.*, *Large-Scale Land acquisition: Implications for Women's land rights in Cameroon*, Canada, International Development Research Centre, 2016, p. 97.

women have access over fall under national land and so once such grants are made, these women can no longer have access to such land either for Non Timber Forest Product (NTFP) or for farming otherwise they will be trespassing on the land, confirming indeed the position that these women were/are tenants at sufferance. A recent study by Fonjong *et al*[57] confirms this situation of the women, as the research revealed that land matters are not women matters and for that reason they are rarely consulted before the lands or commons which they have been exploiting are expropriated or granted to investors. If they had strong rights, no such deals would have been concretised without their voices being heard.

The situation becomes more worrisome when such land is expropriated[58] or leased out as explained above. The compensation paid is not for the land *per se* since the state does not consider the women as owners but mere users, tenants at sufferance who have outlived their stay over national land with the coming into force of the 1974. To confirm this, payments are made only over economic development (houses, farm products, etc) on the land and not for the land itself since the state is seen in this light as the land owner. The men are seen as the over lords over such unregistered land and not the women and for this reason, they receive the compensation to the chagrin of the women who have been farming the land[59]. Even where these women receive compensation, they receive as derivative users and not in their own right, forgetting the fact that it is the woman who loses access to her land and rights over her crops or commons forever.[60]

Although the state gave a window for registration of land by those who had been on the land before 5th July 1974, the women could not register as they were mere users of the land. The men were/are the over lords and so any attempts to register the land in the women's name could have met with stiff resistance by the men[61], even though section 9 (a) of Decree No.

---

[57] Fonjong, *et al., Large-Scale Land acquisition: Implications for Women's land rights in Cameroon,* Canada, International Development Research Centre, 2016, p. 75-78.

[58] See Law No. 85/09 of 4/7/1985 to lay down the procedure governing expropriation for public purpose and the conditions for compensation.

[59] See Fonjong, *et al., Large-Scale Land Acquisition: Implications for Women's land Rights in Cameroon,* Canada, International Development Research Centre, 2016, pp. 114-115.

[60] *Ibid.*

[61] Land is regarded the world over as a symbol of male domination as such, any challenge to this is translated into a challenge to patriarchal control and hence the stiff resistance often met. In Africa, this challenge is often styled as undue western influence and a challenge to tradition. See Palmer. R., "Gender Land Rights –Process, Struggle, Or Lost C(L)Ause?", Robin Palmer Land Policy Adviser, Oxfam, 28 November 2008.

76/165 of 27th April 1976[62] gives rights to members of customary communities whose exploitation pre-dates 5th August 1974 to apply for land certificate over such lands. Besides, even if the women could, they lack time and economic power to follow the cumbersome, time consuming procedure[63] which usually takes over six months notwithstanding the revised statutory laws.

By making registration open for customary communities and members thereof to register their rights as provided for in section 9(a), a big lapse is created which some bureaucrats and state elites have taken advantage of to register such family lands in their names (instead of that of the family) which they use for cattle raring or large scale farming, thereby ousting the women from the land leaving them in bewilderment.[64]

After nationalisation of the land and withdrawing land administration from the hands of the traditional rulers, the state has not directly issued any quit notice to any of these customary communities and by extension the women. Section 17 (2) Ordinance No. 74-1 of 6th July 1974 calls on customary communities whose exploitation and occupation of the land pre-dates 6th August 1974, to continue enjoying their user rights. This indeed is the true picture of tenancy at sufferance for although the state who is the land lord recognises that their land right long expired in 1989, the women continue to occupy just like every tenant at sufferance because no 'quit notice' has been served them as such.

Cameroon has affirmed in the preamble of its 1996 Constitution that everyone possesses inalienable rights and is equal irrespective of creed, sex, ethnicity, etc. It further guarantees and protects ownership rights by stating that 'ownership shall mean the right guaranteed every person by law to use, enjoy and dispose of property. No person shall be deprived thereof, save for public purpose and subject to the payment of compensation under conditions determined by law.' Could the state then be seen to have withdrawn same? Even if it were so, Cameroon's obligations in international law makes the *grundnorm* subordinate laws by

---

[62] To establish conditions for Obtaining Land Certificates as amended and supplemented by Decree No. 2005/048 of 16th December 2005.

[63] See generally on this Fonjong, *et al.*, *Land Tenure Practices and Women's Rights to Land in Anglophone Cameroon: Implications For sustainable Development*, Canada, International Development Research Centre, 2013, pp. 29-30.

[64] See Mope, S., "Land grabbing, Governance and Social Peace Building Issues in Cameroon: case Study of The Roles of Elites in Land Deals and Commoditization in the North West Region. "Paper presented at the International Conference on Global Land Grabbing, 6-8 April 2011.

virtue of article 45 of the 1996 constitution. In this regard therefore, it has the triple pronged obligation[65] to respect human right to own land by refraining from interfering with or curtailing women's enjoyment of their land rights; the obligation to protect which enjoins the state to protect women's land rights against abuses and the obligation to fulfil which obligates the state to facilitate women's enjoyment of land rights by taking positive actions in that respect. Much still needs to be done in this regard notwithstanding the duly ratified international laws. Until then, it may not be wrong to liken the rural woman's rights over land as akin to that of a tenant at sufferance.

As opined by Jayne[66] restrained access to land limits the ability of landless groups of which women are top of the list to graduate from poverty through agricultural productivity growth, which is their mainstay. Achieving equitable access to land is central and an integral part to the protection and enforcement of land rights as without these, these women will never be able to positively defend their claims over land and positively engage and defend themselves in any land disputes.[67]

Conclusion

Land is regarded the world over as a symbol of male domination and as such, any challenge to this is translated into a challenge to patriarchal control and hence the stiff resistance often met. In Africa, this challenge is often styled as undue western influence and a challenge to tradition.

Although the 1974 land reform gave political stability to the state it completely killed the hopes of customary women the majority of whom hitherto had access to land. Although the 1974 reforms were crucial for social transformation which could only be possible with the state playing a central role in land ownership and management, the benefits of this, be

---

[65] Shue, H., *Basic Rights: Subsistence, Affluence, and U.S Foreign Policy,* 2nd edition, Princeton, Princeton University Press, 1996, pp. 52-53; Pogge, T., "Are we Violating the Human Rights of the World's Poor ?", *Yale Human Rights and Development Law Journal,* 14, 2011, 1-33, p.5-6. See also Universal Declaration of Human Rights, Foundation of International Human Rights law, UN https://www.un.org>sections accessed 29th on September 2019.

[66] Jayne. T. *et al.*, "Access to Land and Poverty reduction in Rural Zambia: connecting the Policy issues". Working Paper No. 34, Food security Research Prospect, Lusaka, Zambia, 2002.

[67] Eno. C., "Indigenous acquisition of surrender lands by the Cameroon Development Corporation and livelihood of in-migrants of Fako Division South West Region Cameroon," UnPublished PhD thesis, University of Buea, August 2019, p.31.

that as it may, have adverse implications for women in terms of access to and ownership of land, thereby leaving them as true tenants at sufferance. As the question begs for answer whether women's land rights should be a bother in the face of increasing population, urbanization, technological advancement and of women empowerment? Palmer[68]opines that since land is an economic resource, access to land and/or ownership will foster the bargaining power of women in the domestic arena and create room for security of other socio-economic rights apart from providing food security and nutrition for her family. Her status as a "tenant at sufferance" will deny her this right and the opportunity to use the land as collateral for much needed money which customary/rural women need for farming. In addition, since the land is not hers, she will not bother to care for the land but will want to maximise the use of it not minding the environmental effect.

By not recognising long use over the land as being equivalent to ownership right, mindful of the disadvantage women suffered from patriarchy, the 1974 Land laws failed to give women justice but instead took away some of the rights they had under custom.

The voices of women need to be heard in land administration of Cameroon. Apart from the non-negotiable need for accountability in local land governance as opined by Ribot[69], there is need for networking amongst the different women's group and Non- Governmental Organisations in order to mount the necessary pressure for the desired change of the 1974 laws which are the basic laws on land and in addition to the enforcement of the duly ratified international laws. If rural women are to be taken from the shackles of poverty, their status as "tenant at sufferance" must be redressed by giving some statutory recognition over long use of land.

---

68 Palmer, R., "Working on Land for Oxfam, 1997-2007 or Last Rites for Land Rights", Extracts from a farewell talk by Robin Palmer, Oxfam GB Global Land Adviser.

69 Ribot, J., *Democratic, Decentralisation of Natural Resources: Institutionalising Popular Participation,* Washington DC, World Resource Institute, 2002.

Traditional authorities and land conflict resolution in Nso, Cameroon: A historical appraisal

By

Emile Sunjo

Senior Lecturer of International Relations and Resource Conflicts,
Department of International Relations and Conflict Resolution,
University of Buea, Cameroon
Email: emile.sunjo@ubuea.cm

Abstract

Traditional authorities played an unquestionable role in the management of land and resolution of conflicts that arose from its communal ownership and use in pre-colonial Africa. Nowhere was this role felt more in what is today known as Cameroon than in the grassfields fondoms of the North West region. Using the specific case study of Nso, Bui Division, and based on four interviews and documentary sources, the paper makes a historical appraisal of the factors that drove land related conflicts in the pre-colonial and immediate post-colonial periods. It argues that conflicts over land were caused by the constant rise in the value of land, population pressure, inheritance related struggles, farmer-grazier disputes and the illicit sale of land. Using an array of methods, traditional authorities with the Fon of Nso at the helm managed and resolved many of these conflicts. The paper argues that despite significant challenges like the lack of cooperation from the Mbororos, limited resources and no recorded evidence to make concrete ownership decisions, the traditional authorities did a reasonably good job. This is more glaring especially when we compare with what the civil administrators have been doing in post 1974 era when a new land tenure ordinance all but dislodged the traditional authorities from the process. The paper concludes that in order to reduce the frequency of land related conflicts in Nso and Cameroon in general, traditional authorities should be given a more prominent role.

Keywords: Traditional authorities, land, conflict, land conflict, Nso, Cameroon

Introduction

The role that land plays in the socio-economic development of any society is unquestionable. Land ownership guarantees a sense of security especially in contexts where formal employment and access to other resources are limited. Land resources continue to have major historical, cultural and spiritual significance.[1] The history of Africa is riddled with land dispossession and contestation and has produced a lopsided distribution of land ownership. This has made land to be a primary subject of exploitation, expropriation, conquest and conflict.[2] The result of this is that across Africa, the question of land ownership remains a contentious one especially exacerbated by the arbitrary lines of demarcation drawn by the European colonizers.[3] The nature of land conflicts is a complex one and ranges from inter-personal, through inter-communal to inter-state disputes over ownership of land.[4]

Prior to the annexation by the Germans in 1884, all land in present day Cameroon was communal and was managed by *landlords* designated by the relevant traditional ruler. Once the colonial administration had a foothold into the hinterlands, it began altering the existing customs regarding land ownership and this created disputes and conflicts. The core issue surrounding land in Cameroon is the legal reality that most rural inhabitants are little more than squatters on their own land, with regard to the forests and other land assets which by custom they have logically held in undivided shares ('common properties').[5] The other problem is that while population growth is steady, and with it an increase in the demand

---

1 Odgaard, R. (2006) "Land rights and land conflicts in Africa: The Tanzania case", Copenhagen, Danish Institute for International Studies; Goheen, M. (1988) "Land accumulation and local control: The manipulation of symbols and power in Nso, Cameroon", *African Studies Centre*; Goheen, M. (1992) "Chiefs, sub chiefs and local control: negotiations over land, struggles over meaning", *Africa*, *62*(3), 389-412.

2 Page, B & Sunjo, E (forthcoming) "Land and political settlements: the case of the Bakweri in Fako, Cameroon".

3 Yamano, T. (2005) "Land conflicts in Kenya: causes, impacts, and resolutions", Foundation for Advanced Studies on International Development / National Graduate Institute for Policy Studies FASID Discussion Paper 2005-12-002.

4 Jahun, S. & Bauchi Emirate, Nigeria (2015) "The roles and the challenges of traditional rulers in land conflict resolution and management in Nigeria: a case study of Bauchi State, Nigeria", FIG Working Week 2015.

5 Wily, L. (2011) "Whose land is it: the status of customary land tenure in Cameroon", *Centre for Environment and Development*, Yaoundé

for the land which is stagnant. This demand and an uncertain land tenure system in this mostly rural environment breed conflict.[6]

These conflicts have been compounded by the inability of post-colonial administrative and judicial institutions to find lasting solutions. In pre-colonial and immediate post-independence Cameroon, land management was largely based on customary laws and practices with the various traditional authorities as the custodians of these lands. Official regulations governing land were first introduced by the Germans.[7] In the pre-colonial era, land ownership in Nso was communal with the *Fon* as the custodian. The *fon* in turn devolved these land rights to *landlords* (*Ataangwen*) who managed it on his behalf. In pre-colonial Nso, like in most of Cameroon, land was used principally for subsistence agriculture and settlement construction. Once a parcel of land had been given out to particular family, it remained within that family and was inherited by subsequent generations.[8] Considering that the *fon* was the custodian of the land and the people generally respected his authority, few problems usually arose from land ownership. However, the few cases of land conflict were handled by the traditional council set up by the *fon*. When the British took over the administration of the Cameroons after the defeat of the Germans in World War One in 1916, they introduced a policy of indirect rule. This policy further empowered traditional institutions in the administration of their peoples and lands under the supervision of the British.[9]

The British later decided to apply the land laws of the Southern Province of Nigeria. The Land Natives Rights' Ordinance recognized and safeguarded land occupation in accordance with Native Laws and Customs. Therefore, the rights to manage conflicts over land and in other domains remained largely in the hands of the traditional authorities under the auspices of the *fon* as stipulated in the Land Registration Ordinance passed in 1924. The *fon's* role in land conflict management continued into the immediate post-colonial period.[10] It should be noted that soil fertility

---

[6] Shipton, P. & Goheen, M. (1992) "Introduction. Understanding African land-holding: power, wealth, and meaning", *Africa, 62*(3), 307-325

[7] Menjo F. (2008) "Changing land tenure arrangements and access to primary assets under globalization: a case study of two villages in anglophone Cameroon", *African Development Review, 20*(1), 135-162.

[8] Goheen, M. (1996) *Men own the fields, women own the crops: Gender and power in the Cameroon grassfields,* Wisconsin: University of Wisconsin Press.

[9] Chilver, E. & Kaberry, P. (1967) *Traditional Bamenda: The Pre-colonial History and Ethnography of the Bamenda Grassfields,* Volume 1, London.

[10] Geschiere, P. (1993) "Chiefs and colonial rule in Cameroon: Inventing chieftaincy, French and British style", *Africa, 63*(2), 151-175.

and its suitability for agriculture and settlement had attracted so many non-indigenous people like the Mbororos, Nigerians and others within and without Bamenda during the period from 1922-1974.[11] Such influx of people put pressure on arable and settlement land and the consequence was an increase in land use conflicts. These were largely in the form of farmer-grazer disputes, opposing ownership claims and boundary conflicts.

In 1974, a new Land Ordinance established rules governing land tenure in Cameroon, expropriation procedures for public purposes and the terms of compensation. It stripped the customary legal system of any significant role and civil administrators were given overwhelming powers in managing land conflicts. One would have expected that these administrators would provide lasting solutions to land conflicts. However, there has been a high frequency of re-occurrence. Land conflicts like any other conflict, do not disappear simply through a diktat by a civil administrator. In fact, there has instead been a multiplication of land conflicts since 1974 which raises questions as to the effective role played by civil administrators in resolving the conflicts.

The paper uses a qualitative research strategy to examine the historical role of traditional rulers in land conflict management and resolution in the Nso Fondom of the North West region of Cameroon. It argues that the adoption of the 1974 Land Ordinance ushered in a new post-colonial land tenure system in Cameroon which drastically changed the main actors involved in handling land disputes. The choice of Nso for the paper was a deliberate one. Nso is one of the most highly centralised fondoms in the Grassfields of Cameroon with a highly respected traditional authority. Paradoxically, Nso has witnessed many land conflicts since the 1974 Land Ordinance which was aimed at instilling order in the sector. Nso is the largest chieftaincy in the Western Grassfields of Cameroon[12] and a tribe located in the north east of the North West region. Nso *fondom* approximately corresponds to the administrative area called Bui Division and its ruler is respected both by his people and acknowledged by the government of Cameroon with the status of a first-class chief.[13] There are other *fons* who generally act as advisers to the fon of Nso. Most of them

[11]Kaberry, P. (1959) "Some problems of land tenure in Nsaw, Southern Cameroons", *Journal of African Administration,* 11(1), 21–28; Chilver, E. & Kaberry, P. (1967), *ibid.*

[12]Goheen, M. (1988) "Land accumulation and local control: The manipulation of symbols and power in Nso, Cameroon", *African Studies Centre.*

[13] See decree No. 77/245 of 15 July 1977 governing the organization of traditional chiefdoms in Cameroon.

were once leaders of independent tribes but through warfare or peaceful negotiations; or through shared historical events, came to subordinate the *fon* of Nso.[14]

The paper is divided into three parts. The first part analyses the causes of land-related conflicts in Nso. The second part looks at the structure and changing role of traditional rulers in land conflicts, while the third examines the challenges traditional rulers face in managing and resolving land conflicts in Nso. The paper then draws conclusions from the analysis and proffers a way forward.

1. Causes of land conflicts in Nso

There have been land related conflicts in Nso even in the pre-colonial period. However, the colonial and post-colonial periods have seen an exponential increase in these conflicts. A number of factors account for the occurrence of land conflicts in Nso. These include: the rise in the value of land, population pressure, evolving land tenure system, inheritance disputes, questionable land deals as well as farmer-herder confrontations.

1.1. Exponential rise in the value of land

The value of land in Nso has risen over the years in dramatic fashion as the population has increased. The primary reason for settling in this area was to ensure security from external attacks, for agriculture and for human settlement.[15] The pressure on the land kept increasing as it remained a primary economic asset for the local population. The German victory on Nso in 1906 set the pace for changes that invariably pushed up the value of land. The arrival of the British administration saw an expansion of colonial administrative further raised the value of land especially in the three main urban settlements of Tobin, Mbveh, Shisong and Kimbo (where the fon's palace is located).[16] The primary factor driving the value of land in Nso generally and Kumbo in particular was the need for construction purposes as urbanization was steadily occurring. This demand further increased in 1966 with the creation of Kumbo sub-division. There were many new administrative services set up, an influx of civil servants and a corresponding hike in the demand for settlement

[14]Goheen, M. (1992), *ibid.*
[15]Suiven, JP & Asonsaigha, R (2011) "Conflicting Land uses within the Kumbo Urban Space, North West Region, Cameroon", *African Journal of Social Sciences* Vol. 2, No. 2, July 2011.
[16]Shey Roland, 67 years of age title holder.

land.[17] Land which used to be considered communal property was soon parceled up and the commodification and commercialization process further created tension among different land users.

The high economic value that was suddenly placed on land increased the desire for the rich and powerful to grab land.[18] Gray and Kevane[19]contend that this has led to poor families being driven out of land that had historically been under their custodianship and used for subsistence agriculture. The result is an array of conflicts between families and richer land grabbers. The struggle over land is a contentious one throughout Cameroon but particularly so in the northwest region where social status and wealth are usually measured by how much land one is able to amass.[20]

1.2. Population pressure

The surge in land-related conflicts in Nso can also directly be traced to the population growth and composition. Literature on land conflicts everywhere holds that increasing demographic pressure produces negative impacts on scarce natural resources, with land being the primary one.[21] The population explosion means that land for residential purposes is crucial. There are new housing projects everywhere in the newly designated settlement areas like Bambui, while land is virtually used up in older urban spaces of Tobin, Kimbo, Mbveh and Shisong.[22] Despite the paucity of accurate data on population trends over time, it is a given that there has been a steady increase in the population especially in the post-colonial era. In addition to hosting administrative services, Kumbo, also

---

[17]Goheen, M. (1988), *ibid.*

[18] Gray, L. & Kevane M. (1999) "Diminished access, diverted exclusion: Women and land tenure in Sub-Saharan Africa", *African Studies Review*, 42 (2), pp. 15–39.

[19] *Ibid.*

[20] Sakah, L. (2009) "Gender conflicts and natural resources on the Kumbo Plateau, North West Regions of Cameroon", A paper presented in a post-graduate seminar on Conflict prevention, management and resolution, University of Buea.

[21] Le Meur, P. Y. et al (2006) "Conflict over Access to Land and Water Resources within Sub-Saharan Dry Lands: Underlying factors, conflict dynamics and settlement processes", *GRET-FAO LEAD Final Report*; Moyo, S (2008) *African land questions, the state, and agrarian transition: Contradictions of neo-liberal land reforms*, Dakar, CODESRIA; Moyo, S. et al. (2000) "Land reform and changing social relations for farm workers in Zimbabwe", *Review of African Political Economy*, 27 (84), pp. 181–202; Njeuma, M. & Awasom N. (1990) "The Fulani and the political economy of the Bamenda grasslands: Opportunity and conflict, 1940–1960", *Paideuma*, 36, pp.217–233; Yanou, M. (2009) *Access to land in post-apartheid South Africa: An African perspective*, Bamenda, Langaa Books.

[22]Suiven, JP. & Asonsaigha, R. (2011), *op.cit.*

has a number of religious organisations such as churches, schools and hospitals which have attracted new settlers. The population grew from 45,914 inhabitants in 1953 to 50, 0000 in 1959 and 56,243 in 1971. The last official population and housing census of 2005 put the population of Kumbo town alone at 127,538.[23] This represents a growth rate of about 7.05% from the figures in 1970s. Current estimates put the population at 200,000 inhabitants. The growth in the numbers and increasing diversity in the population increased the propensity for conflict and competing claims for the same piece of land became commonplace. Many non-indigenes who settle in Nso sooner or later, often want to acquire plots of land for building purposes. Given that the surge in the population was not accompanied by a corresponding increase in land supply due to its fixed nature, the result was a dramatic rise in conflicts over land ownership. The pressure on land due to population growth has not only been limited to the main urban centres, but also in villages within the urban fringe like Njavnyuy, Ndzen Njii, Kikaikom, Kikaikelaki, Kitiwum, Meluf, Kai and Melim.

1.3. The evolving land tenure system

In Cameroon like in other parts of Africa, the land tenure systems have witnessed several changes which invariably lead to competing claims for land ownership.[24] Prior to colonial rule, land tenure was based on customary law in Nso with the *fon* as the custodian of all lands. The *fon* and his traditional council, landlords, village heads and the *nwerong* (a powerful cult for men in Nso society) made all decisions regarding land with the understanding that they were simply custodians as all land was said to be communally owned.[25] The authority and legitimacy of the customary institutions in land affairs was unquestionable and land wasn't seen as a commodity. All non-indigenes and missionaries who needed land for settlement were simply required to provide a token to the local landlord in appreciation for the gift of nature. There were inherent lapses in this system since the land allocations were not registered. There were cases where the

---

23 *Ibid.*

24 Le Meur, P. Y. et al (2006), *op.cit.*

25 Goheen, M. (1996) *Men own the fields, women own the crops: Gender and power in the Cameroon grassfields*, Madison: University of Wisconsin Press.

same piece of land would be allocated to different parties and this would result in dispute.[26]

These customary practices were gradually phased out during colonial rule. The British through their indirect rule in Anglophone Cameroon did reserve significant control of land policy in the hands of traditional authorities. Through the West Cameroon Land and Native Rights Ordinance, the British recognised the rights of communities to land ownership with the traditional ruler as the trustee of all land within his area of jurisdiction. Some colonial officials and missionaries however regarded the land tenure systems in Africa as 'primitive and in need of change'.[27] The key decisions which completely altered the land tenure system happened in the post-colonial era: the 1974 Land Ordinance 74-1 and 74-2, which still dominate the current laws in Cameroon. These new laws unified the land tenure regimes of the two former colonial trusteeships which had morphed into the two federal states (East Cameroon and West Cameroon) between 1960/61 and 1972.[28] Like many similar pieces of legislation across Africa at the time they significantly strengthened state power over land.[29] This was justified by casting doubt over the development potential of communal land tenure. In short, the state claimed ownership of all unoccupied land and all unregistered land (whether occupied or not). Land was divided into four main categories: Public Land, Private Land, State Land and National Land. Traditional rulers were recognized only as custodians not as owners of land. The law also established the bureaucratic system by which individuals could acquire a plot of land from the government with an accompanying land certificate.[30]

The new land tenure system brought representatives of the central government: senior divisional officers (SDOs) and divisional officers (DOs) into the spotlight as they were now responsible for setting and

---

[26] Menjo Baye, F. (2008) "Changing land tenure arrangements and access to primary assets under globalization: A case study of two villages in anglophone Cameroo", *African Development Review*, *20*(1), 135-162.

[27] Peters, P. (2013) "Conflicts over land and threats to customary tenure in Africa", *African Affairs*, Volume 112, Issue 449, October 2013, Pages 543–562, https://doi.org/10.1093/afraf/adt047

[28] Javelle, AG. "Land registration in Cameroon" http://www.focusonland.com/fola/en/countries/brief-land-registration-in-cameroon/_(25 November 2019)

[29] Njoh, J. (2000) "Continuity and change in Cameroonian land policy", *Planning Perspectives*, 15, 3, pp. 241-265.

[30] Javelle AG "Land Registration in Cameroon", *op.cit.*

chairing divisional Land Consultative Boards. This board plays an important role in the settlement of land disputes. Many people however don't trust these government appointees in handling their land matters, and have been described as 'over-zealous and corrupt.'[31] These administrators became influential in land matters which had been obtained through customary land arrangements. The consequence was a backlog of land disputes which the administrators simply didn't have the competence to examine. The new land tenure system didn't also completely erase the customary means of acquiring land. Consequently, while there was a codified legal system for redressing land disputes in Nso, the acquisition process remained largely customary as many people never bothered to procure land certificates either on previously occupied land or land obtained in the post 1974 period.[32]

The land reforms clearly resulted in competing land tenure systems. While the Nso traditional authorities and institutions continued to allocate land and address conflicts over it following customary law, government officials did so through regulations derived from the 1974 Ordinance. This situation of dual rules and institutions caused confusion rather than clarify and streamline the land acquisition and ownership process. Anecdotal evidence suggests that from 1974, parties in land conflicts usually moved from customary to statutory land administration institutions to overturn unfavourable decisions. This ambiguity and uncertainty in the land acquisition process benefitted the most powerful to further their land-related interests in Nso to the detriment of the most vulnerable in society.[33]

1.4. Inheritance-related causes of land conflicts

Land conflicts in Nso have also been caused by factors relating to inheritance and succession rights. This usually occurs mostly in families with opposing claims over land that had been acquired by a deceased relative. Inheritance in Nso is based on the patrilineal succession system that has been practised for centuries.[34] Male children are expected to inherit land from their parents, brothers and other extended family

---

[31] Tohnji, W. (2006) "Chiefs (traditional rulers) in Anglophone Cameroon and modern governance 1961–2000", PhD thesis (unpublished).

[32] Fisiy, C. (1997) "State dislocation of customary management systems: Land colonization on the slopes of Mount Oku, North-West Province of Cameroon", *Law and Anthropology*, *9*, 124-145.

[33] Goheen, M. (1996), *op.cit.*

[34] Nzalie, J. (2011) *The law on succession to property in Anglophone Cameroon*, Yaoundé, ARIKA.

members.[35] The rise in the value of land earlier discussed together with other factors has made this inheritance system to be a source of conflicts over land in Nso. This is because there are always many relatives waiting on the side-lines to inherit the same piece of land. This is common especially in cases where a deceased father leaves behind many sons who all have a legitimate claim to inherit his land.

These competing claims over inheritance rights persist even in situations where there is a customary process of allocating the land to a specific son considered the heir to their late father. In many families and villages in Nso, family heads, village heads and other traditional authorities controlled vast expanses of lands which were handed over to succeeding generations through oral wills.[36] While this process was scrupulously respected in the pre-colonial and early colonial periods, it has become fraught with competing claims in the post-colonial era as the value of land has skyrocketed while the supply of land has remained fixed. This together with factors discussed earlier, has broadened the scope for inheritance-related conflicts over land to occur. Many families have been dragged into land conflicts and potential male successors struggle to position themselves to be in a favourable position to acquire and exploit inherited land. Potential successors thus engage in different manoeuvring techniques to tilt the system to their favour. The outcome is usually the twisting and subverting of existing inheritance rules which increases the propensity for conflicts over succession within families. There are currently many family lands at the centre of disputes in Nso as a result of such inheritance claims.

1.1. Questionable land deals

The commodification and commercialisation of land has engendered many dubious land sales which often result in conflict. As earlier explained, land was a communal property in the pre-colonial era and its transfer from one user to another did not attract any monetary compensation. The situation gradually changed with the introduction of a monetary economy and increased pressure on land as discussed above. By the end of the colonial period in 1961, land had become a key economic asset and a source of finance for those who had access to and control over

[35] Paul Lukong, 80 years old Nso elder.

[36] Nzalie J (2008) "The structure of succession law in Cameroon: finding a balance between the needs and interests of different family members", Unpublished PhD thesis, University of Birmingham.

it.[37] The economic crisis that hit Cameroon and other African countries in the 1980s provided a fertile environment for land sales by landowners who had been affected by a drop in cash crops such as coffee. Many persons who held family and community lands in trust took advantage of this and illegally sold these lands. Such conditions produced conflicts especially when these land deals were done without the consent and approval of relevant family or community members. Once families discover the transaction, they battle to recover their family lands while those who bought them equally fight to retain their new properties.

In many cases, such lands are even sold to multiple buyers. It has been argued that most of these multiple sales are done by family heads in villages such as Yungkui (Meluf) and Kingomen.[38] Some individuals also position themselves as middlemen in land transactions and entice custodians of family lands and landowners to sell their lands through them. Once the transaction is completed, these opportunistic individuals disappear while their client is left reeling from the raging conflict over the authenticity of the land transaction. These opaque land deals have often created boundary disputes because the sales usually do not involve the neighbours in the negotiation to properly demarcate the boundaries. This thus puts the new owners at loggerheads with the neighbours who contest the boundaries and claim that the new owner has encroached into their plots. The situation is compounded by the fact that boundaries lines are hardly drawn by surveyors. Instead, inhabitants have over the centuries based their boundary lines on specific geographical features, oral history and on trust and good faith which explained the communal nature of pre-colonial Nso culture.[39]

1.5. Farmer-grazier disputes

Farmer-grazier disputes are a major cause of land and other natural resource conflict not just in Nso but in the wider northwest region of Cameroon.[40] Their continued occurrence results in human insecurity, food

---

[37] See Page, B & Sunjo, E (forthcoming) for an extensive discussion of this; see also Nnoko-Mewanu, J. (2016) "Who is not at the table: Land deal negotiations in Southwestern Cameroon", Unpublished PhD thesis, Iowa State University.

[38] Suiven, JP & Asonsaigha, R (2011), *op.cit.*

[39] For more on oral history in Nso, see Chem-Langhëë, B & Fanso, V (1997) "Social categories, local politics and the uses of oral tradition in Nso, Cameroon", *Paideuma*, 43, 313-327.

[40] Nnoko-Mewanu, J. (2018) "Farmer-herder conflicts on the rise in Africa", *Inter Press Service (IPS) News Agency* Retrieved from https://www.hrw.org/news/2018/08/06/farmer-herder-conflicts-rise-africa

shortages and environmental challenges.[41] The phenomenon of farmer-grazier conflicts in Nso is often caused by the growth in cattle and human population, unregulated urbanisation, increased commercial and agro-pastoral activities as well as sensitisation and enforcement of conservation projects.[42] While farming has been the mainstay of the local population for centuries, pastoralism in this area is traceable to the migration and settlement of Fulani pastoralists around 1950.[43] The first set of Fulanis settled in villages such as Tan (Jakiri) and Mbiame. British colonial agro-pastoral policy in Southern Cameroons aimed at bringing in more Fulanis pastoralists because they paid cattle tax and also provided meat and milk.[44] This policy of accommodation led to a growth in cattle population from 10,000 in 1922 to 91,782 in 1940.[45] These were mostly the Aku who came into the area with the highly productive and disease-resistant white zebu cattle from Nigeria. The crackdown on the Union des Populations du Cameroun (UPC) in French Cameroun also caused a rapid entry of cattle herders into Nso from present-day West region of Cameroon in the 1950s.[46] Their arrival marked the beginning of an unprecedented encounter between indigenous farmers and Fulani pastoralists.

The growth in livestock population led to a rise in crop damage by the cattle and thus a surge in farmer-grazier conflicts. Mbih argues that the failure of the post-colonial state to address this issue between the 1960s and 1980s made the situation dire.[47] The situation was further compounded by the droughts of the 1970s and 1980s[48] and the economic

---

[41] Mbih, R. (2020) "The politics of farmer–herder conflicts and alternative conflict management in Northwest Cameroon", *African Geographical Review*, 1-21, DOI:10.1080/19376812.2020.1720755

[42] Mbih, R. (2015) "Agro-pastoral landuse transformation: Implications and perspectives in the Norwest region of Cameroon", (Unpublished dissertation), University of Missouri-Kansas City.

[43] Boutrais, J. (1995) *Haut terres d'elevage au Cameroun*, Paris: ORSTOM.

[44] Blench, R. (2010) "Conflict between pastoralists and cultivators in Nigeria", Review paper prepared for DFID. Nigeria. Retrieved from http://www.rogerblench.info/Development/Nigeria/Pastoralism/Fadama%20II%20paper.pdf.

[45] Njeuma, M., & Awasom, N. (1990) "Fulani and the political economy of the Bamenda grassfields, 1940–1960", *Paideuma*, 36, 217–233.

[46] Terretta, M (2013) *Nation of Outlaws, State of Violence: nationalism, grassfields tradition, and state building in Cameroon*, Ohio: Ohio University Press.

[47] Mbih, R. (2020), *op.cit.*

[48] Pelican, M. (2006) *Getting along in the Grassfields: Interethnic relations and identity politics in northwest Cameroon.* Halle, Saale: Universitäts-und Landesbibliothek Sachsen-Anhalt; Pelican, M. (2008) "Mbororo claims to regional citizenship and minority status in North-West Cameroon", *Africa, 78*(4), 540-560.

crisis in Cameroon that led to the imposition of privatisation and liberalisation as part of the Structural Adjustment Program. Many people who lost their jobs saw agro-pastoralism as an alternative means of livelihood also piled up more pressure on already diminishing land for these purposes, leading to a spike in conflicts. Many villages such as Berlem, Meluf, Kov-Ndzeen, Nkuv, Ngongba, Kingomen, Simonkov–Tadu, Tan and Wvem which host both Fulani pastoralists have thus been dragged into a vicious cycle of farmer-grazier conflicts.

2. The structure and methods used by traditional institutions in land conflicts in Nso

2.1. The structure of traditional institutions in Nso

Following the 1974 reforms on land ownership in Cameroon which greatly curtailed the role of traditional rulers in land governance was decree No. 77/245 of 15 July 1977 governing the organization of traditional chiefdoms.[49] As earlier discussed, land was communally owned and held in trust by traditional authorities at the helm of which was the *fon.* In his capacity as an institution of governance, the *fon* had regulatory powers over land.[50] He controlled all the major lands and also settled major land conflicts within and without his *fondom.* For instance, the demarcation of farming-grazing lands, mission lands and lands for government structures were all done by the *fon.* Prior to settling in Nso, a newcomer had to request and obtain permission from the fon before formally approaching any of the landlords (*Ataagwen*).[51]

Directly below the *fon* was the Council of the Seven notables known as the *Vibais.* This council plays an advisory role to the *fon* on land and other matters. These *Vibais* are *Shufais* or clan heads, whose membership in the advisory council has a complex ancestry. They include *Shufai* Ndzendzev, Tahnkum, Doh, Doh, Run, Tsenla, Lun and Yuwar. It should be noted that over the years and at the discretion of the *fon*, some *shufais* have been appointed with the caveat that they do not become members of the advisory council.[52] They equally advise the *Nwerong* society on land

[49]CRTV (2018) "Creation of traditional chiefdoms: Minister of Territorial Administration outlines procedure". Retrieved on 29/05/2020 from http://www.crtv.cm/2018/06/creation-of-traditional-chiefdoms-minister-of-territorial-administration-outlines-procedure/

[50] Kaberry, P. (2005) *Women of Grassfields*. Routledge.

[51] Chem-Langhëë, B., & Fanso, V. G. (1997), *op.cit.*

[52] Fisiy, C., & Goheen, M. (1998) "Power and the quest for recognition: neo-traditional titles among the new elite in Nso', Cameroon", *Africa*, *68*(3), 383-402.

conflicts matters, promoting the use of pacific rather than antagonistic means of arriving at a consensus. The *Nwerong* is the next structure charged with land conflict issues. Although the primary responsibility of this society is to regulate and balance *the fon's* powers, it is also the main security arm of Nso culture and enforces decisions taken by the *fon.*[53] Membership into this society is reserved for males from primarily one social category: the nsheelav (retainers or palace attendants). Together with the *fon*, the *vibais* and the landlords (*Ataagwen), nwerong* fully resolved land conflicts in Nso. The British colonial government through the Native Authority Ordinance recognized and promoted the functioning of these institutions in Nso. The 1974 ordinance on land tenure and the 1977 decree on the classification of chieftaincy institutions in Cameroon completely altered this structure. Appointed government officials were thrust entrusted with managing and resolving land conflicts in their areas of jurisdiction using a single template for the highly heterogonous cultural landscape in the county.

2.2. The role of traditional authorities in land conflict issues

Historically, traditional authorities have resolved land conflicts in Nso through the imposition of sacred sanctions on the defaulter and negotiated settlements in less than certain circumstances. Despite this generic approach, each type of land conflict often requires a specific means of settlement. When the conflict was over a disputed boundary line, the traditional authority had the obligation to resolve it in an amicable and mutually acceptable ways.[54] In the event that both parties to the conflict failed to resolve the dispute on their own, one of the claimants would then use the appropriate channels to report the matter. In his capacity as the custodian and regulator of land, the Fon would convene a session of the Ataangwen to hear the case. Both parties would be invited to present their arguments on the dispute, after which the council would deliberate on the matter. In order to arrive at a decision, the team would have to visit the boundary to ascertain the claims. Usually, elders designated by the *fon* and the landlords of the respective claimants would be members of the delegation. In a case pitting a certain Leinyuy and Kongnso,[55] in Shisong village, the traditional authority headed by the Nwerong secret society asked both parties to take an oath to determine who had breached the

[53] Mzeka, N. (1990) *Four Fons of Nso': Nineteenth and Early Twentieth Century Kingship in the Western Grassfields of Cameroon* (Vol. 3), Spider Publishing Enterprise.

[54] Yilaka, A. (1981) "The phenomenon of change in Nso"'.

[55] Names are anonymised to protect the identity of the persons involved.

boundary.[56] According to Leinyuy, the nwerong placed a calabash filled with palm wine and asked both parties to pour it into a hole that had been dug at the boundary and then drink from it. After the oath-taking, the committee adjourned and the claimants asked to report to the fon's palace in two weeks. Kongnso fell ill shortly after and could not report to the palace on the said date. His illness was thus interpreted as a sign that he was guilty of violating the boundary. The case was thus ruled in favour of Leinyuy and the team demarcated the boundary with peace plants. Kongnso on his part had to atone for lying to the gods. He brought a goat, fowl, kolanut and palm wine to the nwerong society and was forgiven and later regained his health.

Traditional authorities also resolved land conflicts arising from opposing claims on the same piece of land. Although land was historically not bought and sold in Nso, opposing land claims did exist and so before the introduction of the 1974 land laws, the traditional authorities were fully involved in resolving such conflicts. A good case is the dispute between Bime and Jumbam in Tobin. Both claimed a piece of land located in Tobin, the current administrative capital of Bui division. Bime reported the matter to the traditional authorities and explained that after his secondary education he travelled out of the country and only returned seven years later. Upon his return, Jumbam was already farming his piece of land and claiming ownership.[57] The two parties unsuccessfully tried to find a solution to the dispute and so Bime reported the matter to the landlord. Despite all his efforts, the landlord could not also make both parties to agree on a solution and thus referred to the case to the *fon*. The first step taken by the *fon* was to temporally suspend all activity on the said piece of land. After carrying out preliminary investigations, the *fon* summoned both parties before the council of elders, the nwerong and the landlords. The council further sent a team to investigate the matter and decided to place a traditional injunction on the land. This injunction not only reinforced the earlier suspension but also forbade any trespassing on the piece of land.[58] The council decided to engage a negotiated settlement and after further consultations, the council reconvened. After an intense debate and deliberation, it passed its verdict in favour of Bime. However, Jumbam was persuaded to adhere to the verdict in order to avoid future claims. The council was able to prove to him through several witness testimonies that the piece of land actually belonged to Bime. The foregoing thus proves that traditional rulers were able to use pacific

[56] Interview, Leinyuy, 78, Retired teacher, 5 April 2017.
[57] Interview, Berinyuy, 80, Retired builder, 7 April 2017
[58] Interview, Fai Lukong, 75, Traditional Ruler, 8 April 2017

methods to settle land ownership disputes. While this is just one case, many of such conflicts existed and continue in to the 21st century.

Land use disputes also attracted the attention of traditional rulers. The high frequency of these disputes reveals the evolution of the population structure and thus the land use patterns. Many of the villages in Nso are host to nomadic Mbororo (graziers) community. The indigenous farming communities often had to find ways of accommodating and integrating these Mbororos. Over time, there was an astronomical increase in human and animal populations whereas land remained fixed and even deteriorated because of poor farming and grazing practices. In the search for more arable and grazing land, farmers and graziers often came into confrontation with each other. This at times resulted in violent land conflicts. For instance, Kibungla of Nkuv village reported a case of crop destruction by cattle to the landlord of his community.[59] After investigation, a certain Oumarou found to have been the owner of the cattle that had destroyed the crops. The landlord then convened a meeting but Oumarou failed to turn up after two invitations and Kibungla took up the matter to the *fon*. The *fon* set up a committee which went down to the field and brought back the findings to the palace. Both parties were later invited to the palace and the case was settled and a compensation package imposed on Oumarou. The fon further tasked Oumarou to fence his grazing land to avoid future cases of cattle destroying crops of farmers in the village. Usually when such disputes were successfully resolved, the landlord would ask both parties to embrace themselves and a common meal of *fufu* corn and grilled chicken (*khati khati*) was served. While this is just an example pitting two individuals in a single village, many of such land use disputes often occurred between Mbororo graziers and farming communities in villages such as Berlem, Kov-Ndzeen, Ngongba, Kingomen, Simonkov-Tadu, Tan and Wvem.

Land disputes resulting from a clash of competence between the traditional authorities and the civil administration in the post-1974 era have also become common. The said 1974 ordinance defined the post-colonial land tenure for the entire Cameroon two years after a referendum had been organized to scrape the federal state. Accordingly, all land which was titled became state land in complete disregard of the existing communal land ownership system.[60] This meant that Nso traditional institutions were dispossessed of their privilege to administer land and

[59] Interview, Kibungla, 82, Farmer, 13 April 2017.
[60] See Page, B & Sunjo, E (forthcoming).

resolve conflicts arising from its ownership and exploitation. A new chapter was opened in land conflict resolution, as traditional and state institutions started competing over who had the competence to hear such conflicts.[61] Instead of taking their land matters to the traditional authorities, many inhabitants began resorting to the Divisional Officer and the Land Consultative Board. This reduced the influence of the *fon, nwerong, ataangwen* and the Council of Seven in the management of land conflicts. The traditional institutions were not ready to be completely outmoded. They thus, in total disregard of the new dispensation, continued to hear land related cases in Nso. This was possible because of the indigenes' belief in the effectiveness of these institutions and their desire to protect their customary rights over what they considered as 'communal lands'.[62] For instance, Amomniteng, a Kumbo town inhabitant reported a land dispute with a certain Wirngo to the Traditional Council and after hearing both parties, the council ruled in favour of Amomniteng.[63] Wirngo rejected the outcome and later took the matter to the Divisional Officer for Kumbo sub division to obtain what he expected would be a fair decision. What emerges from this example is that the advent of a new post-colonial land legislation led to a decline in the role of traditional authorities in the management of land disputes. Although in many instances they operated in complete disregard of the land laws, in many instances they collaborated and continue to collaborate with state institutions in the resolution of land conflicts. This perhaps is a tacit recognition of the indispensability of these institutions in land conflict issues.

2.3. Challenges faced by traditional authorities in resolving land conflicts

In trying to resolve land conflicts, traditional authorities inadvertently caused the breakdown of societal cohesion. Many of these conflicts often generate animosity between not just the individuals involved but their immediate families or clan members. Losing a land dispute had financial, material and social implications which were not easy to accept. As such enmity was created at times for generations between the families of the

61 Goheen, M. (1992) "Chiefs, sub chiefs and local control: negotiations over land, struggles over meaning", *Africa, 62*(3), 389-412.

62 Fisiy, C. (1997) "State dislocation of customary management systems: Land colonization on the slopes of Mount Oku, North-West Province of Cameroon", *Law and Anthropology, 9*, 124-145.

63 Divisional Archives Kumbo, Letter by Divisional Officer to Denis Wirngo and George Amomniteng relating to their land dispute, 27 April 1990.

parties involved in the conflict. Given that the role of traditional authorities is first and foremost to rally all their subjects in the spirit of African solidarity, such breakdown as a result of land related disputes proved challenging to the traditional authorities who often do not want to be perceived as blatantly favouring one party of the other. There are stories of aggrieved parties having to relocate from their village to other parts of Nso in protest of the outcome of a land dispute.[64]

The attitude of the Mbororo graziers in particular proved to be a significant challenge for traditional rulers in their task of resolving land conflicts. Most of the graziers regarded and continue to do so as an impoverished lot. They considered their cattle to be more of high economic value than the farmers' crops.[65] Such attitude significantly contributed to the recurrence of land use disputes in Nso. Each time these disputes were reported to the traditional institutions, the graziers most often never turned up for the hearing or did so at their convenience and usually on days when they knew the farmers would have to be on their farms.[66] Even when they eventually showed up, they tried as much as possible to corrupt the landlords and other relevant traditional authorities with bribes in an attempt to get them rule in their favour.[67] Given their usually poor economic state, many of these traditional authorities found it difficult to reject some of the enticements from the cattle herders.

An acute inadequacy of the necessary resources to engage in the task was also a major hindrance to the ability of traditional authorities in resolving land conflicts.[68] Land conflict management and resolution doesn't only require the technical expertise but also requires financial resources. The resources were required for transporting those involved in

---

[64] Goheen, M. (1989) *The Earth Shall Give Judgment: Land, Leadership and Political Legitimacy in Highland Cameroon.* African Studies Center, Boston University, Vol. 143.

[65] Pelican, M. (2008) "Mbororo claims to regional citizenship and minority status in North-West Cameroon", *Africa*, 540-560; Dafinger, A., & Pelican, M. (2006) "Sharing or dividing the land? Land rights and farmer-herder relations in Burkina Faso and Northwest Cameroon"', *Canadian Journal of African Studies/La Revue canadienne des études africaines*, *40*(1), 127-151.

[66] Kaberry, P. (1959) "Some problems of land tenure in Nsaw, Southern Cameroons", *Journal of African Administration,* 11(1), 21–28; Ngwa, N. E. (1990) "Land use dynamics and restructuring on some sectors of the Grassfields plateau (Cameroon)", *GeoJournal*, 20(3), 203–208.

[67] Njeuma, M., & Awasom, N. F. (1990) "The Fulani and the political economy of the Bamenda grassfields'1940–1960", *Paideuma*, 36, 217–233.

[68] Fonjong, L., Sama-Lang, I. F., & Fombe, L. F. (2012) "Implications of customary practices on gender discrimination in land ownership in Cameroon", *Ethics and Social Welfare*, *6*(3), 260-274.

the field investigations and other logistics. Nso is a vast geographical entity with limited accessibility to most of the areas where these conflicts often occurred. As a result, some of the decisions made by the traditional authorities were based on anecdotal evidence rather than field visits by the competent authorities. In addition to this difficulty, many land deals were not recorded and so ownership and boundary lines were usually based on vague or ambiguous understanding of the circumstances by the traditional authority involved.

Conclusion

This paper makes a historical appraisal of the role of traditional authorities in land conflict resolution in Nso, Bui Division of Cameroon. Nso was one of the most highly centralised and well organised fondoms in pre-colonial grassfields of Cameroon. The traditional ruler was seen as a source of unity, inspiration and the law. In Nso like in most of pre-colonial Africa, land was communally owned and so was not transferable from one owner to another based on the exchange of money. Families and clans were simply apportioned a parcel of land by the landlord or the fon, who held the land in trust for the entire tribe. The penetration of the British colonial administration in the early 20th century began to alter this status quo, especially as there was an influx of nomadic Mbororo pastoralists into the area from French Cameroun and Nigeria. They were encouraged by the British to migrate to Nso in order to provide a source of protein from cattle milk and beef. This influx, together with other factors like population growth, inheritance struggles and farmer-grazier disputes resulted in numerous land-related conflicts. Cognizant of their historically powerful role in Nso society, traditional rulers had to assume the responsibility of resolving these conflicts using various means which ranged from negotiation and mediation to oath taking and the placement of traditional injunctions. Despite the consolidation of colonial administration, traditional authorities in Nso retained their status as the custodians of land and so continued to resolve conflicts arising from its ownership and use. This was largely due to the British colonial policy of Indirect Rule in tropical Africa.[69] This completely changed in 1974 after the earlier reunification of British and French Cameroons into a federation

[69] Mamdani, M. (1999) "Historicizing power and responses to power: indirect rule and its reform", *Social research*, 859-886; Geschiere, P. (1993) "Chiefs and colonial rule in Cameroon: Inventing chieftaincy, French and British style", *Africa*, *63*(2), 151-175.

and the abolition of the federation in 1972, paving the way for a harmonisation of land law throughout the country.

The said 1974 ordinance effectively stripped all traditional rulers of any substantive powers they had in managing land and resolving conflicts arising from its ownership and use. Appointed Divisional and Sub Divisional Officers were given the task of resolving the conflicts with traditional authorities only playing a marginal consultative role in the Land Consultative Boards. A 1977 decree further undermined and subordinated traditional authorities in land conflict resolution, as it described them as 'auxiliaries of the administration'.[70] In retrospect, one can argue that in resolving land conflict, traditional authorities in Nso faced a number of challenges such as some decisions which created enmity between aggrieved parties, the uncooperative attitude of the Fulani pastoralists and an inadequacy of resources to engage in the difficult task. It should be noted that since traditional authorities were effectively dislodged from land conflict resolution, Nso has witnessed tremendous population growth and changes in land use pattern. The disputes over land have thus increased manifold, and the administrators who represent the republic are often considered as alien to local realities and so cannot effectively resolve some the conflicts which have a cultural bearing. A large majority of the population in Nso and the grassfields of Cameroon remain more loyal to traditional authority which they consider as the more legitimate governance structure.[71] Many of the administrators have been accused of fomenting rather than resolving land related conflicts especially between graziers and the indigenous farming population. In particular, they are accused of receiving bribes from cattle herders in cash or kind which either delays the resolution of the conflicts or tilts them in favour of the Fulanis.[72] Based on such arguments which highlight the weaknesses of the current land conflict resolution regime and the important role that traditional authorities play in local development, the paper concludes these traditional authorities should be effectively reintegrated into land management.

70 Cheka, C. (2008) "Traditional authority at the crossroads of governance in Republican Cameroon", *Africa Development*, *33*(2).

71 *Ibid.*

72 Mbih, R. (2015) "Agro-pastoral landuse transformation: Implications and perspectives in the Norwest region of Cameroon", (Unpublished dissertation) University of Missouri-Kansas City.

The impact of the Boko Haram crisis on development in the Far North region of Cameroon

By

Kiven James Kewir

Associate Professor of Conflict Resolution,
Department of Political Science and Comparative Politics, University of Buea,
Research Hub Director for Central Africa, African Leadership Centre Trust,
Nairobi, Kenya & Guest Lecturer, Department of Political Science,
University of Bamenda
Email: jameskewir@yahoo.com

Abstract

Since 2012, the Far North Region has been a target for the Boko Haram terrorist group. The crisis orchestrated by the attacks of the terror group and fighting with the military has had far reaching implications for development in the region. The purpose of this qualitative study was to examine the impact of this crisis on development in the Far North Region of Cameroon. Using data obtained through desktop research, the paper shows that the crisis has had a serious impact on the local economy but also on the national economy. It has also had far reaching social consequences with women and children being particularly affected. To resolve the crisis, it is recommended that more should be done to address the socio-economic needs of the population that have made the region attractive for BH activities including recruitment and armed attacks.

Key Words: Boko Haram, Terrorism, Development, socio-economic needs, Impact

Introduction

This paper explores the impact of the Boko Haram (BH) conflict in the Far North Region of Cameroon on development. The Far North is one of Cameroon's ten regions. It shares borders with Chad's Ndjamena to the East and Nigeria's Maiduguri to the West. The peculiar geography of the Far North, specifically as a border region and with considerable volume of cross-border movement of goods and persons, makes the region an important economic zone, as well as a staging post for regional trade and relations with Chad and Nigeria. This however equally exposes Cameroon to regional security risks, including the 'Contagion Effects', linked to the persistent security problems in Chad and North-Eastern Nigeria. Specifically, repeated attacks by BH and the inflow of refugees from Nigeria in the Far North Region of Cameroon have disrupted the social life of inhabitants and the habitually intense flow of trade with the neighboring Nigerian settlements since 2012[1]. The extremist group has drawn support from the local population by exploiting the regions vulnerabilities akin to those in North-Eastern Nigeria. Using a qualitative approach, the study examines the causes (structural, proximate and conflict-sustaining), economic and social consequences of the crisis. The paper is qualitative and employs both primary and secondary sources of data to interrogate the history, economic and social consequences of the conflict since 2012.

1. The Context of Cameroon

Cameroon is a Central African country which shares borders with six (06) countries including Nigeria to the West. The 1,690 km^2 border separates historically and geographically linked areas including in the Far North Region of Cameroon that has been devastated by BH attacks. Politically the country has not experienced a democratic change in government since independence. Socially, the country has a fast growing population with a high rate of unemployment and growing poverty including in the Northern regions. It is one of the most diversified economies in the Central African sub-region and a major trade hub for other countries in the area.

---

[1] Guibbaud, P., 2014, BOKO HARAM : Le Nord-Cameroun dans la tourmente ?, Groupe de Recherche et d'Information sur la Paix et la Sécurité (GRIP), Bruxelles

[2] Lizzie Williams & Mark Shenley, 3rd edn., 2012, Nigeria, USA, The Globe Pequot Press Inc, p. 3

The colonial history of Cameroon is unique in several respects. It is the only country on the continent that was governed by three colonial powers (Germany, Britain and France). The territory also experienced significant changes during the colonial era. Finally it is contested whether it was actually a colony given that the term was never officially used to describe it under successive administrations. During the First World War, the territory was seized from Germany, under which it was called a protectorate (1884 – 1916) and divided between the United Kingdom and France after the War. German Kamerun as it was called, included parts of Gabon, Congo, Central African Republic, Chad, and Nigeria.[3] It is not clear what criteria was used to divide the territory with a long stretch extending from the coast to lake Chad was given to the United Kingdom as a League of Nations Mandate and the rest to France under the same terms. In the aftermath of the Second World War, these became a United Nations Trust Territories under UK and French administrations.

Part of the British portion referred to as Northern Cameroons became part of Nigeria following a United Nations Plebiscite in 1961 whither the other part the Southern Cameroons was associated to French Cameroon in a Federal arrangement following another plebiscite in the same year[4]. This territory today forms parts of Borno, Adamawa and Taraba states in Nigeria. These changes resulted in a situation where people that were linked by culture and those that had been linked by history and custom, were separated. Towns such as Gulumba, Banki and Dikwa in Borno State, Nigeria have consequently continued to experience intense trade with the neighboring communities in Fotokol, Kolofata Amchide and Kerawa in the Far North region of Cameroon. This together with the geography of the area makes the border highly permeable including to crime and illicit trade[5] which intensifies with disruptions in formal trade.

Cameroon is a highly centralized unitary state, and faces important governance challenges. Corruption[6] and poor accountability are

---

[3] The Commonwealth, 'Cameroon : History,' accessed on 13 February 2018 at http://thecommonwealth.org/our-member-countries/cameroon/history

[4] Anyangwe, C., 2009, Betrayal of Too Trusting a People: The UN, the UK and the Trust Territory of the Southern Cameroons, Bamenda, Langaa RPCIG.

[5]Crisis Group, 2016, Cameroon: Confronting Boko Haram, Crisis Group Africa Report N°241.

[6] Agence Francaise Press, 2016, "Boko Haram : aux origines de la secte ", Accessed on 13 February 2018 at http://www.jeuneafrique.com/depeches/336885/politique/boko-haram-aux-origines-de-secte/

characteristic of public services[7]. Although the economy is diversified when compared to neighboring Central African countries, most of the population lives on agriculture and trade in agricultural products. In the Far North of the country, agriculture is the predominant source of livelihoods. Most of the people are commercial cattle or sheep herders or farmers. In addition to animal and farm produce locally made goods such as pots are also traded in the markets[8]. The demand for these goods is strong in neighboring towns of Nigeria that have been largely under the influence of BH in the last decade.

The Far North Region that has been directly affected by the Boko Haram Crisis is culturally[9] and geographically similar to Borno and Adamawa States in Nigeria, home to BH strongholds. The population of the two border areas is composed of Kanuri, Hausas, Mandara, Choa Arabs, Marghi[10] and Fulani tribes. The people share common markets with towns such as Banki serving as major markets for both communities. Islam is also an important part of the religious landscape in both areas. These similarities have made it easy for BH militants to mix with the local population unnoticed and recruit without much difficulty. In addition to the cultural similarities, there is a very high unemployment rate in the Far North region, a large youth population and a high poverty rate. The number of people living below the poverty line increased to 8.1 million from 2007 to 2014, representing a 12% rise. About 56 % of the poor live in the North and Far North Regions.[11] About 74.3% of people in the Far North Region live below the poverty line[12]. All these facilitated recruitment by BH.

The historical, cultural and geographical similarities of the Far North Region of Cameroon with border states of Borno and Adamawa in Nigeria made the implantation of BH in Cameroon predictable. The activities of

[7] Lederman, D., Loayza, N. and Soares, R., 2005, "ACcountability and Corruption: Political Institutions Matter", *Economics & Politics*, Vol. 17, No. 1.

[8] Tilouine, J., 2016, « Cameroun : comment les terroristes de Boko Haram se sont convertis à l'import-export », *Le Monde*, accessed on 12 February 2018 at http://www.lemonde.fr/afrique/article/2016/07/11/cameroun-comment-les-terroristes-de-boko-haram-se-sont-convertis-a-l-import-export_4967769_3212.html

[9] Crisis Group, 2016.

[10] Vaughan, J., 'Culture, History, and Grass-Roots Politics in a Northern Cameroons Kingdom', University of Cincinnati, accessed on 12 February 2018 at: http://onlinelibrary.wiley.com/doi/10.1525/aa.1964.66.5.02a00050/pdf

[11] World Bank, 'Cameroon', accessed on 13 February 2018 at: http://www.worldbank.org/en/country/cameroon/overview

[12] Crisis Group, 2016. P. 3

BH took root and grew on the fertile ground provided by a precarious economic situation in the far North and the near absence of governance structures owing to the highly centralized nature of the Cameroonian state. Boko Haram has benefitted from the rich trade in agricultural produce including in animals and illicit arms trade. It has also been able to recruit from the local population and benefitted from the corruption of local administrative officials.

2. The origin of the Boko Haram crisis in Cameroon

The origin of the Boko Haram Crisis in the Far North can be traced to 2009[13] when it started establishing itself in the area. Although some sources trace its origins to as early as 2006 it was in 2009 that clear evidence of recruitment by BH and proselytization emerged.[14] Its activities in Cameroon can be explained by the radicalization of young people that had studied in North Eastern Nigeria, the presence of BH clerics and members who fled a crackdown by Nigerian forces and the remote presence of Cameroon security services in the Far North Region before 2010. Direct confrontation with the Cameroonian security forces and intensification of BH attacks in the region is linked to a crackdown on the group's activities since 2010.

Key towns in the Far North, namely, the Sub-Divisions of Fotokol, Makary, Kolofata, Mora, Waza, Mayo-Moskota and Hile-Alifa have witnessed the highest number of attacks.[15] The attacks were mostly isolated and localized until the 19 February 2013 when a French family was kidnapped in the Waza National Park. This was the first time the terrorist group kidnapped foreigners in Cameroon. The incident put a spot light on Cameroon as one of the countries affected by the growing control of the fundamentalist group in the neighboring state of Borno in Nigeria.

---

[13] Crisis Group, 2016, p. 8.

[14] Ibid, p. 8

[15] Colantoni, C., March 2015, « L'émergence Boko Haram au Cameroun », INTERSOS

Table 1. Number of BH attacks per Division and Sub-Division in the Far North Region (1 January 2013 – 31 January 2017)

Divisions	Number of attacks	Sub-Divisions	Number of attacks
Diamare	3	Bogo	1
		Meri	1
		Pette	1
Logone and Chari	147	Fotoko	33
		Hile-Alifa	22
		Goulfey	2
		Kouseri	3
		Makary	35
		Waza	43
		Logone-Bimi	3
		Darak	5
		Zina	1
Mayo-Sava	250	Kolofata	157
		Mora	90
		Tokombere	3
Mayo-Tsanaga	88	Koza	5
		Mayo-Moskota	69
		Mokolo	14
Mayo-Danay	3	Guere	1
		Yagoua	1
		Kai-Kai	1
		TOTAL	**491**

Source: Compiled by the author with data from https://www.crisisgroup.org/africa/central-africa/cameroon/boko-harams-shifting-tactics-cameroon-what-does-data-tell-us

The attacks of BH intensified at the beginning of 2015 and caused massive displacement of the population in the border areas. This displacement together with the strong inflow of refugees from Nigeria has had a significant impact on social and economic situation of the Far North Region. Tens of thousands of refugees were received in border towns of Zlevet, Kolofata and Fotokol and this put a strain on the already poor supply of basic services in the area. Among the displaced who moved into

Cameroon were BH converts who actively engaged in proselytization. Some of the refugees in Kolofata engaged actively in recruiting young people by subtly engaging in their discussions and encouraging them to deepen their knowledge of Islam in Nigeria.[16] In 2014, clashes between some refugees who had been trying to force their ideas on the population in the town of Kerawa led to a discovery of an important stock of arms.[17] The resulting intensification of BH attacks following a violent army crackdown led to mass displacement between 2014 and 2016 and disrupted trade and livelihoods. It also led to the shutdown of schools and markets with a devastating impact on vulnerable people including women and children.

Most of the trade in markets that have been specifically targeted by BH is done by women[18]. Women and children have been the most hit by the crisis given that they have also suffered displacement and violence from both BH and security forces. Some of the most affected trading towns by the intensification of attacks include Amchide, Doublé and Gambaru. As early as March 2014, rockets and shells fired from Nigeria destroyed a mosque in Amchide, forcing many to leave the town[19]. The main targets have been markets, brigades and police stations. In addition to the killing and displacement of the population, trade has been seriously affected. Movement between Maiduguri and Banki for example has been disrupted. Many have abandoned their farm and others have lost their cattle. The small but busy market of Doublé's, and popular among travelers on the Maroua-Kousseri road has also seen its activity reduce drastically. Traders who continue to do business in such areas are suspected of having ties with BH[20] by security forces from Nigeria and Cameroon.

Over one thousand families have fled the border areas, moving inward to towns such as Mora. In the Logone and Chari, the localities of Fotokol, Makari and Dabanga have been gradually abandoned by their inhabitants who have sought refuge in Kousseri and Waza. About 400 people left Koumana to settle in Makari, others left from Gore-Mahamat and Bagaram. The Cameroon army provoked some displacement of the populations in Hilé Alifa and Fotokol in anticipation of a major

---

16 Crisis Group, 2016, p.9

17 Ibid

18 **Barbaut, T., Interview on** Voix de la Diaspora, accessed on 12 February 2018 at: https://www.info-afrique.com/5336-boko-haram-enjeux-impacts/

19 L'œil du Sahel, N° 583, 10 March 2014

20 Issa, S. ed., November 2014, Effets Economiques et Sociaux des Attaques de Boko Haram dans l'Extreme-Nord du Cameroun, Maroua, KALIAO

offensive[21]. As at date, the crisis has claimed over 1500 lives and displaced some 155000 people.[22]

The insecurity caused by BH and the violence that has characterized clashes with the Cameroonian and Nigerian armies have therefore disrupted social and economic activities in the Far North especially in communities along the Cameroon-Nigerian border. Repeated terror attacks and the violence have forced many more than a thousand people out of their habitual places of residence with far reaching implications for agriculture and trade. The population already living below the poverty line has remained the main victim of the attacks. In addition to the problem of displacement, the influx of refugees fleeing BH violence in North Eastern Nigeria has also put a strain on the social and economic fabric of the Far North.

3. Causes of the Crisis: contagion and pre-existing socio-economic vulnerability

The causes of Boko Haram's incursions in Cameroon are by no means easy to ascertain given that it was not a strategic part of its intended theatres of operations at inception. The activities of BH in Cameroon however seem to have been favoured by some compelling historical and geographical and social factors. The proximity of the Far North to the State of Borno which is the epicentre of the Boko Haram insurgency, and the cross-cultural ties between the border tribes and the precarious social and economic situation of the Far North have favoured the spread and implantation of BH on Cameroonian territory. This underscores the reality of contagion effect in the case of the Boko Haram crisis in Cameroon; that it, it spread from Northeast Nigeria as a result of geographical proximity, and subsisting socio-economic and cultural ties across border communities. Other factors considered here include pre-existing socio-economic vulnerabilities in the Far North region (weak presence of government services, socio-economic marginalization and deprivation of the Fra North, and the impact of environmental changes and climate change.

---

[21] Issa S. Op cit

[22] CRISIS GROUP, Cameroon: Confronting Boko Haram, Report No 241/Africa, of 16 Nov 2016 https://www.crisisgroup.org/africa/central-africa/cameroon/cameroon-confronting-boko-haram

3.1. Contagion Effect

Several structural factors made the extension of BH activities from Nigeria into the Far North Region of Cameroon highly probable, however the contagion effect plays a strong role. The Far North region has historically served as a corridor for trade and transit between Nigeria, Cameroon and Chad by virtue of its geographical location. It is the northernmost constituent region of Cameroon, located between North-Eastern Nigeria and South-Western Chad. Geographically, it falls within the Sahel region of Africa[23] and is consequently also referred to as the Sahel Region of Cameroon. Like the rest of the Sahel region, the climate is arid and hot with remarkable seasonal variations in rainfall and temperature. In spite of its hash climate, it is one of the most densely populated regions of Cameroon with an estimated population of over 4,000,000 inhabitants. The geography of the Far North therefore makes it one of the most risk adverse regions but also an important trade corridor and potentially viable market.

The over 400Km[24] long and porous border shared with Borno state in Nigeria makes it difficult to contain any activity on either side of the border. The porous nature of the border can be explained by the absence of a physical boundary according to Boggs Classification, the strong cross-cultural linkages between the border communities and the poor management of border areas by the government of Cameroon. [25]' By most accounts, the people living on either sides of the border are common people, particularly those at the frontier-line. According to Kane, the "nearness and connectivity between these same peoples of Cameroon and Nigeria propelled them to see themselves as brothers despite colonial

[23] While some studies do not include the Far North Region in the Sahel (see for example: Virginia Smith, "The Sahel", *www.ce.utexas.edu/prof/mckinney/ce397/Topics/Africa/Sahel/Sahel.doc*), it displays the characteristics of the region and is consequently treated by some including specialized agencies of the UN such as the WHO and the FAO as part of the area.

[24] Afrique Education, 14 December 2016, "Cameroun/Chad/Nigeria : Réouverture des frontières après la quasi-défaite de Boko Haram » https://www.afriqueeducation.com/economie/camerountchadnigeria_r_ouverture_des_fronti_res_apr_s_la_quasi_d_faite_de_boko_haram

[25] Bogg, 1940, distinguishes between (a) physical or natural (boundaries that follow a particular natural feature such as a river, watershed, mountain range, and so on (as cited by Griffiths (1996 :67-68) (b) Geometric (boundaries that follow straight lines, arcs of a circle such as longitude and latitude. (c) Anthropo-geographical (boundaries that relate to various human settlements, culture, and language, and (d) compounded (boundaries that comprise various basic elements mentioned above).

influences." [26] Similarly, Funteh[27] has described the border as "superimposed", in line with the classification of borders by Hartshorne.[28] Border villages of Banki, Dilbe, Bama, Gambaru and Ngoshi in Nigeria for example were formerly located in Colonial Cameroon. The Kanuri tribe, from which BH recruits have mainly been drawn, is present both in Borno State and the Far North Region of Cameroon[29]. This has made communication and access to the Far North region relatively easy for BH. The socio-economic activities of the borders communities take place with little regard for the "artificial borders" inherited from more than a Century of colonial control. The formal and habitual regulation of cross-border trade and transportation is largely absent. In its place, a network of informal trade and travel across the border is widespread. This makes smuggling including of small and light weapons easy and nearly impossible to control.

The porosity of the borders with Chad and Nigeria has hence facilitated intense trafficking in arms, ammunition and drugs. The accompanying radicalization is reinforced by the evolution of certain young people who are for the most part unemployed. The geographical proximity to North East Nigeria and the socio-cultural similarity between the populations of these regions has facilitated the progression of the ideology of Boko Haram and the radicalization of the youths. The border communities, especially the Kanuri have a lot in common, including religion, languages and customs. Generally, there is a correlation between the precarious living conditions of the population and BH violence.

---

[26] Kane (1976 :23-24)

[27] Funteh, M., "Border Shutting and Shrivel of Human and Merchandise on the Nigeria-Cameroon Passage of Banki and Limani," in Issa, S. ed., 2014, Effets Economiques et Sociaux des Attaques de Boko Haram dans L'Extreme-Nord du Cameroun, Maroua, University of Maroua

[28] Hartshorne (1938) divided borders into; (a) Antecedent boundaries, drawn before cultural landscapes are developed. (b) Consequent/ subsequent boundaries; those delimited after such features have already emerged, which coincide with social, economic, cultural, or linguistic discontinuities. (c) Superimposed boundaries drawn after the development of the cultural landscape but without regard to possible cultural boundaries, and (d) Relict boundaries: those that can still be seen in the cultural landscape, even though they no longer have any function of political division, like "Great Wall of China," the "Berlin Wall" that separated East and West Berlin, and "Hadrian's Wall" in the United Kingdom that was built in AD 122 to demarcate the northernmost boundary of the Roman Empire.

[29] IRIN News, 11 August 2017, Young guns: Cameroon's Boko Haram problem, accessed on 14 February 2018 at https://data2.unhcr.org/fr/news/16459

The Far North Region has served as a hideout for BH since 2004. Government repression in the aftermath of the Kanama riots forced some BH militants to seek refuge in the Mandara Mountains[30] in neighboring Cameroon. The geographical position of Cameroons border towns in the Far North Region has also facilitated BH attacks. CRISIS Group for example has observed that "the important trading towns of Amchidé and Fotokol" were "attacked because their geographical position could confer an operational advantage on Boko Haram."[31] BH has also used the border lands as a safe hideout when fleeing from Nigerian government forces.

The most significant entry of the group's militants into Cameroon took place after the clashes in Maiduguri in 2009 during which its founding leader was killed. The terrorist group "set up cells for cells for religious proselytism, logistics and buying and stocking arms."[32] Although the group avoided any confrontation in Cameroon to protect its sources of supply, the contact with young Muslims in the Far North who were already in fundamentalist groups such as Jamaat at-Tabligh and the Muslim Brotherhood, further radicalized them. The radicalization of youths and the problems of unemployment and education that marked the region facilitated recruitment for BH.. Easy access to the border villages in Cameroon was further facilitated by the near absence of government services and poor climate that make life very difficult. Historically, government security forces have had a timid presence in the border areas of the Far North Region. This made incursions by BH very easy. The kidnapping of the French family in the Waza area in February 2013 could not have been possible if the area was under significant police surveillance. As has been the case with North-Eastern Nigeria and similar cases such as Somalia, religious extremism thrives where young people have limited access to education and employment.

---

[30] Heungoup, H., September 2015, « Cameroun : au-delà de Boko Haram, la menace insidieuse du radicalisme religieux En savoir plus », https://www.crisisgroup.org/fr/africa/central-africa/cameroon/cameroun-au-dela-de-boko-haram-la-menace-insidieuse-du-radicalisme-religieux-en-savoir-plus

[31] CRISIS Group, 16 Nov 2016, Report No 241/Africa, https://www.crisisgroup.org/africa/central-africa/cameroon/cameroon-confronting-boko-haram

[32] CRISIS Group, February 2017, "Boko Haram's Shifting Tactics in Cameroon: What Does the Data Tell Us?", https://www.crisisgroup.org/africa/central-africa/cameroon/boko-harams-shifting-tactics-cameroon-what-does-data-tell-us

3.2. Socio-economic marginalization and vulnerability of the Far North

As has been the case in Northern Nigeria, the already poor socio-economic condition of the population in the Far North which has worsened since 2012 is considered a key factor sustaining BH in this part of the country. The Far North region remains the least developed region in the country with very high levels of illiteracy. Food insecurity has also affected a significant part of the population since the start of BH violence[33]. The measures taken by the government to address the problem remain largely insufficient.

The Far North has the highest rate of illiteracy in Cameroon[34]. While the school enrollment rate at the national level reached 84.1% in 2014, it is only 46% in the region with rates of 20% recorded in localities such as Fotokol, Kolofata and Mayo Moskota on the border with Nigeria[35]. This rate is higher for girls who are often refused education or removed from school and sent to marriage at a very early age. The region has a very poor road network and basic amenities such are water are nearly inexistent in most towns. The situation of roads has made moto bikes considered as a facilitating tool for illicit border trade and border crossings at multiple locations by BH militants difficult to control. The large number of motor bike users and the difficulties in systematically registering them makes it almost impossible to associate anyone with a specific bike. As the predominant means of transportation, banning them will be unrealistic and likely to engender more problems between security forces and the population. There is also very limited access to electricity and health centres.

As a response these problems, the government has announced many projects since 2014. These include: a 78.9 billion CFA franc ($143 million) territorial development programme to cover the three northern regions since 2014; a three-year national emergency plan launched in 2015 with a budget of 925 billion CFA francs of which just 42 billion francs was earmarked for the Far North Region; a 5.3 billion CFA franc plan to

[33] World Food Programme (WFP), January 2017, Cameroun, Suivi de la Securite Alimentaire, Bulletin No. 2. ; accessed on 29 August 2017 at ; http://documents.wfp.org/stellent/groups/public/documents/ena/wfp290922.pdf

[34] Journal du Cameroun, November 2016, « Cameroun: développer l'Extrême-Nord pour éradiquer le terrorisme », accessed on 12 February 2018 at https://www.journalducameroun.com/cameroun-developper-lextreme-nord-pour-eradiquer-le-terrorisme/

[35] Crisis Group, 2016, p.3

rebuild schools and hospitals in the region in the same year; and a 102 billion CFA franc project targeting young people across the country announced in December 2016. In spite of these and other promises, only a few new classrooms, feasibility studies, surveys and some construction material for road projects, and the arrival in Maroua of several contractors, have been realized.[36]

By most accounts, the effective resolution of the crisis will require sufficient and effective efforts to address the socio-economic problems faced by the region. As has been mentioned above, these circumstances have made the Far North a fertile recruitment ground. Poverty and illiteracy have played an important role in the radicalization of the predominantly young population. This trend of radicalization will continue under these conditions even with the defeat of BH.[37]

3.3. Government's Military Responses

The government's approach to the BH crisis has perhaps been one of the main sustaining factors. In spite of intelligence reports that suggested, young people were exposed to radicalization by militants from North East Nigeria in 2004 and 2010, the government was reluctant to take any measures, military or otherwise. The kidnapping of a French Family by BH in February 2013 marked a turning point in its activities in Cameroon. The Cameroon government could no longer ignore the group. It could be considered a difficult situation given that Cameroon has not handled such a problem before. Following the first kidnapping of foreign nationals in 2013, the government quickly resolved to militarizing the region. The choice of approach took little account of the factors that had led to the event of February 2013. Although BH was able to secure the release of its members that had been imprisoned in subsequent negotiations, more suspects were captured by Cameroon's security forces. The general treatment of suspects as terrorists without evidence or a court ruling has exposed most of those arrested to torture and other inhumane treatment by security forces[38]. The release of people kept in custody and tortured has

---

[36] IRIN News, September 2017, « Le retard du nord du Cameroun en fait un terreau fertile pour Boko Haram », accessed on 13 February 2018 at https://www.irinnews.org/fr/analyses/2017/09/06/le-retard-du-nord-du-cameroun-en-fait-un-terreau-fertile-pour-boko-haram

[37] IRIN News, September 2017

[38] Ebosse, Y., « Bonne Cause, Mauvais Moyens : Atteintes aux Droits Humains et à la Justice dans le Cadre de la Lutte Contre Boko Haram au Cameroun », http://www.camer.be/45458/11:1/crimes-de-guerre-le-cameroun-dans-le-viseur-de-la-cpi-cameroon.html

contributed to the radicalization of some, and further facilitated recruitment by BH. Although the government took some socio-economic measures in late in 2014[39], these are not as visible as the military effort and have yet to reach a level significant enough to yield the desired results.

The pressure from France and the spotlight that the incident put on Cameroon also made handling the situation more complicated. The negotiations that eventually took place and the payment of a ransom allegedly made[40] to release the hostages must have been interpreted by the group as a sign of vulnerability. Similarly, the release of 10 Chinese hostages and the wife of Cameroon's Deputy Prime Minister was obtained through negotiations with BH.[41] This perhaps explains why BH embarked on targeting more foreigners in Cameroon.

Some political elites allege that the activities of BH in Cameroon are politically engineered by some elites of the affected region as a tool they can use to capture power[42]. The Elites of the North have reacted to this by rejecting the allegations as false. The Speaker of the National Assembly, an elite of Mada in the Mayo-Sava Division of this region dismissed the accusations as a campaign strategy for political appointment by the authors[43]. In spite of these counter accusations, suspicion has remained rife. The growing distrust is symptomatic of the neglect of dialogue at all levels as part of the response to the problem. It is therefore understandable that such suspicion was especially rife at the height of the crisis with both important military casualties and civilian casualties largely attributed to the excesses of security forces.

---

[39] CRISIS Group, 3 September 2015, « Cameroun : la menace du radicalisme religieux » Africa Report No. N° 229, CRISIS Group, p. 26

[40] BBC News, 27 April 2013, "Nigeria's Boko Haram 'got $3m ransom' to free hostages", accessed on 25 August 2017 at http://www.bbc.com/news/world-africa-22320077
See also Langlois, J., April 2013 , "Boko Haram paid $3.15 million ransom to free French family of seven", https://www.pri.org/stories/2013-04-27/boko-haram-paid-315-million-ransom-free-french-family-seven-video

[41] Kindzeka M., "October 2014, Cameroon Receives 27 Boko Haram Captives", https://www.voanews.com/a/cameroon-reports-boko-haram-hostages-freed/2480467.html

[42] RFI, 7 September 2014, « Cameroun: querelles politiques autour de Boko Haram dans le Nord », http://www.rfi.fr/afrique/20140907-cameroun-bisbilles-politiques-le-nord-sujet-boko-haram

[43] Shema, E., September 2015, « Cavaye Yeguie Djibril dénonce ceux qui veulent «la partition» du Cameroun », http://www.journalducameroun.com/cavaye-yeguie-djibril-denonce-ceux-qui-veulent-la-partition-du-cameroun/

4. Impact of the crisis on development

The border crossings in the Far North Region were habitually very busy up to 2011 in spite of their poor management. The geographical location of the region which links it to Nigeria and Chad makes the Far North important for trade with these countries.[44] The sharp drop and fluctuations in trade volumes is symptomatic of the consequences of the BH related violence in the region. In addition to trade, the tourism sector that is one of the most important in this part of Cameroon has also been seriously hit. Other areas that have been significantly affected include agriculture, education and public administration. The effect on all these sectors has had far reaching implications on the already precarious living conditions of the population the area and the public treasury. The increase in government spending on security and the loss of revenue from the region has been considerable. These effects will be examined here.

4.1. Effects on Regional Trade

While poorly organized, border crossings, particularly in the North, are habitually busy. Most parts of Northern Cameroon depend largely on the supply of goods to and from Nigeria. About two thirds of fuel (popularly known as Zua Zua) sold in the Northern regions originates in Nigeria. Other goods that are commonly imported from Nigeria include; loin cloths, moto spare parts, bicycles, motorcycles, sandals and other plastic goods and vegetable oil. Before December 2011, trade flows were estimated in the hundreds of millions USD. This situation changed significantly from 2012 with figures falling sharply.

An estimated 145,000 metric tons of goods per year were imported from Nigeria to Cameroon through the Limani-Banki Border between 2000 and 2010. In the same period, Nigeria received an estimated 112,000 metric tons of goods from Cameroon through this route. Exports from Cameroon include; imported rice, rice paddy from the SEMRY project in Maga, cotton, cereals, fish, cows, sheep, groundnuts, onions and garlic. According to the Cameroon Cotton Society (Société de Développement du Coton du Cameroun, SODECOTON) entered into a trade agreement with Nigerian affiliates in the 1980s.This agreement opened the way for Cameroon cotton to be exported to Nigeria where the demand for cotton

---

[44] Gassida, 2010. Les hébergements marchands de la ville de Maroua 1950-2008. Mémoire de DIPES II Département d'Histoire, ENS, Université de Maroua, p. 102

has been very high.[45] In addition to the high demand, the price of cotton in Nigeria is about three times higher than on the Cameroonian Market. Local producers have also smuggled their cotton into Nigeria to benefit from the attractive price and high demand. Fadimatou for example shows that two-thirds of all the cotton cultivated in Mayo-Tsanaga and Mayo-Sava was smuggled into Nigeria.[46]

Trade in fish has also been important in this cross-border area. About 93 percent of the fish caught in the Far North was exported to Nigeria through the Limani-Banki route[47] up to 2011. Significant exports of cattle, sheep and fowls to Nigeria from the Logone and Chari Division were also common during this period. Like cotton, the exportation of cattle is also favoured by the high prices in Nigeria. The buying price of cattle in Nigeria is almost double that in the Far North of Cameroon.

Most of the fuel consumed in the Far North Region is imported from Nigeria. According to Funteh over 67% of fuel consumed in the Far-North Region of Cameroon is smuggled from Nigeria.[48] Although most of the fuel is smuggled, it plays a very significant role in the local economy. Higher prices of fuel usually drive prices on other commodities up in the Far North and other parts of Cameroon. Official estimates consequently tend to underestimate the amount of fuel that enters the region through Nigeria. Some accounts however situate the market share of Zua Zua in the far North Region at about 90 percent[49] of fuel consumption. A disruption in the flow of fuel cannot be without consequence for the local economy.

Since 2012, trade has been significantly disrupted by growing insecurity from BH activity in the Far North and especially at the border markets that used to be important trade hubs for both Cameroonian and Nigerian businesses. The situation has affected traders, farmers and government

---

[45] Funteh M., 2014, "Border Shutting and Shrivel of Human and Merchandise on the Nigeria-Cameroon Passage of Banki and Limani", in ISSA S. ed., November 2014, Effets Economiques et Sociaux des Attaques de Boko Haram dans l'Extreme-Nord du Cameroun, Maroua, KALIAO

[46] Fadimatou, M., 2011, Crise cotonniere et exportation clandestine de coton entre L'extreme-Nord du Cameroun et le Nord-Est du Nigeria :1974-2011, MA dissertation in History, University of Maroua.

[47] Bello, A. ; Dikwe, Hamso, Dissia, A., 2013, La SEMRY : DE 1971 A 2012, DIPESS II dissertation in History, ENS, University of Maroua.

[48] Funteh M., March 2015, "The Paradox of Cameroon-Nigeria Interactions: Connecting between the edges of opportunity/benefit and quandary", *International Journal of Peace and Development Studies*, Vol 6 (3)

[49] Ibid

revenue collection services. The temporal closure of the border and the markets has had an impact on customs revenue. The principal Customs office of Fotokol for example collected 2, 180, 000 Francs CFA in the first half of January 2012 against 19, 000, 000 Francs CFA during the same period in 2011. Similarly, the principal office of Limani raised 50,000,000 Francs CFA in 2012 against 100,000,000 Francs CFA in 2011 during the same period. Smuggling increases when the border is shut and there is a further drop in exports and imports [50]with a serious impact on customs revenue. The main targets of BH attacks are popular and crowd filled places such as markets, public buildings and security posts. Important markets like those of Maiduguri and Banki have therefore been major targets. The effervescence of Banki along with the increased police presence made it a key target[51].

The crisis has also had an impact on agriculture and livestock. Onions, millet, peanuts, corn and other farming products that are constantly exported to Nigeria constitute an important source of revenue for many Cameroonian economic operators. Cattle traders have suffered a similar fate. It has been impossible to cross the border in periods when attacks intensify or when the borders are closed. This leaves most cattle traders with no other source of income. Since 2012, the trade in goods through the Banki-Limani and other major routes has dropped by more than 50%, reaching about 90 percent during peak periods of the conflict. The tightening of security along the border after its closure and the threat posed by BH make even smuggling very risky. When the border is completely closed, business activities across the two borders virtually come to a standstill.[52]

4.2. Effects on Tourism

The Far North region is home to some of Cameroons most priced tourist sites and cultural attractions. It was the first destination for tourists from Europe and America until 2012[53]. 13 percent of Cameroons' touristic

---

[50] Kindzeka, M., 2014, "Border trade between Cameroon and Nigeria at a standstill", http://www.dw.com/en/border-trade-between-cameroon-and-nigeria-at-a-standstill/a-17481473

[51] Pérouse de Montclos, M-A., 2012, " Boko Haram et le terrorisme islamiste au Nigeria : insurrection religieuse, contestation politique ou protestation sociale ?" Questions de Recherche / Research Questions, N° 40, juin 2012.

[52] Kindzeka, 2014

[53] Laleix, G., 22 September 2016 « Cameroun : relancer le tourisme sinistré par l'insécurité »

sites are found in this region[54]. Since 2012, tourism sector in the Far North Region has been seriously hit by BH related insecurity.

National tourism statistics for 2007 show that out of a total of 364 tourist sites in Cameroon, 67 are in the Far North[55]. The attractive landscape of the Region made it the best tourist destination in the country and businesses in the sector up to 2011. The Rhumsiki landscape, the Waza National Park and the flood plains of the areas in the Logone valley are among some of the most popular tourist attractions in Cameroon.

With the rise in BH attacks since 2012, the occupancy rate of hotels has dropped from 50 percent to 10 percent[56]. In addition to the difficulties in the hotel sector, the crisis experienced by the tourism sector has also affected trade in handicrafts[57]. Most of the touristic sites in the Far North are now deserted for most parts of the year as tourists fear being kidnapped by BH or trapped in violence. Following the kidnapping of a French family in February 2013[58] and that of a French priest in November 2013[59], the performance of the tourism sector dropped sharply. In the Waza area for example, out of 1906 arrivals only 1403 nights were recorded. With the escalation of the crisis in 2013, the situation worsened. 1179 arrivals were registered against 975 nights in the year 2013. The impact of this drop on other the economy can be appreciated by looking at the changes in the figures for value added tax (VAT). The average VAT per year for the Waza camping area between 2005 and 2013 was 8, 882,

---

http://www.rfi.fr/emission/20160922-cameroun-relancer-le-tourisme-sinistre-insecurite

[54] March 2015, « Ce que l'insécurité aux frontières fait perdre à l'économie camerounaise » http://www.journalducameroun.com/ce-que-linsecurite-aux-frontieres-fait-perdre-a-leconomie-camerounaise/

[55] Djanabou Bakary, "Insécurité transfrontalière, perturbation des échanges et léthargie des marchés » in ISSA S. ed., November 2014, p. 86

[56] Ministry of Economy, Planning and Regional Development (MINEPAT), 2015 « Impact de la crise sécuritaire aux frontières sur l'économie camerounaise » MINEPAT

[57] Comité catholique contre la faim et pour le développement-Terre Solidaire (CCFD-Terre Solidaire), April 2015, Aide d'urgence pour les populations fuyant Boko Haram au Nord Cameroun, http://ccfd-terresolidaire.org/projets/afrique/cameroun/aide-d-urgence-pour-les-5009

[58] France 24, April 2013, "French family kidnapped in Cameroon describes ordeal", http://www.france24.com/en/20130423-french-family-kidnapped-hostages-cameroon-released-moulin-fournier

[59] France 24, December 2013, "Georges Vandenbeusch (photo), the French priest kidnapped in northern Cameroon last month, has been released, the office of President Francois Hollande said on Tuesday", http://www.france24.com/en/20131231-french-priest-vandenbeusch-cameroon-boko-haram-kidnap

950 Francs CFA[60]. The VAT average for the year 2013 was 1, 654, 338 Francs CFA, representing a loss of 7, 228, 612 Francs CFA.[61]

4.3. Worsening poverty and socio-economic vulnerability in the Far North

The Far North Region registers the highest rates of poverty in Cameroon[62] with respect to all indicators of the Multidimensional Poverty Index (MPI)[63]. This is important for understanding the context within which BH has remained a threat for several years now.

According to household surveys 2, 3 and 4 conducted by the National Institute of Statistics, 74.3 percent of people in the Far North were poor in 2014 against 65.9 in 2007 and 56.3 in 2001. The North follows with 50.1 in 2001, 63.7 in 2007 and 67.9 in 2014[64]. By most accounts, BH has benefitted from the situation in the Far North[65]. Poverty makes the region a fertile ground for recruitment by BH stands under these circumstances as a major employer. The situation has unfortunately worsened since the outset of the crisis in 2012. With the already remote infrastructure destroyed in many villages and many displaced from their villages, there is hardly any other source of work for young people.

In addition to destroying villages and markets, BH also attacked farms. Agriculture is the main source of income for over 80% of the population. The destruction of farms, the displacement of the population in many villages has not only increased food poverty that is favoured by poor climatic conditions but also other forms of poverty. According to the European Commission, "180,000 people are in need of immediate food assistance in the Far North Region."[66] An estimated 80 percent of the

---

60 Gonné, B., 2014, « Kidnappings, crise du secteur touristique et ralentissement de l'aide au développement », in Issa S. ed., November 2014, Effets Economiques et Sociaux des Attaques de Boko Haram dans l'Extreme-Nord du Cameroun, Maroua, KALIAO, p. 102

61 Ibid

62 National Institute of Statistics (INS), 2014, Réalisation de la quatrième Enquête Camerounaise Auprès des Ménages (ECAM 4), Yaounde, INS

63 United Nations Development Programme (UNDP), Multidimensional Poverty Index (MPI), http://hdr.undp.org/en/content/multidimensional-poverty-index-mpi

64 National Institute of Statistics (INS), 2014

65 Camer News, 16 August 2016, Boko Haram : Extrême-Nord, la Région la Plus Pauvre http://www.camernews.com/boko-haram-extreme-nord-la-region-la-plus-pauvre/#JOjj8X7qJU421GYy.99

66 European Commission, May 2017, « Cameroon », ECHO Factsheet, accessed on 21 August 2017 at http://ec.europa.eu/echo/files/aid/countries/factsheets/cameroon_en.pdf

population in the region "is either poor or very poor, with limited access to basic services and essential food commodities."[67] The Catholic Committee Against Hunger and for Development Terre Solidaire, has described it as a situation of generalized poverty[68]. With an already highly unemployed young population, the growing poverty due to destroyed livelihoods has therefore made the region a fertile recruitment ground for BH.

The Far North is the least developed region in Cameroon. The region has a large deficit of basic socio-economic infrastructure, as well as opportunities for training/education and economic opportunities, particularly for young people. This rather fragile situation, coupled with governance gaps, is a determining factor in violence, which can rapidly degenerate under certain circumstances[69]. The literacy rate of the region is 26 percent, far below the national average of 71 percent[70]. The average years of schooling are 4.2 years against a nation average of 6.7.

With respect to professional training, only 5 percent of the population in the Far North has obtained formal training which falls far below the national average of 27 percent[71].The already dire rate of education has been made worse by the deliberate attacks on schools by BH. These attacks suggest that BH sees schools as a threat to its objectives. Since 2015, over 181 schools have been closed by the government[72] for security reasons. Government High School Tourou for example was closed for 2 years and only reopened in September 2016[73]. In addition to the high level of illiteracy, the near absence of government services, the cultural ties of most of the population with the North East of Nigeria, the repercussions

---

67 Ibid

68 Comité catholique contre la faim et pour le développement-Terre Solidaire, April 2015, « Aide d'urgence pour les populations fuyant Boko Haram au Nord Cameroun », http://ccfd-terresolidaire.org/projets/afrique/cameroun/aide-d-urgence-pour-les-5009

69 European Union, 2016, « Document d'action de fonds fiduciaire de l'UE à utiliser pour les décisions du comité de gestion », https://ec.europa.eu/europeaid/sites/devco/files/cameroon-resilience-eutf-18042016_fr.pdf

70 Equal Access, 2016, "Cameroon", http://www.equalaccess.org/country-programs/cameroon/

71 Ibid

72 **Mbou S., September 2016, «** Fermeture d'écoles dans l'Extrême-Nord Cameroun », http://www.kalaranet.com/fermeture-d-ecoles-dans-l-extreme-nord-du-cameroun/

73 Cameroon Info.net, September 2016, « Le lycée de Tourou rouvre ses portes après 2 ans de fermeture », https://www.cameroonweb.com/CameroonHomePage/regional/Le-lyc-e-de-Tourou-rouvre-ses-portes-apr-s-2-ans-de-fermeture-387558

of the instability in Chad, the smuggling including trafficking in small arms and light weapons and the geographic terrain that makes it easily accessible from most part of Borno state have predisposed the Far North to BH activity[74]. The work of many public agencies including, clinics, public schools, customs and police was also disrupted by BH violence. The town of Kerawa (Mayo Sava department) was temporally occupied by BH in October 2015[75]. Balochi and Achigachia (Mayo Tsanaga department) were also temporarily occupied by BH.

Education has been dealt a heavy blow. In a region with high rate of illiteracy, the attacks perpetrated on public schools have made running schools an uphill task for local authorities. In addition to schools, several markets and public infrastructures have been destroyed. The destruction represents a significant economic loss for the government and adds to the heavy cost of security. According to the IMF, the crisis cost the government 1 to 2 percent of its GDP in 2015.[76]

The insecurity that has characterized BH incursions and the escalation of violence following the counter-offensive by the Cameroonian army have clearly disrupted cross border trade, farming, social life and the normal conduct of public administration. BH related terror has led to a mass exodus towards the relatively secure areas of the Far North Region. The crisis has exacted a heavy toll on government revenue from the region and deepened the poverty in the region. Together with the closure of schools in many localities, these problems have made the already precarious situation of the population much worse.

---

[74] CRISIS Group, 16 November 2016, "Cameroun : faire face à Boko Haram » Africa Report No. 241, CRISIS Group, https://www.crisisgroup.org/fr/africa/central-africa/cameroon/cameroon-confronting-boko-haram

[75] Le Figaro, October 2015, « Cameroun: Boko Haram prend la ville de Kerawa », http://www.lefigaro.fr/flash-actu/2015/10/23/97001-20151023FILWWW00203-camerounboko-haram-prend-la-ville-de-kerawa.php

See also AFP, October 2015, « Boko Haram : au moins 55 morts lors d'attentats et de combats à la frontière », accessed on 19 August 2017 at :
http://www.france24.com/fr/20151024-boko-haram-nigeria-cameroun-attentats-combats-frontiere-kerawa

[76] Invest in Cameroon, February 2015, « Cameroun : le FMI estime à 1 à 2% du PIB, l'impact de la guerre contre Boko Haram sur les finances publiques » http://www.investiraucameroun.com/gestion-publique/0305-7371-cameroun-le-fmi-estime-a-1-a-2-du-pib-l-impact-de-la-guerre-contre-boko-haram-sur-les-finances-publiques

4.4. Internal Displacement and Refugees

Since the outset of the conflict in the Far North, thousands of people have been displaced and the region has also received thousands of refugees fleeing BH violence from Nigeria. Over 198, 899 people were displaced in the Far North Region as a result of BH violence[77] at the end of 2016. The numbers have continued to rise. The Displacement Tracking Matrix (DTM) conducted by the International Organization for Migration in March 2017 shows that BH attacks inside Cameroon have displaced 223 000 Cameroonian Nationals[78].

In addition to the growing problems from internal displacement, the Far North region has been host to 64,000 refugees from Nigeria who are living in the Minawao camp in the Mayo-Tsanaga Division. The management of the refugee crisis has put a strain on the local administration that already faced governance problems prior to the start of the crisis. With the inflow of refugees are associated security concerns as BH militants are believed to infiltrate the camp[79]. The conditions in the camp are also very poor. Among others, there is a lack of adequate health care, food and water. About 41 percent of the camp's population is considered to be food insecure. Growing food around the camp to complement food supplies is very difficult due to the arid soil. The refugee crisis and the internally displaced persons have therefore put an extra strain on the already precarious food problems in the region

5. Impact of Counter-terrorism operations

The counter-terrorism strategy adopted by Cameroon is based on what can be considered a military approach. While this has been effective in ending the scale of attacks witnessed in 2015 in towns like Kerawa and Kolofata it does not address the root causes of the conflict. The weakening of BH following the collaborative military assault on its positions from all affected countries is therefore unlikely to result in the eradication of the

---

[77] International Organisation for Migration (IOM), November 2016, « Près de 200 000 personnes sont déplacées à l'intérieur du Cameroun »,
https://www.iom.int/fr/news/pres-de-200-000-personnes-sont-deplacees-linterieur-du-cameroun

[78] European Commission, May 2017, « Cameroon », ECHO Factsheet, accessed on 21 August 2017 at
http://ec.europa.eu/echo/files/aid/countries/factsheets/cameroon_en.pdf

[79]AFP, November 2014, "Refugees fleeing Boko Haram flood Cameroon camp", accessed on 17 August 2017 at: http://www.dailymail.co.uk/wires/afp/article-2836282/Refugees-fleeing-Boko-Haram-flood-Cameroon-camp.html

terrorist group. Cameroons counter-terrorism strategy seeks to achieve the following: put an end to meetings and public drinking after 6pm; increase the number of controls whistle blowing; increase significantly the presence of the military in the region; ensure effective control of trade in goods; monitor mosques and control children and women.

The governor of the Far North banned drinking in public places from 6pm since July 2015. This ban also included gathering in other public places including mosques. The government has also created vigilante groups to work with security forces. In addition to this, efforts have been made to increase the number of soldiers significantly. There are over 8,500 soldiers stationed in this region currently. The sale of goods has been restricted to license holders only. Further, all registered businesses are required to have a fixed location. One of the most innovative measures has been the systematic search of children who are increasingly used to carry out suicide attacks by BH. Another measure that could hardly be expected has been the banning the burqa by the governor of the region following the double bombing by veiled women in Fotokol on 13 July 2015. Finally, the government has increased surveillance at mosques[80]. For this to be effective, a mapping of mosques was carried out.

The military approach adopted has contributed in reducing the number of attacks especially using armored vehicles and 4WD vehicles equipped with heavy weapons. This approach has however been very expensive and is unlikely to completely remove the threat. The tactics of BH have changed since the a coalition of forces backed by the Economic Community of Central African States (ECCAS) and the Lake Chad Basin Commission members was formed to address the crisis since February 2015. To be effective, the counter terrorism measures will need to focus more on addressing the socio-economic problems that facilitated the implantation of BH in the region. Such an approach will be better suited to ending the asymmetric approach currently employed by making the recruitment of young people very difficult.

---

[80] Succès C. T. January 2012, « Boko-Haram paralyse l'activité économique dans le Nord-Cameroun », http://www.nkul-beti-camer.com/ekang-media-press.php?cmd=article&Item=3081&TAB=1&SUB=0

Conclusion

This chapter identified the root causes of the BH crisis to include the historical ties with the neighbouring population in Nigeria, weak presence of government services, geographical and environmental complexities. The proximate causes include the activities of BH members from Nigeria and the handling of cases of kidnapping. Three main factors have contributed to sustaining the activities of BH in the Far North. These are the military approach adopted by the government, the alleged complicity of the political elites and the continued socio-economic deprivation of the population.

The crisis has had a serious impact on the local economy but also on the national economy. It has also had far reaching social consequences. Women and children have been particularly affected. Many young girls have dropped out of school in a region where education and female education in particular is already a challenge. The disruption of cross-border trade has seen a drop in customs revenue and fall in the quality of life of residents. The closure of markets has destroyed livelihoods. Schools have also been either closed for long periods or destroyed completely. The closure of schools and the displacement of students have further limited access to education in the region. The disruption of agriculture has also increased food insufficiency. Many farmers have been forced to abandon their farms while some have seen their crops destroyed by BH militants. Livestock farmers have also lost their animals to BH or have been forced to leave them behind. The decline in education, employment and the increasingly limited access to healthcare has particularly affected vulnerable groups including the youth, women and children.

The security approach adopted together with the violence perpetrated by BH has created serious governance problems. Many government services have been either closed or rendered non-operational. The predominance of the military and hard security concerns has resulted in the erosion of human rights and a surge in corruption and smuggling. In spite of efforts to address the concerns raised by the population on the erosion of civil liberties by military excesses, there is visible damage on the state of civil military relations. The predominantly security/military approach adopted has hence fallen short of guaranteeing the security of persons and property necessary for the socio-economic advancement of the region.

The role of non-governmental organisations in the promotion and protection of human rights from 2016 to 2020: The case of the on-going Anglophone crisis in Cameroon

By

Patience Sone

Associate Professor of Law,
Department of English Law, Faculty of Laws and Political Science,
University of Buea, Cameroon
Email: pattysonem@gmail.com

Abstract

The gruesome and sustained violation of human rights in Cameroon is alarming and a call for concern, especially since 2016 when the current phase of the Anglophone crisis[1] began. Several legal and institutional measures have been taken by the government of Cameroon to curb human rights violations in the country but these seem ineffective. This has led the researcher to investigate the role played by non-governmental organisations (NGOs) in ensuring the promotion and protection of human rights during this period when, arguably, Cameroon has recorded one of the highest rates of human rights violations since independence. This article is based on a detailed study, including interviews, was done on the activities of selected NGOs which have been very active in monitoring, documenting and reporting human rights violations during the crisis. The findings reveal that these organisations have recorded significant achievements in their work, by bringing to the limelight the situation of human rights violations in the country despite the numerous challenges they face in their functioning. Based on the findings, the paper highlights some positive policy recommendations that may help improve their important role in promoting and protecting human rights in the country.

Key words: NGOs, human rights, Anglophone crisis, Cameroon

---

[1]The Anglophone problem centers on issues of identity, marginalization, and discrimination they are faced with. It has its roots from the 1960 while the Anglophone crisis emerged in 2016 following the lawyers and teachers strike actions in the process of exposing the problems and requesting the guarantee of their rights.

Introduction

According to the Universal Declaration of Human Rights of 1948,[2] rights are universal, indivisible, and inalienable. They are an independent body of rights endowed on human beings by virtue of their humanity. A comprehensive approach to the promotion and protection of human rights suggests that everyone should be treated equally with dignity and should enjoy simultaneously all rights, freedoms and social justice in a given society. Despite their theoretical justification, however, human rights refer to a wide continuum of values or capabilities thought to enhance human agency or protect human interests.[3] The fundamental assumption is that each human being is a moral and rational being who deserves to be treated with dignity. Hence, human rights are predicated on the principle of respect and protection.

It is important to note that human rights are not just first and second-generation rights as canonised in the twin 1966 human rights treaties[4] but also include third-generation rights, such as the right to development, as propagated by the 1993 Vienna Declaration and Program of Action[5] as well as the 1986 Declaration on the Right to Development.[6] This development came about after a period in which world powers gave very limited attention to the promotion of the right to development. All these rights have received significant attention, been incorporated into the United Nations human rights system as legal norms and are included in many national constitutions and legal systems. This is the case of Cameroon, as demonstrated in the preamble of the Cameroon Constitution of 1996 as amended in 2008.

As will be discussed later in this paper, the primary responsibility for the promotion and protection of human rights, as advocated in the triple-

---

[2] The Universal Declaration of Human Rights (1948) enshrines civil, political, economic, social and cultural rights and was intended to be the precursor to a single, universal human rights covenant.

[3]Burns, H. Weston, March 20, 2014, Encyclopedia Britannica. Available at: https://www.britannica.com/topic/human-rights. Accessed on 10/10/2019.

[4]The International Covenant on Civil and Political Rights (ICCPR) and the International Covenant on Economic, Social and Cultural Rights (ICESCR).

[5] Vienna Declaration and Program of Action, adopted by the World Conference on Human Rights, in Vienna on 25 June 1993.

[6]Declaration of the Right to Development. Adopted by the UN General Assembly Resolution 4/128 on December 4th, 1986.

pronged theory of human rights,[7]lies with the state through its National Human Rights Institutions. In Cameroon, the state has set up a plethora of bodies charged with promoting and protecting human rights. These include the National Commission on Human Rights and Freedoms, presently known as the Cameroon Human Rights Commission, the National Bilingualism Commission, the National Anti-Corruption Commission, courts and tribunals, law enforcement agencies and their personnel, including the Police. Human rights obligations are binding not only on the state but on every actor at every level, including the family which is the basic unit of every society. Other duty bearers include civil society organisations,[8] especially NGOs,[9]which should act as watchdogs for human rights violations in Cameroon and elsewhere.

NGOs[10]are intended to act as a bridge between the population and the state, in identifying and addressing the basic needs of the population such as safety, security, food, water and housing, derived from the Human Needs Theory propagated by John Burton.[11]They should raise awareness with the state and the entire community towards addressing these

---

7The Triple Pronged theory was propagated by Henry Shue in 1980. It dwells on the States' responsibilities or duties imposed on them after ratifying the International human rights treaties. The duties are the duty to respect, protect and fulfil the basic and fundamental rights endowed on the citizens.

8A civil society organisation generally refers to an association which is neither state nor a family grouping that plays a positive and active role in social, economic and cultural activities. Civil society is multifaceted and forms the greater part of non-state actors in Cameroon. Since the enactment of Law No. 90/53 of 19 December 1990 relating to Freedom of Association, as amended and supplemented by Law No. 99/11 of 20 July 1999, the growth of civil society has strengthened over the years. Civil society, in the context of Cameroon, can be used as a blanket term to refer to several non-state actors such as common initiative groups (CIGs), faith-based organisations (FBOs), non-governmental organisations (NGOs) and community-based organisations (CBOs). As a result, the term 'civil society organisations' can be used to describe non-state actors or associations in Cameroon, whose focus is the general welfare of the population. It is worth noting that it is an older concept than NGOs.

9 Non-governmental organisations are regulated by Law 99/14 of 22 December 1999 governing NGOs. According to Article 2(1), NGOs are created and approved to participate in the execution of missions of general interest. It is a non-profit, voluntary citizens' group which is organised at local, national, regional and international levels. See David Lewis, "Nongovernmental Organizations, Definition and History", The London School of Economics and Political Science, 2010.

10 Groups are initially registered as associations; that they evolve into NGO status over time.

11 Burton John, *Conflict, Basic Human Needs*, New York, St Martin's Press, 1906. Burton holds that citizens' basic needs must be met for them to attain self-actualisation and to avoid conflict in society.

concerns to enhance peace and security in the country. For our purposes, these include the Center for Human Rights and Democracy in Africa (CHRDA); Human is Right Cameroon (HSR-Cmr); Modern Advocacy, Humanitarian, Social and Rehabilitation Association (MAHSRA); Federation of Female Lawyers (FIDA); South and North West Task Force (SNWOT); Blessing Associates for Women And Children (BAWAC); and Authentique Memorial Empowerment Foundation (AMEF), Finders Initiative Group (FGI), among others.

The paper focuses on the role of non-governmental organisations in the promotion and protection of human rights in Cameroon, in the specific context of the socio-political crisis rocking the Northwest and Southwest regions of Cameroon from 2016 to 2020. In October 2016, the Anglophone problem was brought to the limelight by English-speaking lawyers and teachers who highlighted the marginalisation and assimilation suffered by Anglophones in Cameroon. Government agents and the leaders of the Consortium,[12] which acted as the mouthpiece of the suffering masses in English speaking Cameroon, failed to reach a consensus on resolving the grievances. This was due to the differences in ideology and approach. These differences turned violent and culminated in the gruesome rights violations visible today. This has drawn the attention of different stakeholders, all of whom are duty bound to promote and protect human rights in the country.

This paper focuses on the activities of NGOs in a climate of widespread human rights abuses and the meagre efforts undertaken to address them. NGOs have a particular role to play because victims of human rights violations have very limited access to justice and redress due to their ignorance and vulnerability. The findings reveal that gathering and disseminating information on human rights violations, as well as educating the population on how to avoid situations of human rights abuse, are part of the promotion and protection role of human rights NGOs in Anglophone Cameroon. They have only had limited success, however, because of the institutional strength and impunity of those committing the violations. Like corruption, human rights violations and abuses thrive in an atmosphere of clandestine activity and a lack of institutional and procedural transparency.

[12]It referred to the Anglophone Civil Society Consortium. The composition was made up representatives of various trade unions from basic to higher education, some lawyers including transporters.

In Cameroon, the government has been accused of frequent rights violations in the areas of freedom of expression, press freedom, freedom of assembly, as well as the rights to life and fair trial. The latter includes excessive judicial delays, arbitrary arrests and unduly prolonged periods of pre-trial detention. Some notable victims of rights violations of the above excesses are Albert Mukong,[13] Maurice Kamto,[14]Felix Nkongho and Fontem Neba,[15] just to name a few. Some of them were and are political activists with conflicting political objectives against the government.

In order to properly understand the role of the NGOs in the promotion and protection of human rights, this paper will, first of all, analyse the evolution of the institution of NGOs in Africa and Cameroon in particular. It will identify the normative framework regulating human rights in Cameroon and examine the role of some NGOs in the promotion and protection of human rights. These specific NGOs were selected because they have been active in these roles in Anglophone Cameroon since the crisis erupted in 2016. The findings are based on interviews the researcher had with the various organisations and highlight their challenges. The paper ends with some recommendations to address the challenges faced by NGOs in carrying out their work.

1. Evolution of the institution of NGOs in Cameroon

The concept of political liberalisation, which acted as part of the globalisation process that was unleashed in Africa following the collapse of the Cold War,[16] led to political reforms including the promotion and

---

[13]He was a political activist who was always at loggerhead with the Government. This caused him to be arrested and detained constantly.

[14]He is a political leader of MRC party. He was arrested and detained for organizing a peaceful match past without obtaining authorization from the States officials .

[15]Both Nkongho and Neba were some of the leaders of the Anglophone Civil Society Consortium who were arbitrarily arrested and detained for propagating the Anglophone problem.

[16]The Cold War was a period after the Second World War, between 1947 and 1991, which was characterised by political tension and an arms race between the Eastern Bloc (the Soviet Union and its satellite states) and powers in the Western Bloc (led by the United States and including the European Allied Powers and others). These two blocs never engaged in an all-out war but provided support to proxy wars. There was growth in authoritarian rule in Third World countries and failing economies, among other things. The end of the Cold War brought a wave of democracy which saw the ousting from power of many authoritarian governments and demand for democracy and respect for human rights.

protection of human rights.[17] At the end of the Cold War, there was a need for rapid development in many countries across the world. In Western countries especially, this led to collaboration between the state and religious associations in the provision of humanitarian aid to less privileged regions.[18]

In Africa, civil society and especially human rights NGOs, have allowed people in the community to group themselves into associations to have a stronger, collective voice, as individual voices are often ignored and rights to protest against oppression is subdued. J.C. Alexander[19] suggests that civil society organisation can be seen as a "solidarity sphere, in which a certain kind of universalising community comes to be culturally defined and to some degree institutionally enforced."

Civil society organisation has grown over the years in Cameroon, following the 1990 Law on Freedom of Association.[20] This law is set under international human rights instruments and the 1996 Constitution of Cameroon. In a bid to strengthen organisations in the country, and to foster development in different sectors,[21] the government has instituted several laws which regulate different facets of society. Civil society is divided into different facets which group themselves according to their size, character, composition and most importantly, their purpose.

NGOs are the most prevalent part of civil society in Cameroon. They are regulated by Law No. 90/053 of 19 December 1990 relating to Freedom of Association, amended and supplemented by Law No. 99/11 of 20 July 1999, Law No. 99/014 of 22 December 1999 to govern NGOs and Decree No. 2001/150/PM of 13 May 2001 relating to the organisation and functioning of the technical commission in charge of NGO activities. Article 3 of Law No. 99/14 sets out the various areas in

---

[17] Appiagyei-AtuaKwadwo, "Human rights NGOs and their role in the promotion and protection of human rights in Africa", *International Journal on Minority and Group Rights*, vol.9 No. 3, 2002, pp. 265-289.

[18] Dieudonné Kimaka, « Le Cadre Juridique des Organisations Non-Gouvernementales au Cameroun », 2009. Available at: http://www.mireilletchiako.files.wordpress.com/2015/03/cadre-juridique-des-ong-au-cameroun.pdf&ved=2ahUKEwimgLOTo13cAhVMJ8AKHUGbD_oQFjAAegQIBBAB&usg=A)vVaw2HsCK_g2D98FEBVRW4LLD. Accessed on 10/10/2019.

[19] Jeffrey C. Alexander, *The Civil Sphere*, New York, Oxford University Press, 2006, p 31.

[20] See Law No. 90/053 of 19 December 1990 dealing with Freedom of Association .

[21] Temngah J. Nyambo, "Legal Framework of Civil Society and Social movements", in YenshuV.E (ed.) *Civil Society and the Search for Development Alternatives in Cameroon, Oxford, African Books Collectives,* 2009, p. 47.

which NGO status will be granted: legal, economic, social, cultural, health, sports, education, humanitarian sectors or in matters of environmental and human rights protection. To be granted NGO status, however, an organisation must be a "duly declared association or duly authorised foreign association backed by at least three years of effective contribution."[22]

2. Procedure for the legalisation of NGOs

For an association to be legalised in Cameroon, the following documents and procedures must be fulfilled: the article of association (the by-laws); founding members including the executive members and photocopy of their identification cards (at least 5 executive members for a start); minutes of the last 3 meetings. The above three documents should be bounded in a single booklet and replicated into three copies. These documents including an application (signed by the head of the organisation) declaring the intention to create such an organisation citing the laws, objectives and the headquarter of the organisation, are be submitted to the SDO's office with the sum of 45,000frs. Normally, the applicant is expected to wait for a maximum of one month for the authorisation to be granted. Most often due to administrative bottlenecks, one may wait longer than the expected period to get the authorisation from the SDO's office. However, once the authorisation is granted, the organisation goes operational.

The determination of effectiveness is left to the discretion of a "commission responsible for the technical study of approval applications and for monitoring the activities of NGOs."[23] After NGO status is granted to an organisation, it gains a legal personality of its own and acts in its name and capacity. The Technical Commission in charge of the activities of NGOs was created by Article 7 of Law No. 99/14 but only came into existence in 2001. As at 2010, the Technical Commission had granted NGO status only to 26 organisations[24] despite receiving several applications each year. This law has given rise to NGOs whose focus is the promotion, protection and implementation of human rights standards. These NGOs are usually independent of the government and they ensure

---

[22] Article 4 of Law No. 99/14 of 22 December 1999 to govern Non-Governmental Organisations.

[23] Article 7.

[24] Speech delivered by Dr Chemuta Banda (Chairperson of the NCHRF) on Peace, Security and Human Rights in the Central African Region, at the African Sub-Regional Meeting of the ACP-EU Joint Parliamentary Assembly, Yaounde, 28-29 April 2010.

the protection, promotion and implementation of human rights through diverse means, methods and activities. It can be said that human rights NGOs, especially at the national level, complement human rights promotion and protection where the government's actions fail or are inadequate.

NGOs have been active in the human rights domain for a long time. They were formally recognised and empowered by the United Nations in Article 71 of the United Nations Charter which states that "the Economic and Social Council may make suitable arrangements for consultation with NGOs which are concerned with matters within its competence. Such arrangements may be made with international organisations and where appropriate, with national organisations after consultation with the members of the United Nations concerned."[25] Under this provision, NGOs can be granted consultative status with the United Nations Economic and Social Council (ECOSOC). This procedure was initially governed by ECOSOC Resolution 1996/31 of 25 July 1996.[26]

3. Normative framework safeguarding human rights in Cameroon

International human rights law recognises civil, political, economic, social and cultural rights as well as the right to development as integral parts of our domestic human rights framework. It is important to state that as a monist state, once these treaties are duly ratified, they are automatically incorporated into national law and override national legislation on the relevant theme.[27]There are many ratified international, regional and national human rights instruments which empower human rights NGOs in the promotion and protection of human rights in the country.[28] It is worth mentioning that the Cameroon Constitution which

[25] Article 71, Chapter 10, Charter of the United Nations (1945).

[26] United Nations Economic and Social Council Resolution 288 B (X) was superseded by ECOSOC Resolution 1296 (XLIX) of 25 May 1968. The current terms of reference of the Committee are set out in Resolution 1996/31 of 25 July 1996.

[27]Article 45 of the Constitution of Cameroon (1996) as amended in 2008.

[28]Some of them are the International Covenant on Economic, Social and Cultural Rights (1966); the International Covenant on Civil and Political Rights (1966); the Declaration on Social Progress and Development (1969); the Convention on the Elimination of All Forms of Discrimination Against Women (1979); the Convention Against Torture, Cruel, Inhuman and Degrading Treatment or Punishment (1954); the Convention on the Rights of the Child (1989); the Vienna Declaration for Program of Action (1993). At region level: the African Charter on Human and Peoples' Rights (1981); the Protocol to the African Charter on Human and People's Rights on the Rights of Women in

is the umbrella law of the land embodies all the necessary rights that need to be promoted and protected as outlined in the preamble of the constitution and by virtue of article 65 of the constitution, the preamble is part and parcel of the constitution.

4. The role of non-governmental organisations in promoting and protecting human rights in Cameroon

Non-governmental organisations generally play a vital role in the promotion and protection of human rights in Cameroon. They serve as secondary bearers of this duty, remind the state of its obligations and highlight lapses in the respect, protection and fulfilment of human rights. These are achieved through human rights monitoring, investigation, documenting and reporting.

Monitoring human rights is the process of systematically tracking and assessing state performance against clear benchmarks and targets. The process requires data collection and analysis, involving not only official statistics but possibly also field observation, investigation and even fact-finding delegations.[29] In addition, NGOs play a vital role in monitoring human rights by organising seminars and campaigns to raise awareness and expose abuses of human rights in a country.

Some of the roles they perform include indicating whether a State is meeting its obligations or not, providing a basis for holding the State accountable, as well as identifying the source and nature of human rights violations. They equally identify the problems involved in realising the enjoyment of human rights. They identify priorities for action and make suggestions on the allocation of resources. Furthermore, they support legislative advocacy and policy formulation, engage in public awareness and education campaigns, and promote principled policy-making that incorporates a human rights perspective and processes that facilitate public accountability. The results they obtain from monitoring are often used to pursue actions to obtain remedies from the courts and they provide the basis for reports and submissions to national and international bodies.

Africa (2005); the African Convention on the Rights and Welfare of the Child (1990). At the national level: the Cameroon Constitution of 1996; the 1983 law protecting the rights of persons with a disability; the 1992 law protecting the rights of prisoners; and the 1990 Liberty Laws.

29 Manuel Guzman and Bert Verstappen, "What is Monitoring?", *Human Rights Monitoring and Documentation Series*, vol. 1, 2001.

NGOs are engaged in the collection, verification, and dissemination of information on human rights abuses. Local human rights NGOs are better placed to have such information because they are closer to people than local or international human rights organisations in the country. In a bid to collect relevant information for exposing human rights abuses and violations, they 'work with a loop of international and domestic ties between NGOs, local social movements, foundations, the media, churches, intellectuals, parts of intergovernmental organisations and branches of government'.[30] Based on the views of Claude Welch[31] that "without the flow of the NGO-system, the UN would come to a halt," it is clear that NGOs play an important role in enhancing the human rights mandate of the UN. Also, Baehr[32] posits that "the thematic mechanisms of the UN rely almost exclusively upon information from NGOs."

In Cameroon, local human rights NGOs collaborate with international NGOs such as Amnesty International, International Crisis Group and Human Rights Watch to provide information on human rights violations in the on-going crisis in Anglophone Cameroon. Recent reports published by some NGOs[33] have helped to expose the human rights situation in Cameroon. This has led the international community to caution the government to investigate and ensure the proper protection of human rights of its citizens.[34] All of these activities have led NGOs to be described as 'watchdogs' incharge of monitoring and assessing the situation of human rights protection in Cameroon.

Center for Human Rights and Democracy in Africa (CHRDA)

The Center for Human Rights and Democracy in Africa is an apolitical, non-governmental organisation created with the mandate of protecting and promoting human rights and democracy in Africa. It was created in 2005, has its headquarters in Buea and has an office in Bamenda. CHRDA

---

[30] Keck M. & Kathryn E. S., *Activists Beyond Borders: Advocacy Networks in International Politics*, New York, Cornell University Press, 1998, p. 9.

[31] Welch Claude, 'Introduction', in Welch Claude (ed.), *NGOs and Human Rights Promise and Performance*, University of Pennsylvania Press, 2001, p. 5.

[32] Beahr Peter, *Non-Governmental Human Rights Organisations in International Relations*, Palgrave, Macmillan, 2009, p. 37.

[33] CHRDA and Raoul Wallenberg, Center for Human Rights. "Cameroon's unfolding Catastrophe: Evidence of Human Rights violation and crimes against humanity", Montreal, Concordia University 2019. Also available online at: www.chrda.org and www.rwhrc.org accessed on 20/02/2020.

[34] This is evidently seen when both the national and international organizations enjoined the government to set up an independent commission of inquiry to investigate the Ngarbuh massacre which the government did.

is split into the following operational departments: Human Rights, Legal, Humanitarian Affairs, Gender, Democracy, Communication and Projects.

The Center has over the years been actively engaged in activities geared towards respecting human dignity by providing philanthropic aid to orphanages in the Southwest Region of Cameroon.[35]It works with children living with disabilities and organises seminars aimed at combating corruption, hate speech,[36] promotes digital rights and fights gender-based violence.

In the wake of the Anglophone Crisis affecting the Northwest and Southwest Regions of Cameroon, CHRDA has noted an alteration of gender roles among local communities. Owing to the indiscriminate male massacres, sexual violence, the unlawful use of force, psychological violence, summary and extrajudicial executions, arbitrary arrests and detention, CHRDA has lobbied and advocated for the respect and protection of fundamental human rights of the civilian population. CHRDA has also reached out to Internally Displaced Persons (IDPs)[37], bringing food and non-food items as well as basic WASH &Dignity Kits. They also visited the Ogoja refugee camp in Nigeria in 2018 which hosts about 50,000 refugees who fled the violence in Anglophone Cameroon.

In February 2020, the Chief Executive Officer of CHRDA was one of the first authorities in the country to vehemently condemn the gruesome massacre that occurred in Ngarbuh village, in which over 20 people died. He publicly condemned the act and advised that the perpetrators be held accountable.[38]

In a bid to foster and mainstream the role of women and to build women's capacity, CHRDA has organised seminars and workshops aimed at mainstreaming the role of women in conflict resolution and peacebuilding as well as civil rights and advocacy. This was marked by the unprecedented First Annual African Women Solidarity Peace Forum, held from 31July to 2August 2018. During this event, CHRDA equally organised a training-of-trainers for civil society organisations working on

---

[35]CHRDA specifically donated food items to the Hotpec Orphanage Centre at Mile 14 (Dibanda) in 2018.

[36]'Combatting Hate Speech in Cameroon', a seminar organised at PAID-WA in November 2018.

[37] The organisation has visited hundreds of IDPs in Malale Village several times in 2018 and 2019.

[38] See the report available at: hrw.org/news/2020/0.

gender-related activities, public campaigns and for women's rights and advocacy in online and offline fora.

As a mechanism to prevent conflict, radicalisation and violent extremism, CHRDA organised a two-day sensitisation campaign aimed at combating hate and dangerous speech in Cameroon, from 16 to 18 November 2018. This event brought together many stakeholders including the Consul General of Nigeria to Cameroon for the Northwest and Southwest Regions, representatives of the university community, state agents, youth leaders, media activists and other CSOs. This activity ended with the adoption of a 10-point declaration which intimated state representatives, bloggers and citizen journalists to shun the use of hate speech, especially within a crisis. The Gender Taskforce of CHRDA also organised workshops in the Northwest and Southwest Regions on combating gender-based violence. CHRDA organised these seminars to sensitise the population on the need to foster peaceful co-existence in society and the importance of securing the rights of all, regardless of sex or any other status in society.

These actions have resulted in positive changes: CHRDA's actions have kept the international community informed of the grave human rights situation and have resulted in pressure being brought on the government to curb human rights abuses and work towards a peaceful resolution to the socio-political crisis. CHRDA's efforts have led a reduction in the number of extrajudicial killings, arbitrary arrests and detentions, forced displacement, burning of villages and torture. The Legal Department of CHRDA has championed the campaign for the release of detainees arbitrarily arrested in Buea. So far, more than 300 detainees have been released thanks to the relentless efforts of CHRDA.

Women and girls have also received skills training to build economic resilience and generate funds, keeping them off the streets and from indulging in unhealthy practices in a bid to fend for themselves. CHRDA has also given training in sexual and reproductive health in the light of a surge in unplanned pregnancies among women and girls. Above all, CHRDA has been at the fore for monitoring, documenting and reporting human rights violations since the start of the crisis.[39]

Human is Right Cameroon (HSR-Cmr)

Human is Right (HSR-Cmr) is a renowned human rights NGO that operates in the domain of promotion and protection of human rights,

---

[39] Available at: www.chrda.org and www.rwhrc.org accessed on 24/02/2020.

especially the rights of the vulnerable persons and groups. The organisation was established in 2012 because of the growing rate of human rights violation in prisons, prolonged pretrial detention, denial of the right to fair trial and access to justice. It is based in Buea, Southwest Region of Cameroon and has offices in most chief towns in the Region notably in Fako, Kupe Muanenguba, Manyu, Meme and Ndian Divisions. HSR-Cmr staff are knowledgeable and passionate about issues relating to human rights and the rule of law in Cameroon.

Since its inception, HSR-Cmr has worked to expose the reign of terror in the region, with the accompanying breakdown in the rule of law and violations of fundamental human rights and liberties. Its work focuses on the following specific rights, which the population has been unable to enjoy for some time in the Region: life, property, education, access to justice, freedom of movement and expression as well as a decent and secure living environment.[40]It does this by identifying instances of rights violations, gathering information from the field, reporting the specific violations and their intensity to the relevant authorities and to the affected population itself. This is done for purposes of awareness and for prompt remedial action to be taken. SHR-Cmr embarked on a campaign to expose human rights atrocities committed by both private individuals and public authorities without fear or favour.

The organisation has a special mission for protecting the fundamental rights of vulnerable groups. It runs a prisoners' rights project aimed at facilitating access to justice for detainees who have been in prolonged pretrial detention in the South West Region. In 2019 for instance, SHR-Cmr staff used their expertise to handle the case of Awungafack Clinton, a 14-year-old boy who was arrested and detained since 2017 without remand warrant at the Buea Central Prison. His situation was ameliorated when the organisation filed a habeas corpus petition, following which the court ordered his release.[41]

SHR-Cmr often organises seminars and capacity building workshops to educate the population and human rights defenders on the importance of upholding the values of human rights. Training also includes the

[40] HSR-Cmr, "The reign of terror and the breakdown of rule of law and violation of fundamental human rights and liberties in the South West Region in July 2018". Available at: www.hisrcameroon.org. accessed on 20/10/2019.

[41] Information derived from an interview granted by the Director of the South West Regional head office of the organization based in Buea on 30/10/2019.

relevant instruments and mechanisms available for the protection of human rights in the country.

South west North west Women Task Force (SNWOT)

SNWOT is a ground breaking organisation made up of female committed leaders of the Southwest and Northwest origin. It was created in Buea in June 2018. Its headquarter is in Buea and has focal points in Bamenda, Douala and Yaounde where some of the members are resident. As part of its major objectives, SNWOT is determined to contribute towards efforts to end indiscriminate rape, other forms of gender based violence including abduction, kidnapping of women and girls, and Cameroonian citizens.[42] They are out to end the destruction of livelihood, burning of schools, property and disruption of access to education.

SNWOT has stood at the front during the Anglophone crisis in condemning all the human rights violations happening in the regions. Following a focus group discussion I had with some of the members in Buea on the 20/01/2020, they stated that in August and September 2018, SNWOT carried out two major lamentation campaigns both in the Southwest and Northwest regions respectively. The campaigns were preceded by media sensitisation on peace and violence against women and girls in times of war. Physical campaigns were also organised to women's groups for mobilisation of the women. These campaigns were followed by training workshops where members were given skills in peacebuilding and the need to promote and protect their rights. The outcome of the training was the development of a position paper on the crisis, which was delivered in Yaounde to Diplomatic Corps, the media, civil society and the public on the 10th of December 2018.

Prior to the National Dialogue, SNWOT organised preconsultations with women in the North west and South west regions, where their views were sampled on the issues of war, peace and governance. These were submitted to the prime minister during his pre-dialogue consultations. SNWOT also took part in the National Dialogue where members presented the views of women on all issues including the form of the state, post conflict reconstruction, rehabilitation of separatist fighters and other issues. SNWOT has been very successful. It has received international recognition for its work which has led to trainings on mediation and

[42]See the Website *Journal du Cameroun*, 17/07/2019. https//www.Journalducameroun.com. The organisation launched a 'black Wednesday' to protest against violence in Anglophone regions where women and children are being brutalised and killed by the military and armed men.

peacebuilding. It has also received support from grassroots women, who today are more willing to support their work in the conflict ridden zones of the Northwest and South west regions.

The members reiterated that their lamentation for peace and the position paper, which called for ceasefire and dialogue contributed to high level discussions for a national dialogue. They declared that their organisation held a consultation session with Leymah Gbowee, the Nobel Prize winner and renowned Liberian activist in Yaounde in 2019 at the office of the UN women. Moreso, more women's coalitions are being created for peace inorder to enhance peace, respect for human rights and stability in the country.

Modern Advocacy, Humanitarian, Social and Rehabilitation Association (MAHSRA)

MAHSRA is keen to advance human rights, especially involving women and children as vulnerable groups. Its headquarters are in Mile 6 (Nkwen) in the Northwest Region with offices and staff in other towns in the Region and went operational in 2009. It works in collaboration with other bodies in addressing issues relating to human rights, peace and equal opportunities for all. In commemoration of International Women's Day in 2018 for instance, MAHSRA worked with the British and Canadian High Commissions in Cameroon to present a programme supporting the right to development for women in the region in the domains of health, agriculture, provision of water and sanitation.[43] This was done in a bid to empower women with information and finances inorder to improve their living standards and status in the community.

MAHSRA has organised many seminars and workshops to sensitise women and children, specifically widows and orphans,on their rights and how to live a dignified life in society. It has worked to inform traditional rulers, administrators and the general population of the negative effects of exploiting and trafficking orphaned children in the Region. They also educate the community on the inheritance rights of widows, who often suffer from discrimination in this disregard.[44]

---

[43] MASHRA, "MASHRA advocacy call on the Development Rights of Vulnerable Women in Commemoration of Women's Day", official website March 8, 2018. http://mahsra.org/index.php/information/89-news-items/333-mahsra-s-advocacy-call-on-the-development-rights-of-vulnerable-women-in-commemoration-of-women accessed on 20/10/2019.

[44] High Commission of Canada in Cameroon, "Protecting Widows and Orphans in Northwestern Cameroon", official website, November 2015.

The organisation has been vocal in condemning the human rights abuses that are recurrent in the Region since the start of the Anglophone crisis. It has been reporting on the security and human rights situation in Anglophone Cameroon, which has witnessed a continuous rise in instances of violent confrontation between the military and armed groups. The occurrence of abductions and kidnappings, unprecedented human rights violations, destruction of property and institutional values, tribal and political hatred, and armed banditry is well-known thanks to MAHSRA's reporting activities.[45]

5. Challenges faced by NGOs in the promotion and protection of human rights

In a study carried out by Leslie Fox,[46] he notes that NGOs often lack efficient structures, qualified personnel, adequate funding, lack of a system of evaluation of their performance and some of their activities are hampered by administrative bottlenecks. However, most of them are still ongoing and determined to pursue their objective of promoting and protecting the rights of citizens. The three organisations, whose activities are discussed above, informed the researcher of the numerous challenges they face in carrying out their human rights activities generally and, more specifically, during the Anglophone crisis. These are discussed below.

It is worth remarking that after the end of the Cold War, even though most African countries have signed numerous human rights treaties and instituted bodies for the protection and promotion of human rights, there continue to be gross violations of rights across Africa and in Cameroon in particular. This is generally due to the absence of effective democracy in these countries, which means that human rights institutions are not given the freedom and leverage to do the work for which they were created. As a result, they are unable to work effectively and achieve their objectives, and so serious human rights violations continue to occur across the continent.

https://www.canadainternational.gc.ca/cameroon-cameroun/eyes_abroad-coupdoeil/YUNDE-WO.aspx?lang=eng accessed on 21/10/2019.

45 MASHRA, "The Anglophone's Mindset in Conflict", official website, March 2019. http://mahsra.blogspot.com/2019/03/the-anglophones-mindset-in-conflict.html accessed on 25/10/2019.

46 Leslie Fox, *A study of NGOs in the Republic of Cameroon and Cote d'Ivoire*, Washington D.C., World Bank Occidental and Central Africa Department, Population and Human Resource, 1993, p. 90.

The government views the NGOs discussed above as being anti-establishment because they expose human rights abuses, even though these are committed by both state and non-state actors. They equally face financial challenges because although human rights advocacy is free, the methods they use are not cheap. Findings reveal that organisations such as SNWOT, MAHSRA, Human is Rights, etc, could not accomplish their objectives adequately in the promotion and protection of human rights due to lack of finance to drive through their agenda. Instead, they incurred huge financial costs in running programmes and field operations. As not-for-profit organisations, this poses a major problem in attaining the full vision of their activities especially when it comes to accessing all the communities and victims affected by the crisis.

Another problem is the limited nature of qualified staff working in the organisations. As not-for-profit and underfunded organisations, most of them rely heavily on volunteer staff who may not be very skilled in the area of human rights. Qualified personnel who seek employment often require high salaries from these organisations, which are forced to recruit less qualified staff who are then offered job training opportunities in the area of human rights. Other limitations these organisations face include ineffective follow up in cases of violations and abuse and the constant intrusion of the armed forces in the execution of their duties. In addition, there is no specific legislation in Cameroon to protect human rights defenders in the exercise of their duties and this aspect prevents them from being too vocal about human rights violations in the country for fear of an arrest.

There is a noted lack of collaboration and partnership between active human rights NGOs. For instance when SNWOT carried out the lamentation campaigns both in the Northwest and Southwest regions due to the gruesome killing, kidnapping, destruction of properties, etc, no male or any other NGO joined or supported them. This makes it difficult to form a strong alliance and a single voice in promoting and protecting human rights in Cameroon. Many organisations are crafty and stingy with ideas, which hinder collaboration with other organisations. In addition, some civil society organisations are uncoordinated and unaffiliated and therefore cannot liaise effectively with government institutions. As a result, most are not aware of the legal and institutional frameworks available for the protection of victims. This in effect taints the level of protection which can be offered to victims.

The restrictions imposed on all civil liberties in Cameroon following the 2014 law on the repression of acts of terrorism has prevented the organisations from carrying out public protests to denounce the rampant gross human rights violations (such as arbitrary arrest, illegal detention, molestation, abduction, forceful disappearance, etc.) of human rights defenders, including journalists and other civilians in the country.[47]

Furthermore, human rights NGOs experience a lack of collaboration from state authorities such as judges, mayors, Divisional Officers, Senior Divisional Officers and members of the forces of law. This prevents them from effectively carrying out their human rights work, especially in detention centres. They are regarded by these officials as opponents and not partners in the development of the country.

Having said that, sometimes they receive assistance and protection from state organs in the execution of their work. For instance, the National Commission on Human Rights and Freedoms, which is the National Human Rights Institution (NHRI) of Cameroon,[48] has the obligation to liaise with these organisations to further the protection and promotion of human rights in Cameroon. This has been done through activities carried out by the Commission in collaboration with NGOs. These activities include educational campaigns and the follow up of reports on human rights violations submitted to them by NGOs, among others. In line with the Paris Principles,[49] the Commission works in close collaboration with organisations that are affiliated to it, to facilitate their human rights agenda. They also assist in the release of human rights defenders who are illegally detained, as well as train and educate the staff

---

[47]Available at: https://www.chrda.org/chrda-13-civil -society-organisations-appeal-and-urge-au-to-engage-in-resolving-the-anglophone-crisis-in-cameroon/, accessed on 09/02/2020.

[48] Besides the NCHRF, NGOs also liaise with other government institutions such as the Department of Human Rights and International Cooperation in the Ministry of Justice and the Inter-Ministerial Committee for the follow-up of decisions and/or recommendations of international and regional human rights promotion and protection mechanisms located in the office of the Prime Minister. This was outlined in the Ministry of Justice's 2014 National Action Plan for the Promotion and Protection of Human Rights in Cameroon.

[49]Principles relating to the Status of National Institutions (The Paris Principles). UN General Assembly Resolution 48/134 of 20 December 1993. The Principles on the Methods of Operation provides in paragraph (g) that, "in view of the fundamental role played by the Non-Governmental Organisations in expanding the work of the national institutions, develop relations with the Non-Governmental Organisations devoted to promoting and protecting human rights, to economic and social development, to combating racism, to protecting particularly vulnerable groups (especially children, migrant workers, refugees, physically and mentally disabled persons) or to specialized areas."

of such organisations. In addition, there exist international instruments such as the UN Declaration on Human Rights Defenders and regional mechanisms such as the African Commission on Human and Peoples' Rights. The African Commission is the first regional human rights body to create a specific procedure to deal with the protection of defenders' rights,[50] and has been instrumental in the protection of this group of persons.

Human rights defenders are those who act "individually and in association with others, to promote and strive for the protection and realisation of human rights and fundamental freedoms at the national and international levels."[51]Human rights civil society organisations are indispensable in assisting the State to ensure the full respect of fundamental freedoms, democracy and the rule of law. There have been heightened demands for better protection of human rights over the years due to political uprisings and autocratic strongholds. Human rights defenders are put in a position where they must do more to ensure that states respect their duty to promote, protect and fulfil the rights and freedoms of their citizens, even though this may cause the organisations to be seen as working against political regimes.

In Anglophone Cameroon, human rights NGOs focus their activities in urban areas and have failed to expand and create a similar impact in rural areas where gross human rights violations are continuously committed by state and non-state actors against the civilian population.

Conclusion and recommendations

The State bears the primary responsibility to promote, protect and fulfil the human rights of citizens. However, this duty is also shared by civil society organisations, in particular NGOs. The latter act as watchdogs, who often investigate, monitor and report human rights violations by state and non-state actors to bring justice to the victims of human rights violations. They equally seek accountability from the State and enforce the role of the rule of law. Findings reveal that CHRDA, SNWOT, MAHSRA, Human is Right and FGI have contributed enormously in bringing to the lamplight, the human rights violations that have been perpetuated on the

---

[50]Resolution ACHPR/69 (XXXV) on the Protection of Human Rights Defenders in Africa and Resolution ACHPR/Res. 199 XXXXII) 07 on the situation of Human Rights Defenders in Africa. Available at: www.achpr.org/sessions/50th/resolutions/196. Accessed on 20/10/2019.

[51]See Article 1, UN Declaration on Human Rights Defenders (1999).

inhabitants of the two English speaking regions since the crisis started in 2016. Findings also expose the numerous harassment and threats the NGOs have been facing especially from the government authorities when carrying out their activities in the field as human rights defenders and promoters. The government has failed to encourage their activities as human rights defenders of the civilians who have been vulnerable during the crisis period but they are instead construed as traitors of the states. All of these help to limit their ability to effectively push for a safer environment in which human rights are fully respected in times of conflict such as the crisis in the Northwest and Southwest regions of Cameroon.

Cognisant of the challenges faced by human rights NGOs, this paper strongly posits that the State should seek ways and means to work positively with NGOs in promoting and protecting human rights of the citizens especially the vulnerable civilians. This can be achieved by strengthening the relationship between the National Commission on Human Rights and Freedoms (presently called the Cameroon Human Rights Commission) and civil society organisations. Human rights experts should offer their services to NGOs for an improved contribution towards service to humanity and in an effort to make the world a more peaceful place. Since financial constraints are a major obstacle in their activities, people of goodwill are encouraged to fund the efforts of human rights NGOs, including businesses which should see this as part of their corporate social responsibility in the service of humanity. There should be a strong collaboration and partnership between NGOs who are human rights defenders to work for the common good of the population in promoting and protecting their rights void of any form of bias.

A bird's eye view of the vocational training law reform in Cameroon

By

Monkam Cyrille

Senior Lecturer of Civil Law,
Department of French Private Law, Faculty of Laws and Political Science,
University of Buea, Cameroon
Email: monkam.cyrille@ubuea.cm

Abstract

To work is the most desirable action that every citizen wants to embark on. Most often, this action is submitted to the acquisition of skills that can be done through an appropriate training. The sector of vocational training is organized in Cameroon by a new law that is critically assessed by this paper. The article argues that the vocational training law reform is commendable since it has provided the country with a new vision in equipping trainees with modern tools and in preparing them to the working environment. The law also sanctions entities that will operate out of it. This vision can be observed through the various innovative measures in the law. However for the effectiveness of the reform, much still needs to be done in terms of guarantee of the application of the law by the State and the appropriation of the law by the stakeholders. Failing to comply with these requirements will give room to the expansion of unscrupulous training entities out of the cost of trainees.

Résumé

Le désir de tout citoyen est de s'engager dans un emploi. Mais très souvent, l'envie de travailler s'accompagne des qualités professionnelles qui peuvent s'obtenir à travers une formation adéquate. Le secteur de la formation professionnelle est organisé au Cameroun par une nouvelle loi dont le présent article se propose d'évaluer. L'article relève que la réforme de la formation professionnelle est loisible compte tenu de la nouvelle vision qu'elle propose. En réalité, elle équipe les apprenants des outils modernes devant leur permettre de s'intégrer dans le monde professionnel et sanctionne les acteurs qui vont opérer en dehors de celle-ci. Cette vision s'observe à travers les nouvelles mesures mises sur pied. Toutefois, pour que la réforme produise son efficacité, l'Etat doit garantir l'application stricte des règles édictées et les autres acteurs doivent se réapproprier la loi. En l'absence de ces conditions, les centres de formation véreux continueront de se propager au détriment des apprenants.

Introduction

The right to work is a fundamental socio-economic right[1] that has been preserved in most of the international instruments on the protection of Human rights[2] alongside the Cameroon constitution[3]. Specifically, Section 6 (2) of the International Covenant on Economic, Social and Cultural Rights 1966 highlights the appropriate steps to safeguard the right to work by providing: "*the steps to be taken by a state party to the present covenant to achieve the full realization of this right shall include technical and vocational guidance and training programs, policies and techniques to achieve steady economic, social and cultural development and full and productive employment under conditions safeguarding fundamental political and economic freedoms to the individual*". In furtherance of this, the International Labour Organization (ILB) Recommendations on Human Resources Development: Education, Training and Lifelong Learning[4] states that members should "*ensure that vocational education and training systems are developed and strengthened to provide appropriate opportunities for the development and certification of skills relevant to the labour market*". The fact that socio-economic rights are open-ended and indeterminate is problematic since each State is left to interpret the standards as they see fit.[5] It appears from these instruments that the right to work is fully achieved through vocational education and training that seem to be a direct means for living a dignified and decent life by performing an accepted lawful activity.

Notwithstanding the 'vocational school fallacy' that was[6] and continues to be[7] rampant in developing countries, Cameroon had long taken into

[1] V. Mantouvalou, *The Right to work: Legal and philosophical perspectives*, Oxford, Hart Publishing, 2015; for the Book Review, B. Mak, "The Right to work: Legal and philosophical perspectives", *Industrial Law Journal*, Vol. 45, Issue 3, September 2016, pp. 465-475.

[2] See the Universal Declaration of Human Rights of 1948; the International Covenant on Economic, Social and Cultural Rights of 1966, African Charter on Human and Peoples' Rights 1981; and ILO conventions and recommendations.

[3] The preamble of the constitution of 18th January 1996.

[4] R.195, Human Resources Development, Recommendation 2004.

[5] See N. Jheelan, "The enforceability of socio-economic rights", *European Human Rights Review*, Issue 2, 2007, pp. 146-157.

[6] See P. J. Foster, "The vocational school fallacy in development planning", *Education and Economic Development*, London, Cass & Co., 1966, pp. 142-166.

[7] See J. Lauglo, "Revisiting the vocational school fallacy: A tribute to Philip Foster", *Comparative Education*, Vol. 46, Issue 2, pp. 223-235.

consideration safeguard measures by enacting vocational training laws[8] that culminated with the enactment of the Labour Code 1992.[9] By so doing, the State fulfilled its international obligations in line with the 'triple pronged human rights theory'[10] that requires States to respect, protect and fulfill the human rights of its citizens as well as those of aliens living within its territory.

As a permanent task and in order to cope with current economic trends, a cabinet meeting was convened by the Prime Minister in May 2016 on the professionalization of education and training.[11] This was as a follow-up of one of the resolutions of an International Economic Conference held in Yaounde under the theme "*Investing in Cameroon, land of attractiveness*"; and which adopted a resolution calls for "*accelerating the professional training of technicians and engineers, so critical to the country's industrialization, especially for anchor projects and our agricultural economy*". During the meeting, three interventions sealed the pace for a combined vocational training policy in Cameroon. Firstly, the Minister in charge of Employment, after a diagnostic assessment of government's policy on apprenticeship[12] recommended that "*the legislative and regulatory framework should be updated, sources of financing identified, a stronger public-private partnership forged, the guidance of young school drop-outs improved and the certification system better adjusted to current realities*". On their part, the Ministers of Higher Education and Secondary Education also explored and explained the implementation of instructions on the professionalization of education. Lastly, the Minister delegate in the Ministry of Agriculture and Rural Development broached on aspects of professionalization of agricultural training. The meeting ended with instructions to all participants to submit their draft instruments in order to strengthen coherence of all governmental training initiatives. This co-ordination action later led to the production of a draft bill on vocational training that was submitted to Parliament, and was voted into law as Law No. 2018/010 of 11th July 2018 to regulate Vocational Training in Cameroon; repealing all other instruments in this regard.[13] It

---

[8] See Law No. 76/12 of 8th July 1976 organizing intensive vocation training and Decree No. 79/201 of 28th May 1979 on the organization and functioning of the intensive vocation training centres.

[9] See Law No. 92/007 of 14th August 1992.

[10] H. Shue, *Basic Rights; Subsistence, Affluence and US Foreign Policy*, Princetown University Press, 1980.

[11] D. Maingari, "La professionnalisation de l'enseignement au Cameroun: Des sources aux fins", *Recherche et Formation*, No. 25, 1997, pp. 97-112.

[12] See Section 45 of the Cameroon Labour code.

[13] See Section 54.

is by this the lone domestic instrument on vocational training. Mindful of the above, section 6 defines Vocational training "*training consisting in imparting knowledge, skills and competences with a view to ensuring a qualified labour force, and based on the qualitative and quantitative needs of employers and workers*".

Against this background, this paper interrogates the guarantee and the employability of workers. It further questions whether the 2018 law affords an opportunity for companies to enhance their productivity and by implication promote the economic development of the country.

This is done with the objective to sensitize the public on innovations in the new law and to warn against potential hurdles that may disrupt its efficacy. In-depth critical content analysis of the law is adopted in a bid to identify the major innovations emerging from it including identifying shortcomings plaguing its effectiveness. The careful reading of the new law leaves the reader with a mixed sentiment due to the fact that the various innovations that emerged from the law are plagued by political and socio-economic factors.

1. Innovative measures

The innovations in the new law start as from its purpose. Unlike the repealed law that was to organize intensive vocational training, the new law has a holistic approach to vocational training. According to Section 1 (1), "*This law lays down the general legal framework as well as the basic guidelines for vocational training in Cameroon*". This first impression demonstrates the importance of tasks that the State is planning to embark on. The seriousness can also be viewed through the creation of the National Council for Career Guidance and Vocational Training. This council shall assist the State in developing and implementing the vocational training policy.[14]

Apart from these innovations, the 2018 Vocational Training Law Reform clearly portrays the legislator's intention to navigate between modernization trends and State's control. The first laudable measure was to extend the organizational scope of vocational training; the second was to adjust the control mechanisms and the third was to reinforce the sanctions against unscrupulous vocational training entities.

[14] See Section 42 (2).

1.1. Extension of organizational scope

In general, Section 10 (1) provides that: "*Vocational training shall comprise: Initial vocational training; Continuing vocational training; and Apprenticeship*". Careful analysis of the new law reveals that the legislator was driven by three main concerns: the quest for endowment of citizens with an opportunity to gain employment and ensuring job security; the reformulation of apprenticeship policy in the more global content of the vocational training policy; and incorporating information and communication technologies in training methods.

Regarding the first worry, that of vocational training, it is stressed that vocational training is at the same time a management tool and a development lever. In practice, the aim of every organization is to outweigh its competitors in terms of rendering better services to its customers to enable the company to sustain itself in the market. In addition, to act as means of providing workers or job seekers with skills more relevant to the evolving needs of the employers and the economy. Therefore, it should be a priority for companies in order to enhance their productivity. More so, vocational training enriches a person for life, be it job seeker or employee and so provides them with competences which are necessary for individual and social development. It further helps in acquiring skills and experience that may facilitate national and international mobility.

All these features of vocational training are presented through the initial vocational training,[15] the continuing vocational training[16] and even the dual training.[17] They may all be carried out within a vocational training entity or a company. Section 18 (2) empowers the State in the context of initial vocational training programme to "*take time-bound measures to correct any imbalances arising or potentially arising*" in that domain. The analysis of these various provisions, in particular Section 17 (2) shows that the State's objective is "*to enable the trainee to acquire, in particular, the specific qualifications enabling him/her to carry out a professional activity competently and safely; the basic general knowledge he/she requires to access and remain in the world of work, and for social integration; the economic, ecological, social and cultural knowledge and skills enabling him/her to contribute to sustainable development; the capacity and readiness for lifelong learning, critical judgment and decision making*".

---

[15] See Sections 17, 18 and 19.

[16] See Section 20.

[17] See Sections 24, 25 and 26.

The second concern, that of apprenticeship, is one of the major innovations of the law since this provision was not envisaged under the previous legislation and in the employment policy.[18] In fact, the two concepts do not receive the same attention under the 1992 Labour Code. Vocational training was almost ignored[19] whereas a chapter with three sections[20] was dedicated to apprenticeship. Sections 22 and 23 of the new law are almost the same with Sections 46 and 47 of the Labour Code. The same observation is correct with Section 6 of the new law in defining apprenticeship and apprenticeship contract clearly reproduces partly Section 45 of the 1992 Labour Code. It appears then from these observations that substantially there is consistency with the legislator's conception of apprenticeship. However, looking at the definition of apprenticeship contract, the similarity with vocational training is unquestionable and it was wrong to treat them separately. As per Section 6 of the new law, apprenticeship contract is "*a contract whereby the manager of an industrial, commercial or agricultural establishment or a craftsman undertakes to provide or ensure, under his/her responsibility, methodical and comprehensive vocational training to a person, and whereby the latter undertakes in return to follow the instruction he/she will receive and carry out his/her assignment for apprenticeship purposes*". The difference may appear when the regulatory instrument is taken in conformity with Section 23 (3). Actually based on Decree No. 69/DF/287 of 20th July 1969 governing contracts of apprenticeship, the absence of complete training will imply that the contract is no longer one of apprenticeship but one of unspecified duration employment. The failure on the part of apprentice supervisor to perform his duty may constitute an opportunity for the apprentice to gain an employment. It is doubtful whether the same reasoning may be adopted in case of vocational training *stricto sensu.*

The other observation about apprenticeship emerges from Section 23(1) on the capacity to be an apprentice and then a worker. According to this provision "*No person aged below 14 years shall be engaged under an apprentice contract*". Taking into consideration the environment, this provision can be considered as a deliberate attempt to undermine the ILO Convention on the Minimum Age for admission to employment at work[21]

---

[18] The current Labour code does not have such an approach.

[19] Section 28 (3) of Labour code implicitly refers to vocational training without any further explanation when it can be read "*The time required for recruitment, traveling, training* [...]".

[20] See Sections 45, 46 and 47 of Labour code.

[21] ILO Convention, C138, 1973.

that prohibits child labour and that maintains the labour capacity at 18 years.[22] The application of 14 years as can be seen in Section 86 (1) of the Labour Code incites in our context the unlawful practice of child labour which is a social evil in Cameroon. But one may differ with the view because before attaining 18 years, everyone must have acquired a particular skill that can help him/her to enter into the labour market.

For the third concern, that of Information and Communication Technologies (ICT) training methods, the law has provided for distance training even though the terms and conditions still need to be laid down by regulations.[23] Distant training or E-learning can be understood as training done through the means of ICT. These methods are commonly used in the era of globalization; the internet access has even acquired the status of human right.[24] The particularity of this training is that trainers and trainees do not need to be present but are able to produce the same results as if they were physically present. But as a limit to this type of training, we must recognize that much still needs to be done for it be popularized, in terms of internet coverage and mastery of ICT tools. Presently, it is out of bounds for many vocational training stakeholders.

1.2. Adjustment of State's control mechanisms

The State is the controller of the whole process of vocational training from beginning to end as it was under the previous legislation.[25] This management and supervision by the state is due to the benefits and harm that vocational training activity can cause to a country. A careful analysis of the law reveals state's control on the creation of vocational training entities, their activities and their financial resources.

At the level of creation, Sections 13 and 14 (1) indicate that public and private vocational training entities shall be set up under conditions laid down by regulations. Section 14 (2) imposes on private vocational training entities the obligation of state approval by the Minister in charge of vocational training before they can operate.

---

[22] Notwithstanding the exceptions raised up in Article 2 of the ILO Convention C138, we opine that Article 3 that fixes the capacity at 18 years should be maintained in the Cameroonian context.

[23] See Section 27.

[24] See the UN Human Rights Council Report, 2011, in *https://www/wired.com 2011/06*, accessed on 20th September 2019; see also the UK Court of Appeal decision in *Regina v. Smith & Others*, [2011] EWCA crim. 1772.

[25] See Sections 25 to 28 of the 1979 Decree.

Concerning the control of training activities,[26] Section 15 (1) provides that "the State shall have technical supervisory authority over private vocational training entities. To this end, it shall exercise pedagogic and administrative control, notably by verifying compliance with standards set by government, facilities training, as well as training programmes and methods". In conformity with this provision, the State lays down vocational training standards[27] and nomenclature,[28] supervises the assessment at the end of training,[29] and approves professional qualifications.[30] It may even in conformity with Section 40 conclude international agreements to foster international cooperation and mobility.

Concerning their financial resources, Section 16 provides that "*subsidies, donations and special tax incentives may be granted to vocational training entities*". In furtherance to this, Section 19 determines their sources of finance and indicates that the modalities of their collection and management shall be laid down by regulation. It is clear that the State does not intent to allow private training entities to be out of its control. This can be justified by two reasons. The first is linked to the origin of funding. They may be considered as public funds when coming from budgetary allocations and special grants and support from local and regional authorities; in that case there is, based on current social and public practices, an urgent need to have an oversight on their activities. The second stems from the fact that vocational training entities may receive sundry contributions among which are contributions from international organizations be they intergovernmental, regional or transnational like the French Development Agency (FDA), the German Transnational Organization (GTZ), the Center for Industrial Development (CID), the African Development Bank (ADB), just to name a few. This international funding needs also to be controlled in order to avoid any interference in the state's affairs or sovereignty. Based on these two arguments and due to the fact that vocational training is an undeniable tool for company competitiveness and for development, one may understand the rigidity of vocational training regulatory framework.

26 The terms and conditions shall be specified in a regulatory text according to Section 15 (2).

27 See Section 35.

28 See Section 36.

29 See Section 37.

30 See Section 39.

1.3. Reinforcement of sanctions

In Cameroon, the illegal proliferation of vocational training entities is part of the reasons that justify the bad quality of training. It is against this background that Section 14 (2) aptly indicates that private vocational training entities may not operate unless approved by the Minister in charge of Vocational Training. Any breach of this requirement is sanctioned.

Unlike Section 33 of the 1979 Decree prescribing the conditions for the organization and functioning of intensive vocational training that provided only for criminal sanctions, Sections 50 and 51 of the new law provide both for administrative and criminal sanctions.

Concerning the administrative sanction which is an innovation[31], Section 50 (1) states "*Any breach in the implementation of the laws and regulations by private vocational training entities shall be punished either with total or partial closure of the entity, on a temporary or permanent basis, or temporary or permanent ban on the suspected official or staff to exercise training activity, according to the nature and seriousness of the offence*". It follows from this provision that there exist several types of sanctions. We have identified four possible sanctions that shall befall on the unscrupulous vocational training entity. They include the partial temporary closure, the total temporary closure, the partial permanent closure and the total permanent closure. Against the defaulter, be it manager or staff, two sanctions are recorded including the temporary ban to exercise the function and the permanent ban to exercise it. In general their objective is to prevent the defaulter establishment or manager to be able to continue with the training activity. On both sides, the choice of a particular sanction will depend on the nature and seriousness of the offence committed. The only certainty is that the assessment of the offence is vested with the administrative authorities. We do hope that such sanctions will not be used by the vested authority as a sword against entities or managers that fail to act in their favour.[32]

Section 50 (2) gives room for receivership in the event of defects in management. In this situation, a private vocational training entity without losing its status is managed on its behalf and at its own risk by public authorities or persons appointed by them in order to preserve the interest

[31] Section 16 of the repealed 1979 Decree imposed disciplinary sanctions on trainees and Section 29 of the same mentioned the withdrawal of approval for private establishments.

[32] See possible obstacles, infra.

of trainees. In practice, the sanction aimed at preventing social disturbances.

Concerning the criminal sanction, Section 51 (1) provides that without prejudice to administrative sanctions, promoters of private career guidance and vocational training entities shall be criminally liable. Section 51 (2) specifies that "*Penalties provided for in Section 321 (c) of Penal Code shall be imposed on promoters of private vocational training entities found guilty of one of the following offenses:*

- opening of a career guidance or vocational training entity without authorization;

- operating a permanently or temporarily closed career guidance or vocational training entity;

- closure of a private vocational training entity in the course of the training cycle, without the prior express authorization of the competent supervisory authority." The abovementioned provision, Section 321 (c) of the Penal Code, sanctions aggravated misappropriation and false pretense committed by "*an offender advertising or who has advertised publicly*". In the event of such occurrence, the penalties prescribed by Section 318 shall be doubled. Section 318 punishes with imprisonment from 5 (five) to 10 (ten) years and with fine of from CFAF 100000 (one hundred thousand) to CFAF 1000000 (one million).

These sanctions may suggest the presumption of good faith on the part of the State in its quest to providing its citizens with a strong and stable vocational training policy. But can this be achieved with all the shortcomings that may challenge its implementation?

2. Possible obstacles to the implementation of the law

The achievement of the realization of objectives of a particular adopted instrument requires the full commitment of both the government and other stakeholders. The viability and sustainability of the law depends on their coordinated and combined actions. However, in addition to some limitations that exist in the law; it has been observed in practice that the new law may fail to achieve its objective within a short period due to social and institutional constraints.

Firstly, the main limitation is that the new law did not transform vocational training as a legal obligation for companies.[33] In a competing

[33] Provisions under chapter one (Sections 1 to 11) posit the vocational training in a general context of the right to work that should be guaranteed by the State, but not imposed on stakeholders.

world, companies cannot do without having well trained employees who can help the organization to assure its sustainability in the market.[34] Therefore, in order to enhance its productivity, vocational training should be transformed in to legal obligation for companies. Even though vocational training has become for the past decades a major preoccupation for managers in Cameroon, there is no compulsory measure in the law, as it is available in other countries for companies to mandatorily comply with the training of their workers. In fact such an obligation was applicable before 2001[35] but the measures were eliminated by the 2000-2001 Tax law, because the funds collected do not really serve for the purposes they were meant for. As a consequence, companies are free either to train their workers or not irrespective of the devastating effects that can be caused to the national economy. It is opined that, in such situations, the best solution would have been to impose such an obligation on companies by including for example in the law the training leave period, the skill balance sheet, the financial participation of employers in training, a specific amount of finance allocated in the capital for the training of each worker, the establishment in each company of internal training policy, just to name a few. We do hope that a well-organized domestic and international financial system as indicated will help companies to fill this gap.

Secondly, the enactment of the law does not guarantee its effective application. The latter requires the establishment of regulatory or implementing texts. The aim here being to clarify the law and provide details on specific issues that were generally mentioned in the law. Without them, the law will lack precision. Precisely, implementation of the law is fundamental to achieving the legislator's intention. There are too many texts for implementation of this[36] (15 in total) that needs to be merged into a single text. Based on this assumption and cognizant of the fact that implementing texts are often belated[37] leaves on with no choice than to question the effectiveness of the applicability of the new law. The proof of this opinion is clearly manifested in Section 53 of the law that provides

[34] See for a case study, E. Njaba Ndelle, *The impact of Vocational Education and Training (VET) on company performance – case study: CDC Bota Limbe*, P.G.D Research Project, Pan African Institute for Development- West Africa, 2015.

[35] There was imposed on companies an apprenticeship tax of 0,3% from company wage mass and 1% for contribution to Employment National Fund (ENF).

[36] The required implementing regulations of the law can be observed through Sections 15, 16, 23 (3), 26 (2), 27, 30, 34, 36, 37 (2), 38 (2), 39 (2), 40 (2), 43, 44, and 49 (3).

[37] See the awaited implementing text for Section 66 of the 1996 constitution on the declaration of assets; same with many provisions of the 2016 Penal code, just to name a few.

for progressive implementation principle by stating that "*Regulatory instruments shall be signed, as and when necessary, for the implementation of this law*". The executive inertia in failing to promptly act for the benefit of establishing such regulations may be injurious to the law. We do hope that all these regulatory instruments will be put in place within a reasonable period of time in order to avoid any lapses in the application of the law.

Thirdly, there is the persistent problem of management of public and even private establishments or entities in Cameroon. Sections 13 and 14 empower the public and private vocational training entities with the training mission. Section 15 (1) on its part arrogates to the State the technical supervisory authority. It is then clear that all these entities are endowed with public missions and will be managing public funds. However, it has been constantly observed that such entities have not been properly managed. This may be justified by the crisis of values that has affected almost all the segments of the society. In fact, it is extensively documented that the socio-political and economic environment is tainted by gross misfortune like corruption, misappropriation of public funds, tribalism, nepotism, just to name a few. These social evils may constitute a serious barrier to the achievement and effectiveness of the missions entrusted to these entities by the new law as has been experienced in many other institutions.

Finally, the precarious situation of job seekers coupled with the insufficiency of workers' financial means to meet up with personal vocational training cost also constitute a serious obstacle for the efficiency of the law. In fact, Section 49 (2) of the law states that "*Funding for vocational training shall be derived from: [...] own resources of the training entities, obtained through income generating activities and applicable training fees*". This provision should be read together with Section 21 which provides "*Where a worker benefits from employer-sponsored vocational or further training, it may be agreed that the worker continues to serve the employer for a specified period based on the vocational or further training cost*". It follows from these provisions that the trainee, be it job seeker/apprentice[38] or worker is required to pay a training fee. This requirement may constitute an obstacle to access to vocational training facilities in a country where the financial crisis and the unemployment are rampant and where the Guaranteed Inter-occupational Minimum Wage is 36270 FCFA.[39] The interpretation of the above provision, Section 21, may

---

[38] By waiting the new implementing text in conformity with Section 23 (3), see the Decree No. 69/DF/287 of 20th July 1969 governing contracts of apprenticeship.

[39] See the Decree No. 2014/2217/PM of 24th July 2014 revaluing the Guaranteed Inter-occupational Minimum Wage.

even be seen as trespass to the freedom to work in the sense that the provision imposes on a worker a continuing obligation to perform his duty until the complete payment of the cost of training. It suggests an implicit prohibited resignation clause which is, in our mind an attempt to curtail the worker's freedom. The situation of job seekers is even lamentable because of financial shortage. Most at time, after spending all the family economy in theoretical education, they arrive financially weak for vocational training because of lack of employment due to the general economic situation of the country.[40] If proper measures are not taken against these political and socio-economic obstacles, one may doubt the efficient impact of this law on the labour and economic market.

Conclusion

The intervention of a new legislation always derives from the inability of the previous one to satisfy the current governmental and societal needs either because of its inherent shortcomings or due to the difficulty in responding to the test of time. Cameroon is indeed a country with low employment rate due to multifarious factors ranging from inadequate training of prospective job seekers to the precarious nature of economic fabric. The government's task is to increase the rate of employment by adopting appropriate incentive measures or rules. Can this new law be classified among such measures?

It has been revealed that though the law is laudable in the sense that societal and economic developments depend also on the strength of vocational training policy as it provides access to skills and entry routes into labour market; much still need to be done in order to strengthen its efficiency.

In fact, without the speedy adoption of implementing texts by the government, the applicability of the law will remain jeopardized. To attain the objective of the law, a quick action is then required from the government for its effective application. In addition, a new Labour Code is needed in order to improve the employment policy as a whole and to align its provisions to the new law and to modern employment challenges. Apart from that political action, socio-economic factors like the acceptance of the new vocational training policy by the employers and the sustainability of its cost by jobseekers/workers need to be achieved.

---

40 Several studies have revealed that less than 10% of the population of Cameroon is formally employed; other people evolve in the informal sector.

The new law on the whole, is very comprehensive. It portrays the State's desire to preserve the right to work, a basic human right. Its success or failures would ultimately depend on those responsible for its application. It is opined that these measures be taken in order to assess in the near future the effective impact of the new law on the entire community.

La valeur des emblèmes de l'État

By

Jean Denoël Victor Yves Tsala

Senior Lecturer of Civil Law,
Department of Civil Law, Faculty of Law and Political Science,
The University of Bamenda, Cameroon
Email: yvessenzo@gmail.com

Résumé

L'observation des faits contemporains suscite une inquiétude relative aux grands symboles représentant la fierté, la dignité ou l'honneur des États. En réalité, il est de plus en plus récurrent de voir les emblèmes de l'État malmenés, piétinés ou brulés sur des lieux publics par des individus sans foi ni loi. Face à ce phénomène devenu régulier, il est urgent de s'interroger sur la véritable valeur de ces emblèmes. À l'observation et au regard des textes nationaux et internationaux, un grand nombre de puissances étrangères a accordé une valeur purement symbolique dénuée de tout pouvoir de coercition aux emblèmes. Ceci n'est pas le cas d'autres pays, qui leur accordent une place fondamentale du fait de leur constitutionnalisation. Cette insertion des emblèmes dans la constitution n'est pas exempte de tout calcul. Leur violation est susceptible d'entrainer des sanctions d'ordres administratif, civil ou pénal.

Mots clés : Emblème, valeur, État

Abstract

State emblems are symbols of visual identification, unadventurously chosen to distinguish herself from others, and recognised as such by virtue of her distinctive flag, motto, seals, currency, coat of arms, anthem, etc. Their representation as signs of victory, recognition, unity, respect, honour, celebration and reverence, with its sense of belonging and consequent social, historical, economic, political, ideological identification, are at the heart of political and strategic issues. Therefore, whenever acts are perpetrated against State emblems, the gravity is always instinctively, because one's attachment to these emblems, are of a moral legal nature, a symbolical value of state emblems. However, it is inevitably to talk about their juridical representation, or the legal value of state emblems. In fact, legal justifications are contained in the different constitutional guarantees and enhanced legal protection under constitutional and criminal jurisdictions; suggesting the consciousness inviolability of emblems as an inherent instinctive thing, which precedes the awareness of their legal value, as a fundamental thing.

Key words: Emblem, value, state

Introduction

L'emblème tricolore de la France, représenté dans une « *œuvre d'art* » comme du papier toilette [1]; l'Union Jack en flamme, balancé sur la voiture de Sa Majesté la reine d'Angleterre[2], le drapeau camerounais brulé et piétiné sur la place publique par des manifestants en colère[3]. Les exemples forts récents d'emblèmes des États malmenés ne manquent absolument pas. À chaque fois que de tels actes sont posés, c'est presque instinctivement que la gravité est ressentie. En effet, la question de l'existence ou pas des règles qui sanctionnent de tels actes parait d'emblée secondaire, tant la force de réprobation est grande. Ce sentiment de réprobation est une conséquence de l'attachement à l'égard de ces emblèmes. Cet attachement n'est non plus désincarné. Il découle du sens même de ces emblèmes. En effet, les emblèmes sont des marques d'identité, de singularité, de démarcation d'un État par rapport aux autres. C'est le signe de son originalité, sa souveraineté. Dans ce sens, l'attachement aux emblèmes traduit l'attachement à son pays, à sa nation. Emile Durkheim précise l'importance des emblèmes lorsqu'il écrit : *« (…) sans symboles, les sentiments sociaux ne pourraient avoir qu'une existence précaire (…). Ainsi, l'emblématique, nécessaire pour permettre à la société de prendre conscience de soi, n'est pas moins indispensable pour assurer la continuité de cette conscience* »[4].

Les emblèmes se définissent comme des êtres ou objets visibles, conventionnellement choisis pour représenter quelqu'un ou quelque chose. À l'époque contemporaine, ils renvoient à plusieurs choses à savoir le drapeau, l'hymne, les sceaux et la devise. Ce sont des éléments d'identification visuelle *a priori* d'une entité et qui lui permettent de se

[1] La Fnac de Nice avait lancé un concours de photo en 2010. L'un des candidats avait fait parvenir son œuvre représentant un homme qui semblait vouloir utiliser le drapeau français comme du papier toilette. La garde des Sceaux avait exigé une enquête. Mais le procureur avait classé le dossier en soutenant qu'il s'agissait d'une œuvre de l'esprit. Mais à partir de cette affaire, une polémique était née en France sur la question de la répression de l'outrage au drapeau. Mais cela n'avait pas empêché le ministère de la Justice de prendre, quelques mois plus tard un décret punissant d'une amende de 1500 euros quiconque se rendait coupable d'outrage au drapeau français.

[2] En 1999, deux manifestants lancent le drapeau du Royaume-Uni en flamme sur la voiture de la reine en visite à l'étranger.

[3] Le 8 décembre, pendant la grève des enseignants et anglophones, des manifestants brulent le drapeau du Cameroun et certains vont jusqu'à hisser le drapeau des *« sécessionnistes ».*

[4] E. Durkheim, *Les formes élémentaires de la vie religieuse : le système totémique en Australie*, Paris, Éd. Félix Alcan, 1912 ; p. 330-331.

distinguer d'autres entités qui seraient du même genre. Mais pour l'État, les emblèmes sont des outils d'identification visuelle qui permettent de le reconnaitre au premier coup d'œil en le distinguant des autres. Ce sont aussi des instruments d'affirmation de l'État qui lui permettent de refléter son identité sociale, historique, économique, politique et idéologique.

Dans le sens et le rôle qu'on leur donne aujourd'hui, les emblèmes sont étroitement liés à l'affirmation de l'État moderne à partir de la fin du XVIIIe siècle. Avant cette période, les drapeaux par exemple existaient certes, mais davantage comme des bannières et des étendards liés à une famille, une dynastie, un parti[5]. Les hymnes sont également récents. Les premiers découlent de chants guerriers, soit d'hymnes en hommage au monarque[6].

Les emblèmes sont donc au départ, des signes de reconnaissance. Ils sont aujourd'hui des signes d'appartenance. Ils sont aussi au cœur d'enjeux politiques et stratégiques. L'importance qu'ils revêtent conduit tout naturellement à s'interroger sur leur valeur. Ainsi, quelle est la valeur des emblèmes de l'État ? Avec la montée des radicalismes, les atteintes aux emblèmes et plus spécifiquement aux drapeaux sont de plus en plus fréquentes. Cette tendance rend pertinentes les études sur la valeur des emblèmes de l'État aujourd'hui. À l'observation, La force immatériellement attachée aux emblèmes permet de conclure qu'elles ont une valeur *a priori* symbolique (I) et, si un doute était permis, cette valeur est *a posteriori* confortée par les dispositions légales (II).

I. La détermination de la valeur symbolique des emblèmes de l'État

Par principe, les valeurs relèvent davantage de l'ordre de la morale que du droit. De manière générale, le droit puise dans la morale. Dans cette logique, le respect de certaines normes morales juridicisées semble relever plus d'une obligation morale que d'une obligation juridique. Leur seule évocation impose un respect presque instinctif, une conscience de l'obligation qu'il y a à les respecter. Cette attitude est sans doute la

---

[5] Voir pour détails, J. Rey, *Histoire du drapeau, des couleurs et des insignes de la monarchie française, précédé de l'histoire des enseignes militaires chez les anciens*, Paris : Techener, 1837 ; Dominique Dupart, *« De l'usage d'un drapeau en histoire, ou la parole en couleur. 1789-1830 », Romantisme*, Revue du XIXe siècle 2012, n° 157, p.9-21 ; F. Ruda, *L'hymne et le drapeau : des symboles de l'État en droit comparé*, www.academia.edu.

[6] *Ibid.*

conséquence de la puissance des symboles attachés aux emblèmes (A) et à l'importance des circonstances au cours desquelles ils sont convoqués (B).

A. La puissance symbolique de représentation des emblèmes

La puissance est le caractère de ce qui produit de grands effets. Les représentations symboliques des emblèmes ont un impact considérable lié à la signification qu'ils ont à certains moments. Cette puissance est attachée aux différentes représentations du drapeau (1) ainsi qu'à celles des autres emblèmes (2).

1. Les représentations du drapeau

La présence du seul drapeau est un message plein de signification. Elle emporte parfois davantage plus que des mots. Un message clair, c'est celui qui est passé dès qu'il est implanté sur un territoire en période de conflits : c'est une victoire. Lorsqu'il est remis aux soldats ou aux civils dans certaines circonstances : c'est une reconnaissance nationale.

a) L'implantation du drapeau comme signe de victoire

Le drapeau d'un État est la première marque, le premier signe d'identification de celui-ci. Il signifie l'existence d'un groupe uni par le lien de nationalité. C'est « *le signe manifeste de l'affirmation d'une communauté humaine unique et singulière, d'une population qui s'est muée en peuple et de son aspiration à être reconnu comme telle* »[7]. Ainsi, tous les États au monde possèdent un drapeau unique et officiel qui est leur marqueur matériel et permet par conséquent de les identifier partout dans le monde entier. C'est un « *outil d'identification visuelle* »[8]. Il prouve leur identité et souligne leur existence de même que la présence de leurs intérêts aussi bien à l'intérieur de leurs territoires qu'à l'extérieur. Le drapeau porte très généralement l'histoire du peuple considéré. Dans ce sens, il suggère que la nation véhicule des valeurs considérées comme positives et vertueuses.

Ce sont ces valeurs qui sont portées dans les champs de bataille par les soldats. En effet, la victoire d'un État s'est toujours traduite sur le terrain des conflits par l'implantation de son drapeau. Il donne dans ce sens une indication. C'est l'indication du triomphe de l'État et de ses idées sur

---

[7] E. Derdaele, *« Le drapeau tricolore, un symbole constitutionnel dans tous ses états »*, Communication présentée au VIIIe Congrès de l'Association française de droit constitutionnel, Nancy, les 16 et 18 juin 2011, dans l'atelier n° 1, « Droit constitutionnel et autres branches du droit », présidé par les professeurs Guillaume Drago et Charles Vautrot-Schwartz.

[8] F. Ruda, *op.cit.* p.2.

l'ennemi. C'est pour cette raison que dès lors qu'un territoire est pris, la première chose à faire par les nouveaux occupants est d'enlever les drapeaux des vaincus et de hisser le leur. Une photographie devenue célèbre prise le 23 février 1945 représente cinq marines américaines hissant le drapeau américain sur le mont **Suribachi**, lors de la bataille sur l'île japonaise d'**Iwo Jima** pendant la Seconde Guerre mondiale[9]. C'est en s'inspirant d'elle que Felix de Weldon a érigé la sculpture du **US Marine Corps War Memorial,** située à **Arlington** en **Virginie**[10].

Exemple peut être pris dans l'actualité avec l'Organisation de l'État islamique qui, à chaque fois qu'il conquiert un espace hisse son drapeau. En sens inverse, lorsque les armées irakienne ou syrienne reprennent leurs territoires, elles hissent également leur drapeau[11].

En dehors de le hisser sur le terrain des conflits, le drapeau peut être offert en don. Dans ce sens, il porte une charge importante.

b) La donation du drapeau comme reconnaissance de la nation

L'une des significations les plus importantes du drapeau est sans aucun doute contenue dans le fait de l'offrir en donation. Qu'il s'agisse d'une donation aux civils ou aux militaires, c'est le signe d'une reconnaissance, celle de la nation tout entière.

Les cercueils des soldats tombés sur-le-champ de bataille et même des soldats morts naturellement, mais qui ont passé leur vie aux services de la nation sont toujours recouverts du drapeau et celui-ci est très souvent offerts à leurs proches comme le témoignage de la reconnaissance à eux due. Cette reconnaissance est également due aux personnes non militaires telles que les hauts commis de l'État, les footballeurs et les athlètes lors des évènements sportifs importants. Par ce geste, le message selon lequel ils sont morts pour des choses importantes est transmis de la plus belle des façons. Par ailleurs, à l'occasion d'évènements malheureux qui

---

[9] La photographie réalisée par Bill Genaust a eu un fort retentissant à l'époque. C'est le seul cliché qui a obtenu le prix Pulitzer de la photographie l'année même de sa publication. Elle est considérée comme la photographie la plus diffusée de tous les temps.

[10] L'œuvre représente des marines américaines s'efforçant de hisser le drapeau américain en plein combat.

[11] Par exemple, en 2015, quand l'armée irakienne reprend la ville de Ramādī occupée jusque-là par Daech, le drapeau de l'État irakien est hissé. Pareil en fin d'année 2016, lorsque l'armée syrienne reprend Alep, le drapeau syrien est hissé par les soldats de l'armée régulière syrienne.

affectent la nation entière (catastrophe ayant fait de nombreuses victimes, décès d'un chef d'État), le drapeau est très naturellement mis en berne.

Le drapeau détient une puissance telle que lorsqu'il est entre les mains de l'ennemi, il s'agit d'un échec très important. La reprise des drapeaux entre les mains de l'ennemi passe donc pour être essentielle. Illustration peut être faite du cas du drapeau mexicain entre les mains de la France après la guerre de 1862-1864. Les drapeaux mexicains avaient été pris sur-le-champ de bataille par des soldats français. Le président français, en l'absence de textes clairs réglant le problème des drapeaux de l'ennemi pris sur-le-champ de bataille, avait choisi de les remettre au président mexicain. **Adolfo Lopez Mateos** s'était alors déplacé personnellement pour aller les accueillir à leur descente d'avion et les avait embrassés presque aux larmes.

Cette charge symbolique qui impose le respect au-delà de la contrainte extérieure n'est pas exclusive au drapeau. D'autres emblèmes portent également cette charge importante.

2. Les représentations des autres emblèmes

L'hymne, la devise, les sceaux dégagent une force semblable à celle du drapeau. Ce qui permet de souligner que leur respect semble s'imposer au-delà d'une obligation qui serait imposée de l'extérieur.

a) L'exécution de l'hymne comme action de ralliement aux mêmes valeurs

Un hymne est un chant qui célèbre quelqu'un ou quelque chose. Rattaché à l'identité d'un État, il s'agit d'un chant patriotique, souvent choisi par le gouvernement. Il est toujours connecté à l'histoire du pays considéré. Il est exécuté lors des cérémonies officielles et est très généralement fait dans la langue officielle ou la langue parlée par la majorité de la population.

L'exécution de l'hymne est en général un moment très fort au cours duquel on ressent l'attachement à sa patrie. C'est donc un chant de ralliement. Il porte en principe l'histoire d'un peuple. On attribue aux Pays-Bas le premier hymne chanté. Le *« het wilhelmus »* aurait été écrit entre 1568 et 1572 durant la guerre de quatre-vingts ans et adopté officiellement en 1932. Le *« kimi ga yo »* japonais daterait de plus loin encore sauf qu'il n'a été considéré comme hymne qu'en 1999[12]. En France la Marseillaise a été écrite en 1792 et adoptée en 1795. Elle marque un passage important dans

[12] Japan Policy Reseach Institute, July 2001.

l'histoire de la France[13]. Au Cameroun, il est utilisé officiellement depuis 1948. C'est en 1957 qu'il est adopté. Les paroles composées par **René Djam Afane** avec **Samuel Minkio Bamba** et **Moise Nyatte Nko'o** contient des relents de la colonisation qui seront expurgés en 1970. La nouvelle version rend hommage aux ancêtres et appelle les générations présentes au devoir à l'égard de la nation. **Bernard Fonlon** rédigera en 1978 le texte en anglais[14]. Au-delà de toute la controverse autour de la pertinence du texte de l'hymne national du Cameroun, son exécution passe pour être une obligation lors de cérémonies officielles et l'émotion qui est instinctivement attachée au moment de son exécution est un indicatif de la valeur qui s'y attache. En effet, son exécution n'est pas explicitement prévue, mais au regard de son importance dans la pratique, personne ne songe plus à discuter de sa place dans les évènements.

Afin de conforter le sentiment d'appartenance à la même histoire et au même destin, l'hymne national est enseigné dès les premières classes du primaire. Ainsi, l'enfant grandit avec la conscience d'un lien étroit avec l'État.

Participe de cette même finalité l'énonciation de la devise et l'apposition des sceaux de l'État.

b) L'énonciation de la devise et l'apposition des sceaux comme identité de la nation

Tout comme le drapeau et l'hymne, la devise et les sceaux participent à la singularisation de l'État.

La devise est une phrase courte ou une expression symbolique qui décrit les motivations d'un groupe social ou d'une organisation qui la choisit pour suggérer un idéal, comme règles de conduite ou pour rappeler un passé glorieux. C'est donc un idéal qui est enfermé dans l'expression liberté-égalité et fraternité ou dans celui de paix-travail-patrie.

Sa simple énonciation permet d'identifier l'État qui est incarné. La devise participe donc à l'identification, mieux, à la définition de l'État concerné. Elle lui est dans ce sens intrinsèque. Ce lien donne toute une importance particulière à la devise. C'est le cas des sceaux.

[13] Notamment la révolution

[14] Certains auteurs soutiennent que la version anglaise est un hymne complètement différent de celui qui est écrit en langue française. D'après Thomas Théophile Nug Bissohong, ils auraient en commun un seul ver (voir, *L'hymne national du Cameroun, un poème-chant à décoloniser et à réécrire*, Éditions Clé, 2009, 94 p.).

Les sceaux sont des cachets où sont gravés en creux des signes propres à une autorité souveraine, à un corps constitué ou à un simple particulier, et qu'on applique sur une matière molle, cire ou plomb, afin que l'empreinte en relief ainsi réalisée atteste l'authenticité, l'autorité, la validité des documents sur lesquels ils sont apposés. Dans ce sens, le sceau de l'État est une preuve de la légitimité même d'un acte. Il donne toute sa force à l'acte et son défaut le dépouille de toute force.

La puissance symbolique dont recèlent les emblèmes est davantage amplifiée par l'importance des évènements au cours desquels ceux-ci sont convoqués.

B. L'importance des circonstances de convocation des emblèmes

Les emblèmes ne sont pas utilisés au même titre que toute autre chose. Leur invocation ou présentation doit être faite en des circonstances particulières. Il peut s'agir de célébrer un triomphe important de la nation ou de marquer une révérence pour des raisons diverses

1. La célébration d'une victoire nationale

Les évènements au cours desquels le drapeau est brandi en signe de victoire sont pluriels. Il est aisé de les organiser en évènements militaires et civils.

a) La célébration d'une victoire militaire

Le domaine militaire est sans aucun doute celui dans lequel le drapeau revêt une importance toute particulière. Cette singularité est liée au fait que ce sont les militaires qui sont chargés de protéger le territoire, d'une part, contre les éventuelles attaques extérieures et d'autre part, contre les menaces à la paix à l'intérieur de l'État. C'est donc eux qui, matériellement, sont chargés du maintien de la souveraineté de l'État. Les victoires militaires sont alors celles de toute la nation. Ainsi, lorsqu'un territoire est pris à l'issue d'une bataille, le vainqueur fait trôner son drapeau. Lorsqu'il faut commémorer les victoires, le drapeau est hissé automatiquement et l'hymne national est exécuté solennellement.

b) La célébration d'une victoire civile

Sans que cela soit consacré, le brandissement du drapeau et l'exécution de l'hymne sont faits à chaque victoire qui revêt une dimension nationale. Le drapeau est brandi comme signe de force et de reconnaissance, indifféremment des domaines, intellectuel, sportif, culturel, économique…

dans le domaine du sport, il est devenu rituel qu'après une victoire, qu'il s'agisse de celle d'un individu ou d'un groupe, d'un sportif représentant directement le Cameroun dans une discipline ou évoluant simplement dans le cadre de sa carrière personnelle, ils brandissent le drapeau de leur pays. Pour le cas du Cameroun, il faut se souvenir notamment de **Samuel Eto'o Fils** en 2006 lorsqu'avec son club le FC Barcelone, il est vainqueur de la « *league des Champions* » en Europe. Il recouvre son maillot du drapeau camerounais et fait le tour du stade. Cet acte fera percevoir sa victoire comme celle du Cameroun. Grâce au drapeau, c'est le Cameroun qui remportait la « *league des champions* » cette année-là. Le fait que son coéquipier du FC Barcelone, **Ronaldhino** arbore lors d'un évènement, un costume aux couleurs du drapeau du Cameroun renforce l'affection des Camerounais à son égard. Lorsqu'elle rentre dans l'histoire comme la première femme à remporter la médaille d'or olympique deux fois de suite au triple saut en 2008 à Beijing, l'athlète **Françoise Mbango** fait flotter autour d'elle le drapeau du Cameroun. Moment intense dans tout le pays qui ressent cette victoire de manière générale.

S'ils sont utilisés pour célébrer une victoire nationale, les emblèmes sont également convoqués pour faire des révérences lors des manifestations spécifiques.

2. La révérence aux occasions importantes

Certains emblèmes de l'État sont indissociables des devoirs militaires. Mais le drapeau est tout particulièrement utilisé pour marquer les évènements de tristesse nationale.

a) Les hommages aux héros

Le concept de « *héros* » n'est pas un concept juridique. Il est cependant courant dans le domaine militaire. C'est le Décret n° 76/424 du 16 septembre 1976 fixant les règles du protocole à observer en matière de cérémonies publiques, préséances, honneurs civils et militaires qui détermine les personnes devant bénéficier de ces honneurs. À la lecture de la règlementation en vigueur, on peut déterminer deux catégories. Premièrement, la catégorie de personnes directement habilitées par le décret de 1976 et celle des personnes qui en bénéficient indirectement grâce au décret du Président de la République. Au cours des cérémonies publiques, les éléments clés restent le drapeau et l'hymne national. Rendre hommage ainsi à des personnes est une manière de montrer que leur sacrifice a été fait pour le bien de la nation tout entière et qu'au-delà de la perte que peut ressentir la famille, c'est une perte qui est aussi celle de tout l'État. Le Décret n° 76/424 du 16 septembre 1976 fixant les règles du protocole à observer en matière de cérémonies publiques, préséances, honneurs civils et militaires précise les circonstances qui peuvent permettre l'usage du drapeau et interdit cet usage dans les cas non énumérés par le texte. En dehors des militaires morts en fonction et certaines personnalités publiques limitativement énumérées pour lesquels l'usage du drapeau sur le cercueil est automatiquement prévu, c'est le Président de la République qui décrète pour ce qui concerne les autres. Le drapeau est utilisé *lors du dé*cès du Président de la République en fonction. À cette occasion, les drapeaux et étendards des armées prennent le deuil.

b) La mise en berne en des occasions de tristesse nationale

Mettre un drapeau en berne signifie le maintenir à mi-hauteur de son mat. Le drapeau est mis en berne à des occasions particulières de grande tristesse dans l'État[15]. C'est le cas très généralement d'un deuil national ou d'une tragédie pour lequel l'État décide par un acte formel. Au Cameroun par exemple, le deuil national est décrété par le Président de la République. Dans ce cas, le drapeau est d'abord hissé en haut de son mat, puis abaissé à mi-hauteur ou juste maintenu hors d'atteinte. En France par exemple, le drapeau tricolore a été mis en berne sur toute l'étendue du territoire du 08 au 10 janvier 2015 à la suite de l'attaque de Charlie Hebdo ; du 16 au 18 juillet 2016 à la suite de l'attentat du 14 juillet à Nice. Au Cameroun, le président de la République décrète le 16 octobre 2015 journée de deuil national et les drapeaux sont mis en berne à la suite de la bousculade à la Mecque qui avait fait de nombreuses victimes camerounaises. Le lundi 24 octobre 2016 est déclaré journée de deuil national en la mémoire des victimes du déraillement du train à **Eseka** le 21 octobre 2016. Les drapeaux sont mis en berne sur décret du Président de la République tel que prévu par le décret n° 76/424 du 16 septembre 1976 fixant les règles du protocole à observer en matière de cérémonies publiques, préséances, honneurs civils et militaires.

La valeur qui est attachée aux emblèmes de l'État de manière logique fait en sorte que sa valeur juridique devient évidente.

II. La précision de la valeur juridique des emblèmes de l'État

Cette valeur juridique des emblèmes de l'État est consacrée par la constitution et davantage mise en exergue à travers la répression des atteintes qui y sont faites.

---

[15] Voir loi n° 89/655 du 13 septembre 1989 relative aux cérémonies publiques, préséances, honneurs civils et militaires.

A. La constitutionnalisation des emblèmes de l'État

Les emblèmes de l'État sont, dans bon nombre de pays consacrés dans la constitution. Pour le Cameroun, il serait intéressant de s'arrêter sur l'énonciation constitutionnelle des emblèmes avant d'analyser les conséquences de cette constitutionnalisation.

1. L'énonciation constitutionnelle des emblèmes

« La loi n'est l'expression de la volonté générale que dans le respect de la Constitution »[16]. Ce principe affirmé par le Conseil constitutionnel français réitère la position dominante de la constitution dans l'ordre juridique de la France, une position presque universellement consacrée[17]. Pour intégrer les deux définitions, formelle et matérielle de la Constitution, les Professeurs **Francis Hamon** et **Michel Troper**, proposent de la définir comme *« l'ensemble des règles, quelques soit leur objet qui sont énoncées dans la forme constitutionnelle : elles sont en général contenues dans un document spécial, mais surtout, elles ont une valeur supérieure à celles de toutes les autres normes positives et ne peuvent être modifiées que conformément à une procédure spéciale, plus difficile à mettre en œuvre que celle qui permet de modifier une autre norme, par exemple une loi ordinaire »*[18]. Il convient donc de dire que la constitution renvoie simplement à toutes les règles essentielles à la gestion du pouvoir dans l'État. Y sont contenues les règles considérées comme essentielles à la bonne marche de l'État. Si donc les emblèmes y sont consacrés, c'est dire qu'ils sont revêtus d'une importance particulière.

Certains États consacrent les emblèmes dans le préambule tandis que d'autres les consacrent dans le corpus de la Constitution. Mais compte tenu de la valeur aujourd'hui accordée au préambule de la Constitution dans les États, cette distinction devient peu pertinente. Mais le Cameroun n'a entendu laisser planer aucun doute sur la valeur de ses emblèmes. C'est ainsi que dès l'entrée du corpus de la Constitution, les emblèmes sont énoncés. L'article 1 alinéa 4 dispose dans cette logique que la devise du Cameron est *« Paix-Travail-Patrie »*. L'alinéa 5 dispose que son drapeau *est « Vert, Rouge, Jaune, à trois bandes verticales d'égales dimensions. Il est frappé d'une*

---

[16] CC. Affaire de la Nouvelle-Calédonie, 23 août 1985.

[17] Cette position est bien sûr relativisée dans les États confessionnels. En effet, le texte fondamental reste celui dans lequel Dieu a consigné ses règles. C'est le cas de la Bible ou du Coran. En Iran par exemple, la Constitution est soumise au Coran et à la Sunna.

[18] F. Hamon et M. Troper, *Manuel de droit constitutionnel*, 32e Éd. Paris, LGDJ, Coll. « *Manuels* », 2011, 905 p. Cité par A-M. Cohendet, Droit constitutionnel, *op. cit.* p. 87.

étoile d'or au centre de la bande rouge. » L'alinéa 6 indique que l'hymne national est : *« O Cameroun, berceau de nos ancêtres »*. L'alinéa 7 relève que « *le sceau de la République du Cameroun est une médaille circulaire en bas relief de 46 millimètres de diamètre, présentant à l'avers et au centre le profil une tête de jeune fille tournée à dextre vers une branche de caféier à deux feuilles et jouxtée à senestre par cinq cabosses de cacao avec, en exergue, en français sur l'arc supérieur : « République du Cameroun »* et, sur l'arc inférieur la devise nationale : *« Paix-Travail-Patrie »*, au revers et au centre, les armoiries de la République du Cameroun avec en exergue, en anglais, sur l'arc supérieur : « *Republic of Cameroon* », et sur l'arc inférieur, « *Peace, Work, Fatherland.* » Les armoiries de la République du Cameroun sont constituées par un écu chapé surmonté côté chef par l'inscription « *République du Cameroun* », et supporté par un double faisceau de licteurs entrecroisés avec la devise : « *Paix-Travail-Patrie* », côté pointe. L'écu est composé d'une étoile d'or sur fond de sinople et d'un triangle de gueules, chargé de la carte géographique du Cameroun d'azur, et frappé du glaive de la balance de justice de sable.

La plupart des États d'Afrique débute leur constitution en énonçant les emblèmes. C'est par exemple le cas du Sénégal[19], du Benin[20], du Gabon[21].

Le choix de la constitution pour la consécration des emblèmes de l'État n'est pas fortuit. En effet, plusieurs conséquences découlent de ce choix.

2. Les implications de la constitutionnalisation

Les conséquences du choix de la constitutionnalisation des emblèmes peuvent être relevées aussi bien au plan juridique qu'au plan théorique.

a) Les implications théoriques

La place qu'occupe la constitution dans la hiérarchie des normes confère naturellement une importance considérable aux normes qui y sont consacrées. Dans ce sens, les emblèmes ont le caractère de fondamental. La notion de fondamentalité ne fait pas l'unanimité dans l'identification de certains droits et libertés. Positivistes et jusnaturalistes ne s'accordent guère sur le sens à lui attacher. Dans une posture évidemment jusnaturaliste, les professeurs **M. Robert Badinter** et **M. Bruno Genevois** estiment que « *la fondamentalité ne s'épuise pas dans un texte* »[22]. Pour eux, il suffit qu'un droit ou une règle ait une importance pour revêtir ce

[19] Article 1 de la constitution du 22 janvier 2001 modifiée en 2016.
[20] Article 1 Constitution du 11 décembre 1990.
[21] Article 2 de la Constitution du 26 mars 1991.
[22] R. Badinter et B. Genevois, *« Normes de valeur constitutionnelle et protection des droits fondamentaux »*, *RUDH,* 1990, p. 286.

caractère, sans qu'on ait besoin de consacrer par un texte, fut-il d'une valeur prééminente. Mais dès lors qu'il n'existe pas de critère clair de la fondamentalité, il est difficile de déterminer ce qui en fait partie et ce qui est exclu de la liste. La catégorie devient alors diluée, dénaturée, ce qui impacte sur leur niveau de protection. L'approche jusnaturaliste de la fondamentalité montre alors quelques limites importantes. La logique positiviste est plus restrictive de la catégorie des règles ou choses fondamentales. Ce seraient alors juste celles qui sont consacrées à un niveau éminent de la hiérarchie des normes. Le critère d'identification des choses fondamentales est formel, lié à la nature du texte dans lequel elles sont consacrées.

L'insertion des emblèmes dans la Constitution n'est pas dénuée de calcul. Il s'agit de maximiser leur valeur. Dans ce dernier sens, il est aisé de conclure que les emblèmes sont revêtus des attributs de la fondamentalité.

b) Les implications juridiques

La fondamentalité des emblèmes de l'État découlant de leur consécration constitutionnelle leur permet de bénéficier d'une protection juridique renforcée. Premièrement, ils sont protégés contre tous les organes de l'État (pouvoir judiciaire, législatif et exécutif). Deuxièmement, les emblèmes sont protégés en vertu non seulement de la loi, mais également et surtout de la constitution. Troisièmement, la protection des emblèmes nécessite, pour être assurée contre l'exécutif et le législatif et en application des textes constitutionnels qu'en soient chargées, non plus seulement les juridictions ordinaires, mais également et surtout les juridictions constitutionnelles (à travers notamment le contrôle de constitutionnalité). Quatrièmement, les emblèmes produisent les effets non seulement dans les relations entre les individus, mais aussi dans les relations entre les individus et le pouvoir public. En conclusion, on peut, dans cette étude, mettre l'accent sur deux implications principales à savoir que la fondamentalité des emblèmes emporte une extension du champ d'opposabilité des emblèmes et une extension du champ de leur garantie.

Au-delà de la garantie constitutionnelle des emblèmes, la garantie pénale participe dans une large mesure à leur protection.

B. La protection pénale des emblèmes de l'État

L'usage du drapeau est précisé dans plusieurs textes au Cameroun[23]. Mais les sanctions contre leur violation sont prévues dans le Code pénal. La répression des atteintes aux sceaux de l'État est plus explicitement aménagée au Cameroun tandis que la répression des autres est plus implicite. Spécialement celle du drapeau doit être recherchée avant l'indépendance du Cameroun.

1. La répression des atteintes aux sceaux de l'État

Au Cameroun, la répression des atteintes aux sceaux de l'État est bien explicite. L'article 201 alinéa 1 Code pénal camerounais dispose dans ce sens que « *est puni de l'emprisonnement à vie, celui qui contrefait le sceau de l'État ou fait usage du sceau contrefait* ». L'alinéa 2 du même article précise qu'« *est puni d'un emprisonnement de 10 à 20 ans, celui qui fait usage du sceau de l'État indument obtenu* ».

L'alinéa 3 indique que « *est puni d'un emprisonnement de un à cinq ans et d'une amende de quarante mille à quatre millions de francs CFA celui qui contrevient aux règles relatives à la commande, la fabrication et à l'apposition du sceau de l'État* ».

Pour les peines accessoires, l'alinéa 4 précise qu'« *en cas de condamnation, la juridiction peut prononcer, pour une durée de un à cinq ans, les déchéances prévues à l'article 30* »[24].

La répression de l'atteinte au sceau de l'État est une donnée communément partagée par les États. Ce n'est absolument pas le cas de la répression de l'outrage au drapeau qui n'est pas clairement réprimé au Cameroun.

2. La répression des atteintes au drapeau

La protection pénale du drapeau est une question qui a été largement discutée. Les États en font une appréhension assez différenciée. En effet, la répression du drapeau s'oppose à un droit fondamental à savoir la liberté d'expression. Plusieurs États ont dans ce sens, choisi de ne pas le réprimer. C'est le cas notamment de la Belgique, du Royaume-Uni, de l'Écosse. De même, malgré qu'ils aménagent rigoureusement l'emploi du drapeau, les

[23] C'est notamment le cas de la loi n° 90/042 du 19 décembre 1990 instituant la CNI ; Décret n° 2016/375 du 4 aout 2016 fixant les caractéristiques et les modalités d'établissement et de délivrance de la Carte Nationale d'Identité ; Décret n° 2000/286 du 12 octobre 2000 précisant les conditions d'entrée, de séjour et de sortie des étrangers du Cameroun.

[24] Il s'agit des dispositions relatives aux déchéances.

États unis ne répriment pas l'outrage au drapeau. Ainsi, le drapeau américain a très souvent été brulé symboliquement sur le sol américain. Si à l'époque de la guerre de Sécession, ces actes étaient de mort, à l'époque contemporaine, la Cour Suprême estime que la répression de l'outrage au drapeau est une violation du premier amendement de la Constitution qui protège la liberté d'expression[25].

Mais il faut préciser que si les États ne répriment pas clairement l'outrage au drapeau, il n'en demeure pas moins que celui-ci peut être réprimé de manière détournée. En effet, en invoquant d'autres motifs, l'État sanctionne les atteintes aux emblèmes. Par exemple, au Royaume-Uni, une femme qui avait écrit un slogan pacifiste sur le drapeau américain avant de le piétiner avait été poursuivie et condamnée pour *offense*, deux manifestants qui avaient lancé le drapeau en flamme sur la voiture de la Reine avaient été poursuivis et condamnés pour *atteinte à l'ordre public (breach of the peace).*

Au Cameroun, à la lecture du Code pénal, on peut penser qu'il n'existe qu'une répression détournée des atteintes au drapeau. En effet, si l'usage du drapeau est encadré clairement, l'outrage n'est pas clairement prévu. Certaines dispositions du Code pénal peuvent justement permettre de sanctionner des atteintes qui peuvent en être faites. C'est le cas notamment des dispositions du Code pénal camerounais qui réprime la résistance à l'exécution des lois et règlements notamment l'article 157 du Code pénal camerounais qui réprime la rébellion. Il dispose que *« est puni d'un emprisonnement de trois à quatre ans celui qui,* ***a)*** *par quelques moyens que ce soit, incite à résister à l'application des lois, règlements, ou ordres légitimes de l'autorité publique,* ***b)*** *par des violences ou voies de fait, empêche quiconque d'agir pour l'exécution des lois, des règlements ou ordres légitimes de l'autorité publique ».*

L'article 158 réprime plus fortement cette infraction lorsqu'elle est commise en groupe. L'alinéa 1 dispose qu'*« au cas où l'infraction prévue à l'article 157 est commise par au moins cinq personnes, la peine est de un à trois ans d'emprisonnement et de cinq à quinze ans d'emprisonnement si deux au moins d'entre elles portent des armes ostensibles. Contre tout coauteur qui porte des armes même cachées, la peine est de cinq à quinze ans d'emprisonnement* ».

C'est également l'article 152 qui définit l'outrage comme « *la diffamation ; l'injure ou la menace faite, soit par des gestes, paroles, ou cris proférés dans des lieux ouverts au public, soit par tout procédé destiné à atteindre le public…* »

---

[25] Decision *Texas v Johnson* 1989 ; Decision *US v Eichmann* 1990.

Pour voir une consécration claire de l'outrage au drapeau, il faut remonter à bien loin dans le temps, précisément avant les indépendances. Le texte le plus clair est alors le projet d'emblème n° 3/A adopté le 24 octobre 1957 par l'ALCAM. L'article 2 précise que « *l'outrage ou l'injure envers le drapeau du Cameroun sous quelques formes qu'ils aient été accomplis, qu'ils aient été faits verbalement, par écrit ou par quelque geste que ce soit, seront punis d'un emprisonnement de un à trois mois et d'une amende de 5 000 F CFA à 25 000 F CFA* ».

Comme le Cameroun, certains États répriment les atteintes au drapeau et à l'hymne notamment. En Chine, l'article 299 du Code pénal punit d'une peine d'emprisonnement de 3 ans, d'une mise sous surveillance et/ou d'une privation des droits politiques quiconque se rend coupable d'outrage au drapeau[26]. En Allemagne, le Code pénal punit les atteintes ou les tentatives d'atteinte aux symboles de la République fédérale d'Allemande ou de ses Lander d'une peine de prison de trois ans et/ou d'une amende. Au Japon, l'outrage aux drapeaux étrangers est réprimé alors que l'outrage au drapeau japonais ne l'est pas.

Conclusion

La conscience de l'inviolabilité des emblèmes est un sentiment instinctif, qui précède la conscience de leur valeur juridique. Leur importance s'impose naturellement. Et même dans les États qui par exemple ne pénalisent pas expressément l'atteinte au drapeau ou encore à l'hymne, le sentiment de violer une règle fondamentale est suffisamment fort pour freiner les élans. Dès lors, leur valeur juridique est latente et précède la conscience collective de leur valeur juridique.

[26] Voir Code pénal de la République Populaire de Chine.

Interpretation of the conjunction 'and' in section 1(2)(a) of the matrimonial causes Act 1973 as an indicator of irretrievable breakdown of marriage by courts in Anglophone Cameroon: A critical appraisal

By

Mantinkang Formbasso Lawrence

Senior Lecturer of Law,
Department of English Law, Faculty of Law and Political Science,
University of Ngaoundere, Cameroon
Email: formbassolaw@yahoo.com

Abstract

Family law as a discipline regulates among other issues associated with marriage, the issue of divorce. One cannot talk of a divorce in the absence of a valid marriage. Divorce which is however, an unpleasant termination of a valid marriage of living spouses is often considered by the aggrieved party (the petitioner) as a means of relieve from marital hardship. For the court to hold that a marriage has broken down irretrievably, the petitioner must show proof of one or more of the five indicators of irretrievable breakdown of marriage contained in section 1(2) (a-e) of the Matrimonial Causes Acts (MCA) 1973. As per paragraph (a) of this subsection the petitioner must established that the respondent has committed adultery [and] petitioner finds it intolerable to live with the respondent. This paper set out to examine the interpretation of the conjunction "and" in this paragraph by courts in Southern Cameroon. It is discovered that courts are divided on the interpretation of the conjunction as some decisions hold that adultery and intolerability are independent ingredients which must be independently proved before a degree of divorce is granted while other decisions hold that intolerability is as a consequence of adultery and therefore a successful prove of adultery alone can lead to the grant of a degree of divorce. The paper however, concludes in favour of the decision that intolerability in paragraph (a) of subsection 2 of section 1 of the MCA 1973 is as a consequence of adultery and not an independent ingredient for a petitioner to prove before securing a degree of divorce.

Keywords: Conjunction, Matrimonial Causes Act, marriage, Anglophone Cameroon

Introduction

The Matrimonial Causes Act 1973 (hereinafter referred to as 'the Act'), is an English piece of legislation on issues of divorce and other family related matters. The Act would not have been applicable in Anglophone Cameroon but for section 15[1] of the Southern Cameroons High Court Law (SCHCL) 1955[2], which permits courts in this jurisdiction to apply post 1900 English Laws among which is the Act[3]. Important to note here is the fact that section 11 of the Southern Cameroon High Court Law 1955, which permits courts in the Anglophone Regions of Cameroon to apply English Laws, limits such application only to laws that were in force in England on or before 1st January 1900. Section 11 provides:-

"Subject to the provision of any written law and in particular of this section and of section 10, 15, and 22 of this law:

a) The common law
b) The doctrines of equity
c) The Statutes of general application, which were in forced in England on the first day of January 1900, shall in so far as they relate to any matter with respect to which the legislature of the southern Cameroon is for the time being competent to make laws, be in forced within the jurisdiction of the court".

---

[1] The section provides "the jurisdiction of the High Court in probate, divorce and matrimonial causes and proceedings may, subject to the provisions of this law and in particular of section 27 and to rules of court be exercised by the court in conformity with the law and practice for the time being in force in England."

[2] This law came into force on 31st December 1955 creating the first High Court in the then Southern Cameroons which is today referred to as Anglophone Cameroon. Section 27 of this 1955 Law relates to native law and custom and it warned that no high court within whose jurisdiction a native law or custom is operational should stick to that native law or custom if such adherence will lead to injustice.

[3] It is trite to note that section 15 does not apply to post 1900 English Statutes of general application such statutes therefore are not applicable in Anglophone Cameroon courts e.g. of such Statutes include the Law Reform (Miscellaneous Provision) Act 1970. By virtue of section 1 of this 1970 Act an agreement between two persons to marry one another is not to be considered a binding contract breach of which will give rise to a legal action. Case law in Anglophone Cameroon has long shown that this position of the 1970 Act does not hold in Anglophone Cameroon. See the case of *Ronate Tapong v. Joshua Mobit* Suit N°. BCA/31/74 (Unreported) which follows the decision of the court in *Samuel Esobe Epitime v. Ruth Nange Mbong* (1968) W.C.L.R 41, that a promise to marry is a valid contract breach of which shall give rise to legal action.

From the above provisions, it is clear that courts in Anglophone Cameroon have no powers to apply post 1900 English laws which are not within the contemplation of sections 10, 15 and 22. It would not be wrong to hold that if a provision like that of section 15 of the Southern Cameroons High Court Law 1955 did not exist, the Act would not have been applicable in Anglophone Cameroon and this would have put courts in these Regions in relation to family issues[4] in a very difficult position.

Though Cameroon has a local legislation on family matters[5]. The Act is highly indispensable since our own law[6] is silent on salient issues in family law such as break down of marriage, property adjustment after break down among others. In fact, the 1981 Ordinance, which is a uniform law on family issues throughout Cameroon, made mention of the word *DIVORCE* in its sections 51 and 73 but did not in any where tell us what is either divorce or the grounds upon which divorce can be granted. According to the Act, divorce means dissolution of a subsisting marriage.[7] The Act in its section 1(2) (a-e) spells out the various grounds under which a valid subsisting marriage can be dissolved if the aggrieved party successfully proves his/her case under one or more of these grounds.

This paper is focused on section 1(2)(a) of the Act and attention is on the interpretation of the conjunction **'and'** in paragraph (a) of subsection 2 of section 1 by courts in Anglophone Cameroon. At this juncture it is trite to state in its entirety the provisions of sub section 2(a) of section 1[8]. This subsection provides:-

---

4 Especially with issues or matters touching on breakdown of marriage, property adjustment and custody of children as a result of such breakdown.

5 Ordinance N°. 81/02 of 29th June 1981, which organizes the Civil Status Registration. This Ordinance in a bit to fill the gaps in Law N°. 68/LF/2 of June 11th 1968 on family issues equally fails to address other important family matters as divorce, custody of children after divorce, property rights among others. The Ordinance has been further modified by Law N°. 2011/011 of 6th May 2011 but the issue of divorce under consideration in this article is still not covered by the Ordinance.

6 *Ibid.*

7 Section 2(ii) Matrimonial Causes Act 1973.

8 Other grounds for divorce under section 1(2) include: **b)** that the respondent has behaved in such a way that the petitioner cannot reasonably be expected to live with the respondent; **c)** that the respondent has deserted the petitioner for a continuous period of at least two years immediately preceding the presentation of the petition; **d)** that the parties to the marriage have lived apart for a continuous period of at least two years immediately preceding the presentation of the petition and the respondent consents to a decree being granted; and **e)** that the parties to the marriage have lived apart for a continuous period of at least five years immediately preceding the presentation of the petition.

"The court hearing a petition for divorce shall not hold the marriage to have broken down irretrievably unless the petitioner satisfies the court of one of the following facts, that is to say-

a) *That the respondent has committed adultery and the petitioner finds it intolerable to live with the respondent*"

The word 'and' used in paragraph (a) of section 1(2) of the Act[9] constitutes the core concern of this paper. This conjunction has been variously interpreted by courts in Anglophone Cameroon in certain instances[10] as meaning that a decree of divorce cannot be granted unless and until adultery and intolerability are together proved[11] while in other instances[12] it has been interpreted as meaning that such a decree can be granted based on adultery alone. This paper seeks to critically appraise the interpretation of the conjunction 'and' in section 1(2) (a)[13] of the Act by courts in Anglophone Cameroon as an indicator of the breakdown of marriage. Where necessary references is made to English decisions on divorce relating particularly to the interpretation given to the conjunction '**and**'. The paper will start with a word on divorce (1) and then adultery and finally intolerability (2).

1. Divorce

Divorce[14] represents one of the most vulnerable periods in a couple's life. During this period the concerns are losing their love and equally have a lot of issues to deal with ranging from plain survival to raising children

---

[9] The Matrimonial Causes Act 1973 consists of four parts and three schedules. Part 1 covers divorce, nullity and other matrimonial suits and runs from sections 1 to 20. Part 2 deals with financial relief for parties to marriage and children of family, financial provision and property adjustment orders and covers sections 21 to 40. Parts 3 focuses on protection, custody, etc., of children and runs from sections 41 to 44. Part 4 deals with miscellaneous and supplemental and covers sections 45 to 55.

[10] *Enowchong v. Enowchong* (1968-70) U.Y.L.R.P 65, *Ojong v. Ojong and Jessie Divine* (1968-70) U.Y.L R. 65, *Epo v. Epo* (1972) W.C.L.R. 41, *Veronique Odette v. Njuaka Linus and Agnnes Agbor* (1982) Suit N°. HCSW/7MC/82 (Unreported).

[11] As distinct indicators for divorce.

[12] *Mahop v. Mahop* Suit N°. HCSW/21/mc/78 (Unreported).

[13] It should be noted that adultery which is today considered simply as an indicator for the breakdown of marriage was formerly a ground for the irretrievable breakdown of marriage. See Simon (T. T.): "Evidence of adultery as a cause for divorce under the Civil and Common Law Systems as applicable in Cameroon: A comparative study" in *Annal de la Faculté des Science Juridiques et* Politiques, Tome 18, Université de Dschang, 2016, p. 46.

[14] This is the dissolution of a valid subsisting marriage.

if any of the marriage. This period is marked by high emotions and domestic violence as a lot of anger is often involved[15]. Children where they exist are often caught in the middle. Couples in such situations are faced with the arduous task to make decision to end the relationship in a just and fair manner. A task which is undoubtedly hard to come by in such circumstances[16].

2. Adultery and Intolerability

2.1. Adultery

It is a consensual sexual intercourse between a married person and a person of the opposite sex, not being the other's spouse, during the subsistence of the marriage[17]. From this definition, it is clear that someone can only accuse another of committing adultery if they are legally married and the marriage is still a going concern. The rationale behind this is that a person cannot be guilty of committing adultery if s/he is under courtship or is affianced to the other or was legally married but has been legally divorced. The discussion on the degree or nature of sexual intercourse which will give rise to adultery is not intended in this paper but adultery will be committed irrespective of the degree of penetration of the woman's' vagina by the man's penis[18].

---

[15] See for example the cases of *Gwedoline Abeg Alunjand v. Aloysius Abety Gwandi* Suit No. HCM/016 MC/12 (Unreported) where the respondent Mr. Aloysius Abety Gwandi spend most nights out of the matrimonial home and often threaten the petitioner whenever she questioned the respondents' behavior *and Ajeande Gilian Andeaba v. Mbah Emmanuel Nje* Suit No. HCM/021MC/14 (Unreported) where the petitioner petitioned for divorce under section 1(2) (b) of MCA 1973 as a result of the respondent violent behavior.

[16] Worthy of note is the fact that where children are involved the divorced parties shall nonetheless remain both parents to the children and shall both have the responsibility of rearing the kids. To this end the divorce process must lead to a fair distribution of property as well as custody and support arrangements that are practicable and workable as can be under such situations.

[17] E.N. Ngwafor: *Family Law in Anglophone Cameroon*, (University of Regina Press. Canada, 1993) p. 118.

[18] See Simon (T. T.), "Evidence of Adultery as a cause for Divorce under the Civil and Common Law systems as applicable in Cameroon – a comparative study" *Tome 18, Annal de la Faculté des Sciences Juridiques et Politiques,* Université de Dschang, 2016, p. 47. For a discussion on the nature of sexual intercourse that will amount to adultery.

2.2. Intolerability

This word, being an adjective qualifies a situation or something or a behaviour which is so bad or difficult for someone to bear or accept. Literally speaking and in the context of this paper, the word qualifies a matrimonial behaviour or conduct which is completely unacceptable. Under section 1(2) (a) of the Act the matrimonial behaviour or conduct on which the petitioner can rely to establish that s/he finds leaving with the respondent intolerable is adultery and nothing else. This therefore defeat the import of this provision which is to the effect that the proof of adultery simpliciter is not enough to secure a divorce. The introduction of the requirement of the element of intolerability in the in paragraph (a) of section 1 (2) is a welcome idea since the [would be] respondent can commit adultery and the spouse who would have petitioned the court simply waive the adulterous act of the other spouse. Here, the offended spouse finds the act of the adulterous spouse tolerable. Where the offended spouse feels that s/he cannot continue with the marriage due to the adulterous act of the other, then s/he can petition the court. Here, the petitioner to obtain a divorce on the sole ground that the marriage has broken down irretrievably under section 1(1) of the Act must prove adultery as one of the five indicators for the irretrievable breakdown of marriage under section 1(2) (a-e).

The feeling of the offended spouse which will make him or her find living with the offender intolerable can only be ascertained on a case by case basis. The test to be applied in determining petitioners' feeling is a subjective one. This is to say that there is no standard test for intolerability under section 1(2) (a).

After having considered the above terms the author now examines the various instances where the courts in Anglophone Cameroon have interpreted the conjunction **'and'**. I shall consider the situations where the courts[19] have interpreted the conjunction to mean that a decree of divorce can only be granted if adultery and intolerability are proved (4), (that is where adultery and intolerability must go together) and then where the courts have held that proof of adultery alone will suffice (5) and finally draw a conclusion (6) based on my appraisal.

---

[19] That is courts in Anglophone Regions of Cameroon but where necessary reference shall also be made to English decisions.

3. Instances where divorce was granted only after adultery and intolerability were established

The Matrimonial Causes Act in its section 1(2) (a-e) covers the indicators of irretrievable breakdown of marriage based on matrimonial misconduct. The act of having sex by a married person with a third party who is not his or her legally married spouse is one of such misconducts which has been given the name adultery and is captured by section 1(2) (a) of the Act. The adjective 'Intolerability' found in paragraph (a) of section 1(2) of the Act simply qualifies a matrimonial misconduct (or behaviour) which has been given the name **adultery**. Courts in Anglophone Cameroon have on some occasions as shall be seen much later, held that the two words (adultery and intolerability) are indispensable for a decree of divorce to be granted under this paragraph. To this end therefore, one can safely conclude that the courts have interpreted the conjunction 'and' as meaning that the two words are dependent on each other. Interestingly adultery and intolerability as stated in section 1(2) (a) have been pointed[20] out as two independent requirements needed for one to prove in order to obtain a divorce in court.

The word 'independent' as used herein above equally needs some consideration. If his Lordship[21] and some scholars[22] express the view that adultery and intolerability are independent requirements but continue to hold that a divorce cannot be premised on adultery alone as an indicator of the breakdown of marriage it becomes not only disturbing but also confusing. This assertion beats ones imagination as to what definition (or interpretation) they have ascribed to the word *independent.* Independent in its plain (or literal) meaning refers to something which is unconnected to each other[23]. Taking into account these definitions of independent, adultery alone if successfully proved will provide a relief to a petitioner

[20]Lloyd-Jones J in *Goodrich v. Goodrich* (1971) 2 All E.R 1340.

[21] *Ibid.*

[22] E.N. Ngwafor in his book titled *Family Law in Anglophone Cameroon*, (Canada, University of Regina Press, 1993) on page 126 pointed out that English cases shows that the conjunction 'and' in section 1(2) (a) of MCA 1973 implies that two elements MUST be shown. One of the cases which he referred to as explaining the correct approach of interpreting the conjunction 'and' in section 1(2) (a) MCA 1973 is *Goodrich v. Goodrich* (1971) 2 All E.R 1340 wherein Justice Lloyd-Jones in unequivocal terms pointed out that adultery and intolerability as stated in the section are independent requirements.

[23] See *Oxford Advanced Learner's Dictionary* by A.S Hornby 6th Edition p. 608. On its part Bryan A. Garner, *Black's Law Dictionary*, 9th Ed., West Publishing Co. 2009 at p 838 defines independent in these words "not dependent or contingent on something else, not associated with another."

who sues for divorce under section 1(2)(a). From the foregone it is submitted that intolerability in section 1(2) (a) only arises as a result of the act of adultery and nothing more, therefore not an ingredient to be proved for the purpose of divorce. That said the root cause of divorce under section 1(2) (a) of the Act is adultery and not intolerability.

Courts in Anglophone Cameroon have in a good number of cases blindly followed and are still following the position of Lord Jones in *Goodrich v. Goodrich* which in England is considered as good law. The High Courts and the Courts of Appeal of the North West and South West Regions of Cameroon in following the precedent laid down in Goodrich failed to address their mind to the simple fact that section 1(2) (b) of the Act covers other matrimonial misconducts or behaviours except adultery.

In *Enonchong v. Enonchong*[24], the petitioner (wife) was forced to prove both adultery and intolerability before obtaining a decree of divorce. In this case, the petitioner successfully established a case of adultery against the respondent husband but was unable to secure a decree of divorce under section 1(2) (a) on the grounds that she could not prove intolerability. To establish intolerability, she tendered evidence to the effect that the respondent has been hostile towards her. That the respondent is used to beating her and had in one instance beat and kicked her like a football. That this beating led to the destruction of her rare and expensive lenses. After these second set of facts, the court resolved that she has proven intolerability and a decree of divorce was granted under section 1 (2) (a). A closer look at what the petitioner proved as intolerability shows nothing but bad behaviour on the part of the respondent. Under section 1 (2) (b) which deals with behaviour one will simply restate that behavioural act can either be positive (physical action to another) or negative (passive which is calculated to inflict misery and hardship on another). The act of beating the petitioner in Enonchong's case falls under positive behaviour under para (b) of subsection 2 of section 1 of the Matrimonial Causes Act 1973. My take in this case is that the petitioner did not only prove adultery under section 1 (2) (a) but she also proved that the respondent has behaved in such a way that she cannot reasonably be expected to live with him. This simply shows that she has equally satisfied the purport of section 1(2)(b).

In *Njuaka Veronique Odette v. Njuaka Linus and Agnes Agbor*[25], the petitioner, Njuaka Veronique Odette successfully proved adultery on the

---

24 (1968-70) U.Y.L.R.P 65.

25 (1982) Suit N°. HCSW/&MC/82.

part of Njuaka Linus by tendering evidence to the effect that her husband, Njuaka Linus cohabited with Agnes Agbor and frequently commit adultery with her. The High Court in Buea was not satisfied at this level and went ahead to ask her to prove intolerability. The petitioner in proving intolerability presented the following facts to the court: she informed the court that on their wedding night, the husband Mr. Njuaka slept outside leaving her alone in the matrimonial home. That Mr. Njuaka on one night beat her (the petitioner his legal wife) and burn her clothes because she has refused to share the same bed with him, (the respondent Mr. Njuaka Linus her legal husband), and Agnes Agbor his mistress. After having heard all these, the court concluded that the petitioner (Njuaka Veronique Odette) has proved adultery and intolerability and granted her request for divorce. A closer look on what the petitioner had to tell the court after having proved adultery reveals that she established a distinct set of behaviour other than adultery on the part of the respondent. The act of sleeping outside on their wedding day, the act of beating her for refusing to sleep together with the mistress of the respondent and the act of burning the petitioner's clothes put together constitute bad behaviour[26] which is well stated under paragraph (b) of subsection 2 of section 1 of the Act. Here, it is submitted that the petitioner in this case proved both paragraphs (a) and (b) of subsection 2 of section1 of the Act before obtaining her divorce[27].

It is important to point out here that the test under section 1 (2) (a) to determine whether or not the petitioner finds it intolerable to live with the respondent after the latter's adulterous act is subjective whereas the test under section 1 (2) (b) is objective. It is quite obvious that no reasonable man will remain indifferent to the second set of behaviours established and proved by the petitioners in the cases of *Enonchong v. Enonchong* and *Njuaka Veronique Odette v. Njuaka Linus and Agnes Agbor.* The acts of

---

[26] It should be noted that behavior which can lead to an irretrievable break down of marriage can be positive as in this case (Njuaka) or negative whereby the respondent simple stays indifferent or fails to provide for basic domestic needs of the family such as rents, bills, food and care for the children as was the case in *Ondoa v. Ondoa* suit no HCSW/127 MC/85 (unreported). Wilful refusal to have sexual intercourse with the petitioner will constitute negative matrimonial behaviour and hence a good reason for the marriage to be dissolved absolutely. This was seen in the case of *Phelister Sweri Lobati v. Lawson Late Guillaume.* Suit N°. HCM/001MC/14. The refusal it must be noted should be without any just cause.

[27] The court in Njuak Veronique Odette's case was undoubtedly motivated by the English decisions in Cleary v. Cleary (1974) A E.R 498, Carr v. Carr (1974) A E.R 1193 C.A and *Goodrich v. Goodrich* (1972) 2 A.E.R 1340.

beating, kicking, burning of dresses and forcing a newly married wife to sleep on the same bed with her husbands' mistress constitute behaviours which no wife or husband will reasonably be expected to accommodate.

4. Instances where Divorce has been granted solely on proof of adultery

It is regrettable that the court in *Njuaka Veronique Odette v. Njuaka Linus and Agnes Agbor* (supra) did not pay attention to *Mahop v. Mahop*[28], wherein divorce was granted based on adultery simpliciter. Here the court held that intolerability as stated in section 1 (2) (a) of the Act arises as a consequence of the respondent's adultery and nothing more. In *Elad Hamah Mojoko v. Elad Sam Ekongtang*[29], the court granted a divorce based on adultery alone without making any reference to intolerability. This decision clearly shows that adultery simplicita as a matrimonial misconduct is a good indicator of irretrievable breakdown of marriage. Intolerability as rightly pointed out by Faulks LJ[30] only arises as a consequence of adultery and not an independent fact to be proved by a petitioner who relies on section 1(2) (a) to dissolve his or her marriage.

To hold that intolerability in section 1(2) (a) is as a consequence of adultery, it is important to have a look at section 2(1) of the Act. The subsection provides: "one party to a marriage shall not be entitled to rely for the purpose of section 1(2) (a) above on adultery committed by the other, if after it became known to him that the other had committed adultery, the parties have lived together with each other for a period exceeding or periods together exceeding six months". From these provisions the likely conclusion that can be drawn is that having lived together for a statutory period of six months with the respondent; the petitioner is not in any way hurt by the respondents' adultery. S/he therefore found continuous cohabitation with the respondent tolerable. This subsection is clear. It refers to adultery alone and not any other act on the part of the respondent. This therefore means that other forms of matrimonial misconduct other than adultery are out of the intent of section 2 (1) of the Act.

On the other hand if the petitioner institutes an action against the respondent within six months following the respondents' adulterous act, this will simply point to the fact that s/he (petitioner) in consequence of

---

[28] Suit N0. HCSW/21MC/778.

[29] Suit N0. HCSW/31MC/85.

[30] *Roper v. Roper* (1972) 3 All E.R 668.

the adultery finds it really intolerable to live with respondent. The good law established by the court in Mahop's case and followed, rightly of course, in *Elad Hamah Mojoko v. Elad Sam Ekongtang*, should be practiced throughout Anglophone Cameroon to give effect to the intention of the drafters of the MCA 1973.

Apart from adultery and bad behaviour which can trigger irretrievable breakdown of marriage, desertion is also a matrimonial misconduct which if proven can also lead to the legal dissolution of marriage.

Desertion which is the unjustifiable withdrawal from cohabitation without consent of the other spouse and with no just cause coupled with the intention to remain separated indefinitely is covered by section 1 (2) (c-e) of the Act. For divorce to be granted under section 1(2)(c), the petitioner must satisfy the court that the respondent has deserted the matrimonial home without the petitioner's consent, with no just cause and with the intention to remain separated permanently for two years immediately preceding his/her petition as was seen in *Neh Nkah Yvette v. Jiggi Urbain Tah*[31]. Divorce under section 1(2) (d) will depend on the consent of the respondent[32]. Consent under this paragraph is of essence for a decree of divorce to be granted. If the petitioner is seeking the dissolution of his/her marriage based on desertion under section 1(2) (d) and successfully proved that they have lived apart for two years immediately preceding the presentation of the petition and the respondent withheld his/her consent the decree of divorce will not be granted. For desertion as a ground for divorce under section 1(2) (e) to be justified, the petitioner must prove that they (petitioner and respondent) have lived apart for a continuous period of at least five years immediately preceding the presentation of the petition as was seen in *Iti Devotias v. Techwei George Nyam*[33] . In this case the petitioner adduced unchallenged evidence to show

---

[31] Suit N°. HCM/17MC/09 (Unreported).

[32] The party who has deserted the matrimonial home.

[33] Suit N°. HCM/15MC/13 (Unreported). See also the following cases where divorce was granted based on section 1 (2) (e) *Delphine Lemnui Tamanjong v. Gilbert W. Tangwa* Suit N°. HCM/15MC/10 (Unreported) the parties lived apart for eight years, *Abe Ebede Celestin v. Mendari Etoundi Genevieve Sylvie* Suit N°. HCM/018MC/14 (Unreported) the parties lived apart for nine years, *Helen Kembumbara v. Kem Dominic* Suit N°. HCM/32MC/14 (Unreported) the parties lived apart for five years and *Mbofung Carl Moses funtong v. Chia Gladys Yekelwi* Suit N°. HCM/003MC/14 where the parties got married in 1990 and three years later in 1993 the respondent left for the USA and had not been communicating with petitioner and all attempts by the petitioner to get to the respondent have been in vain. The petitioner testified that the parties have lived apart for twenty years.

that they have lived apart for a continuous period of more than twelve years. It should be noted that a respondent can oppose a decree of divorce where the petitioner is relying on section 1 (2) (e) by invoking the provisions of section 5[34] of the Act.

Conclusion

From above, a healthy understanding of section 1 (2) (a) will hold that the decision in Mahop's case should be considered as the right interpretation of the conjunction 'and'. This decision should therefore serve as a precedent to be followed by courts in the North West and South West Regions whenever a petition for divorce is made based on the paragraph under consideration. From the above appraisal of S.1 (2) (a) of the M.C.A 1973, it is discovered that the muteness of the provision of paragraph (a) of this subsection as to whether the requirement of intolerability should emanate from the fact of adultery alone or from a conduct distinct from the respondent's adultery has given rise to divergent views on the interpretation of the conjunction 'and', and in a very large number of cases the conjunction has been interpreted in favour of the fact that intolerability should emanate from a conduct distinct from adultery. It is clear from the provisions of section 2 (1) of the Act that adultery alone is the fact to be proven under section 1 (2) (a) of the Act. Other forms of conducts that can lead to irretrievable break down of marriage are covered under section 1(2) (b-e). This is to say therefore that intolerability under section 1(2) (a) is as a consequence of adultery and nothing more.

---

[34] This section provide: "A respondent could oppose a decree being granted on the ground that the dissolution of the marriage will result in grave finance or other hardship to him (or her) and that it would in all the circumstances be wrong to dissolve the marriage."

The effect of conflict resolution capacity building on the promotion of peace in Cameroon: Some insights

By

Stanley Tambe Tambe-Ebot

Senior Lecturer of Law,
Department of English Law, Faculty of Laws and Political Science,
University of Buea, Cameroon.
Email: stanleytambe1@gmail.com

Abstract

Peace is so invaluable that it is essential for the success of every human endeavour and necessary for the smooth and proper performance of most activities of life. Peace (the absence of conflict) and conflict in all its forms and ramifications are two worlds apart which can respectively be compared to light and darkness. The former creates a conducive atmosphere for development and the latter sets in to destroy what had been laboured for and creates contention, enmity, misery and death. The very damning challenges created by conflict and the negative impact on people's lives warrant sparing no effort to bring it and its disastrous consequences to a halt quickly. In this context therefore, conflict resolution capacity building is an asset as it helps diffuse conflict. The acquisition of expertise, skills and experience from built capacities is the answer to the settlement of disputes and the maintenance or restoration of peace and normalcy. The aim of this paper is to assess the effect of conflict resolution capacity building on the promotion of peace in Cameroon via the satisfactory resolution of conflicts. The research methodology adopted is the qualitative method. Research materials for this paper were collected from secondary sources. Information and data have been collected from secondary sources such as textbooks, law journals, articles and internet sources. The findings of this research reveal that Cameroon is lagging behind in respect of conflict resolution personnel capacity building and development. She is still in her infancy with regard to the development of conflicts resolution capacity.

Keywords: Approaches, capacity building, conflicts resolution, effects, peace, strategies, styles, tactics, techniques, tips, and tools.

Introduction

The background to the engagement on this research area is the bitter experience of an armed conflict situation and the need to resolve the conflict and restore the situation to normal, by resolving the conflict. The central research problem is that the existence of a conflict is a serious problem in itself, because a conflict can disrupt the life of an individual, a community, a state or even the world, bringing human efforts for decades to naught. Conflict perturbs peace, normalcy, and causes disunity, hatred, fighting, destruction, misery, insecurity and deaths. In the face of these, there is an urgent need to arrest the conflict situation. This requires skill, experience and tact which only trained persons possess. Some research questions that this article seeks to answer are: what are the conflicts resolution approaches, strategy, styles, tactics, techniques, tips and tools used in the resolution of conflicts generally? Also, what are the parameters on which conflict resolution capacity building are based? In order to build the conflicts resolution capacities of students, teachers, legal practitioners, magistrates, heads of establishments, traditional and religious leaders, employers, family heads, investors and businessmen, this paper would discuss the key conflicts resolution approaches, strategies, styles, tactics, techniques, tips, tools and skills, which if carefully studied and put into practice would provide the necessary expertise which affords capacity. The significance of this article is that it would enlighten people about the conflicts resolution approaches, strategies, styles, tactics, techniques, tips, tools and skills.

1. The Approaches of Mary Parker Follett

Similar to the conflict resolution techniques for the Peer Mediation Program (PMP) certification, some other approaches to conflict management were introduced by Mary Parker Follet.[1] Despite the several years that have elapsed since she published her approaches, they are still relevant today. These five approaches to conflict resolution, each has a particular time, place and situation in which it may be applied. But in most cases, the ultimate goal is to: reach a consensus, estimate what is the best and worst outcome for both sides, work out and evaluate what it would cost for protagonists to change their positions, and present them in a pleasant and convincing manner, the need for a change of position if and when necessary and to consider whether a change of viewpoint or position

[1] In her Constructive Conflict Publication in 1926.

would cost a person in terms of loss of face or humiliation and see if that can be avoided, minimized or compensated for otherwise, if it cannot be avoided.

1.1. The Avoidance or Withdrawal Approach

This approach requires that people stay out of conflict and remain neutral on issues of conflict. This approach to conflict resolution is usually employed by persons that have not invested enough or a lot in the conflict to see value in the resolution of the conflict. This approach is often used when the conflict is not critical or is perceived to be beyond the parties' ability to manage. It may also be utilized in minor conflicts where team members have already begun to formulate constructive resolutions.

The aim of this approach is to find the protagonists and to provide incentives to engage them in the process of resolution. A setback of the avoidance approach is that it is usually detrimental to the achievement of a valuable resolution to conflict.

1.2. The Domination Approach

Under this approach, the parties, namely the conflicting parties as well as the third party or intervener are advised to remain singularly focused on one resolution to a conflict. Many individuals involved in a conflict will not readily succumb to the domination engineered by this approach and often fail to recognize the value of alternative approaches to conflict resolution.

This approach should be used only when project success largely depends on the outcome of the resolution efforts. A consequence of this approach is that domination will destroy the good relationship among the parties and will leave accountability for the outcome solely on the conflict resolver. When using this approach, the parties should remain focused on the real objective of the resolution and put the conflict in the limelight. The third party or manager should identify the merits of the dominator's position and seek to demonstrate areas where the dominating party's position complies with conflicting ideas. Let the parties understand and recognize the possibility that they can both "win without anyone losing."

1.3. The Accommodation Approach

The accommodation approach requires that each party should yield entirely to the conflicting point of view. The main objective of this approach is seeking to preserve the personal relationships of the parties, even when it does not benefit project tasks and objectives. This approach should be seldom used and if applied at all, it should be in respect of issues of little relevance to the project success. It may be used as a tool of diplomacy with client sponsors on minor issues. It should never be utilized on any significant issue. In line with the aim of this approach, the parties or manager should emphasize the significance of the project objectives and demonstrate, promote and encourage solutions whereby personal relationships can benefit from the continued success of the project.

1.4. The Consensus Approach

The essence of the consensus approach is to enable the parties reach a mutual agreement and an understanding of each other's position. This approach when judiciously applied, leads to project success, while simultaneously reinforcing personal relationships. It is often the lengthiest resolution to a conflict, but produces the most favourable results. This approach is recommended for serious or major conflicts. For all major conflicts, the parties responsible for a solution should seek to build a consensus among the conflicting parties. It yields the strongest buy-in, for all the parties involved and typically produces the strongest and lasting solution resulting from a unity of the parties' minds, referred to as a consensus ad idem. This is the best approach to conflict resolution. This approach should be employed at all times and may be avoided only when decisions must be made within a very short time frame, since it is time consuming.

In accordance with this approach, consensus should be encouraged even in relatively minor conflicts. The potential synergistic value of this approach is worth the additional time it takes to achieve a true consensus. The goal of any of the groups involved in the resolution of conflict should be to reach decisions that best reflect the thoughts of all group members. This approach is referred to as "reaching consensus". However, many people use this phrase without an understanding of its true meaning. It is easy to be confused about what consensus is and is not. So here are some guidelines. Consensus is not finding a proposal acceptable enough that all the conflicting parties can support and none of them opposes it, nor is it a unanimous vote – consensus may not represent everyone's first priorities. It is not also a majority vote. In a majority vote, only the people in the majority get something. The minority may get something they do not want at all, which is not what consensus is all about. Consensus is not about everybody being totally satisfied. On the contrary, consensus requires time and the active participation of all group members, skills in communication which include skills in listening, conflict resolution, discussion and facilitation and creative thinking and open-mindedness.

1.5. The Compromise Approach

This approach is based on the assumption that no solution can be achieved that will yield complete satisfaction to all the parties involved. The compromise approach attempts to balance personal relationships and project success, when one or both may be compromised in the resolution of the conflict.

This approach is appropriate when the effort involved in resolving differences is not worth the time it will take to do so. This approach should be applied only when each participant has a fundamentally valid position and the differences are insignificant.

Before using this approach, the manager or parties should determine whether a true consensus can be achieved. If possible, then it should be reinforced through the merits of their positions and the conflict should be constructively guided into a free communicating environment where the consensus can be pursued and the compromise approach abandoned.

It should be noted that compromise as a conflict resolution technique discussed under the PMP Certificate Model supra, is similar to "compromise" treated here, as one of Mary Parker Follett's conflict resolution approaches.

2. The Interests-Based Relational Approach (IBRA) Strategy

This conflict resolution strategy respects individual differences, while helping people to avoid becoming too entrenched in a fixed position or posture. In resolving conflict according to this strategy, these guidelines should be observed: make sure that a good relationship is the first priority, as far as possible, ensure that the other party is treated calmly and mutual respect should be promoted. The parties should try to be courteous to one another and remain constructive even under pressure, keep people and problems separate, recognize that the other person is just being difficult. Real and valid differences can be behind conflicting positions. By separating the problem from the person(s), real issues can be debated without damaging working relationships. Also pay attention to the interests that are being presented, listen first, talk second. To solve a problem effectively, you have to understand where the other person is coming from before defending your own position. Furthermore, set out the facts, agree and establish the objective, observable elements that will have an impact on the decision, explore options together, be open to the idea that a third position may exist, and that you can get to this idea jointly. By following these rules, contentious discussions can be kept positive and constructive. This helps to prevent the antagonism and dislike or hatred which so often causes conflicts to spin out of control.

3. The Peer Model Project (PMP) Certification Model Techniques

These techniques are similar to the Approaches of Mary Parker Follett already discussed above. The conflict resolution techniques that are to be discussed below will not only help students and practitioners of conflict resolution in their PMP certification, but also in their daily project life[2].

3.1. Problem-solving

This involves the use of logical thinking to understand the problem. Under this conflict resolution technique, the conflict manager needs to understand the viewpoints of all the conflicting parties. The problem-solving technique has been acknowledged as the best approach for conflict resolution[3]. It also helps in developing trust in the conflict management team, since each party collaborates in trying to explore possible solutions. By utilizing the problem-solving technique, we can achieve a win-win outcome for all the conflicting parties[4].

3.2. Compromise

This technique involves reaching an agreement by each of the conflicting parties giving, losing, forgoing or sacrificing something. Therefore, all the parties do not get all what they want hence, compromise is sometimes also known as a lose-lose solution. However, in cultures, compromise is perceived as a win-win solution. These cultures such as the African and Asian, value the cordial relationship between the parties more than the outcome of the conflict resolution technique. It should be noted that humans do not compromise on issues bordering on values and basic

---

[2] Ruypen Sharma, *Peer Mediation Project (PMP)*, edited and published by Michele McDonough, March 16, 2010.

[3] Project Management Institute, *A Guide to the Project Management Body of Knowledge (PMBOK® Guide)*, Fifth Edition, ISBN: 978-1-935589-67-9., Inc. 14 Campus Boulevard Newtown Square, Pennsylvania 19073-3299, 2013.

[4] *Ibid.*

needs - necessities of life, like food, water, energy, shelter, medication and clothing[5], including power (political, economic), wealth, class or status in society, standard of living, rights and privileges, the need for geographical or physical space, the need to worship (a deity, a god an awesome or venerable personality or thing), and to practice beliefs, religions, cultures, traditions etc.

3.3. Forcing

Forcing is a conflict resolution technique that usually results in a win-lose situation it involves the stronger or dominant party using his authority, power or good offices to decide on the outcome of a conflict regardless of the position or opinion of the participants. In project management, forcing can lead to low morale and dissatisfaction. However, forcing is a very useful technique when there is a need to resolve a conflict urgently, in the shortest possible time. Before deciding to use forcing, the manager or team leader should ensure that the reasoning is discussed with the team at a later team meeting, such as in the Daily Team Meeting (DTM). DTMs can also be used to gauge the morale of the conflict resolution team.

3.4. Smoothing

This conflict resolution technique involves playing down the issue. The key focus of this technique is simply on the positive aspects of removing or at least mitigating or tampering down the negative consequences of the conflict by falsely creating the impression that the conflict is not serious or is non-existent. By using the smoothing technique, the parties would not confront the conflict issues; rather they will treat the problem as if it does not exist. Conflict resolution personnel should avoid using this technique, as it may allow the conflict to escalate or get worse.

3.5. Withdrawal or Avoidance

Withdrawal or avoidance is not actually a conflict resolution technique. Withdrawal or avoidance simply means to withdraw from or avoidance the divergence or problem altogether. Withdrawal or avoidance does not in any way tackle or settle the conflict; rather it allows the conflict room to escalate. Despite its shortcoming, withdrawal or avoidance is useful when there is a healed conflict resolution session and all the parties need

---

[5] *Ibid.*

sometime out to gather their senses and let their hotheads cool off[6]. Conflicts are one of the causes of project management failure.

4. Conflicts Resolution tactics[7]

These include separating facts from emotions, and history from hearsay, testing positions for credibility, suspending judgment for as long as possible, helping the protagonists respect each other and testing and identifying what is acceptable to both sides.[8]

5. Conflicts Resolution techniques and tools

Furthermore, there are certain techniques and tools for achieving a successful consensus. Ultimately, consensus is the best tool for conflict management and resolution, even for moderately important conflicts. Project managers should consider reaching a consensus as opposed to any other approach. So how does one seek to reach a consensus? Below is a set of techniques and tools that will aid project managers to achieve a successful consensus.

5.1. Assuming the role of a facilitator

In nearly every situation, a facilitator is required to bridge the gap between participants in a conflict and provide open lines of communication. Even when the conflict is between the project manager and other team members or client personnel, the project manager can potentially serve as a facilitator; even though in some cases, it may be more beneficial to call a neutral outside source to facilitate more serious conflicts.

5.1.1. Identifying Common Ground

In most cases, participants in a conflict share common objectives or interests, but do not recognize that others share many of the same ideas and convictions as they do. A conflict may sometimes be over a very isolated detail or a sub-section of the bigger picture. To identify a common ground, begin by highlighting where viewpoints are shared and build a foundation of assumptions and objectives that are shared between

---

[6] *Ibid.*

[7] Max A. Eggert & Wendy Falzon, *Resolving Conflict Pocket Book, Management Pocketbooks*, 2005, p. 79. https://www.pocketbook.co.uk/product/resolving-conflict-pocketbook/

[8] *Ibid.*

involved parties. This effort will isolate the points of contention and put them into perspective.

5.1.2. Fully Analyzing Each Position

Having fully analyzed each position, outline the position of each side to the conflict and systematically discuss resolutions on each point. Consensus can only be attached when all the parties involved in the conflict are satisfied that their thoughts have been understood and can then agree on the individual resolution points[9]

5.2. The Techniques of Ernest A. Lewis

Ernest A. Lewis,[10] has provided some conflict resolution techniques which he classified into staying cool in the clutches, cooling off hotheads, preparation, improving your listening skills, inhibitors to listening and mediating conflict. In respect of staying cool in the clutches, Lewis, gives the following conflict resolution tips or tools. Through simulations the conflict manager can imagine his way to success and make the unfamiliar familiar. He must focus on what he can control and play the game rather than concentrate on who wins or loses. He must write down one to three goals that he wants to accomplish that will increase his chance of success. He should share them with someone as he commits to his goals. He should put the paper inside his shoes, pockets or somewhere close. When the game or task is over, he should read his goals and ensure that he held to his commitment.

Regarding "cooling off hotheads" the following tips have been provided: beware of threatening situations and plan how to handle irate individuals. Stand up or sit down slowly and calmly. Listen attentively and do not interrupt. Be polite. Acknowledge how important the issue is and reflect to the parties. For example, "Here's what I heard you say…is that correct? Then offer choices. "Here's what we can do …" Re-explain what you will do with a follow up time and place, as you escort them to the door

---

[9] See Mark Hazleton in his project named "Project Mechanics", *HugeDomains.com*, mark.hazleton@projectmechanics.com conflict resolution techniques – Google News & http://projectmechanics.com/conflict-management/conflict-resolution-techniques.

[10] An Executive Coach and a Consultant in Conflict Resolution, Business Coaching - Executive Coaching - Strategic Action Planning - Team Building - Continuous Improvement - Professional Development.
Copyright © 2009 E.A. Lewis Consulting. Contacts: Tel. 419-345-4254.
Email:ernest@ealewisconsulting.com
www.ealewisconsulting.com/conflict_resolution.htm
Address: Hampton Roads 2438, Bluecastle Ct., Virginia Beach, VA 23454, USA.

or an appropriate person for help. End the conversation politely. Report and document the event.

As it relates to the "Preparation" for the conflict resolution meeting, Lewis prescribes the following tips: Gather the facts, be neutral, and relate the problem to their performance, start by stating the problem as a mutual one to be solved and not a win-lose struggle, get an agreement on this issue before continuing, ask each person to share his version of the problem, stating only the facts and not who is right or wrong. Ask each person to state the other person's viewpoint. Ask each person to suggest a solution or negotiate one. Ask each person to restate their agreement. Schedule a follow-up meeting.

6. Conflicts resolution tips

There are a few more conflict resolution tips that are not mentioned in the PMBOK which are equally important and very handy.

6.1. Tips for Third Party Intervention

These tips may be employed to resolve a conflict, when a third party has to intervene in the settlement of the dispute. If success must be enhanced, the third party intervener must: encourage participants to discuss the problem in a respectful manner, be neutral, never take sides, not pressure or coerce participants to agree. Rather, he/she should encourage them to collaboratively reach an agreement. He/she must understand culture induced behaviors. This is especially true for geographically dispersed teams. For example in information Technology (IT) software Project Management. He also shall ask probing questions to understand the problem.

6.1. Tips for "Improving Listening Skills"

This could be done by developing an active listening posture, eliminating annoying habits, keeping one's emotions in check, asking questions relevant to the conflict and resolution efforts, not jumping into conclusions and staying focused.

6.2. Tips for Dealing with "inhibitors to listening"

Under this sub-head, the following tips should be noted. People do not always say what they mean. They do not always understand their own feelings, so try to help explain to them. It is sometimes difficult to put facts into words. The same words have different meanings for different people. We sometimes hear only what we like to hear and people think about what they are going to say next.

Finally in connection with "mediating conflict" the following tips were prescribed: use the conflict resolution covenant: "we agree to..." attack the problem not each other, focus on the things the parties can do, do not blame the other, collect the facts, own our problems, listen to understand, take the time we need and encourage and respect each other and our ideas[11].

7. The Conflict Resolution Styles of Kenneth Thomas and Ralph Kilmann

In the 1970s, Thomas and Kilmann identified five main styles of dealing with conflict that vary in their degrees of cooperativeness and assertiveness. They argued that people typically have a preferred conflict resolution style. However, they also noted that different styles are most useful in different situations. The conflict resolution styles, identified by Kenneth Thomas and Ralph Kilmann later came to be known as "the Thomas-Kilmann Conflict Mode Instrument" (T-KCMI). The T-KCMI helps a manager to identify which style to turn towards or adopt, when a conflict arises[12].

The conflict resolution styles identified by Thomas and Kilmann are the following:

7.1. Competitive (or Competition)

Persons who prefer a competitive style take a firm stand and know what they want. They usually operate from a position of power, drawn from things like position, rank, expertise or persuasive ability. This style can be used when there is an emergency and a decision needs to be made quickly; when the decision is unpopular; or when defending against someone who is trying to exploit the situation selfishly. This is also described as competition. However, when used in less urgent situations, the competitive style can leave people feeling bruised, dissatisfied and resentful[13].

---

[11] See Lewis'official website, *EA LEWIS Consulting*, http://www.ealewisconsulting.com/Conflict _Resolution.htm

[12] Mind Tools Ltd. (1995-2010) http://www.mindtools.com/pages/article/newLDR_81htm

[13] *Ibid.*

7.2. Collaborative (or Collaboration)

People tending towards a collaborative style try to meet the needs of all persons involved. These persons can be highly assertive, but unlike in competition, they cooperate effectively and acknowledge that everyone is important. This style is useful when there is the need to bring together a variety of viewpoints to get the best solution; when there have been previous conflicts in the group; or when the situation is too important for a mere trade-off[14]. It may also be referred to as collaboration.

7.3. Compromising (or Compromise)

Persons, who choose a compromising style, try to find a solution that will at least partially satisfy everyone. The compromisers are expected to give up or relinquish something. Compromise is useful when the cost of the conflict is higher than the cost of losing ground, when equally strong opponents are at a standstill or stalemate and when there is a deadline looming[15]. It may also be considered as compromise.

7.4. Accommodating (or Accommodation)

This style indicates a willingness to meet the needs of others at the expense of a person's own needs. The accommodator often knows when to give in or submit to others, but can be persuaded to surrender a position even when it is not warranted. This person is not assertive but is highly cooperative.

Accommodation is most appropriate when the issues matter more to the other party, when peace is more valuable than wining or when one wants to be in a position to benefit from the "favour" one gave. However, people do not always return favours. Generally, this approach is unlikely to produce the best outcomes.

7.5. Avoiding (or Avoidance)

People tending towards this style seek to evade the conflict entirely. This style is typified by delegating a controversial decision, accepting default decisions and not wanting to hurt anyone's feelings. It can be appropriate when victory is impossible, when the controversy is trivial or when someone else is in a better position to solve the problem. However, in many situations, this is a weak and ineffective approach to take. This is otherwise known as avoidance.

---

[14] *Ibid.*

[15] *Ibid.*

Once the different styles are understood, the user may select the most appropriate strategy or combination of strategies for the situation encountered. One can also think about his own instinctive approach and learn how to change it, if necessary.

Ideally, an approach that suits the situation, resolves the problem, respects the parties' legitimate interests and mends damaged working relationships should be preferred. It should be noted that the conflict resolution styles of Thomas and Kilmann discussed above namely the competitive, collaborative, compromising, accommodating and avoiding are otherwise referred to as competition, collaboration, compromise, accommodation and avoidance styles respectively should be preferred.

Step One: Set the Scene. If appropriate to the situation, agree on the rules of the interest based relations (IBR) approach or at least consider using the approach yourself. Make sure that people understand that the conflict may be a mutual problem, which may be best resolved through discussion and negotiation rather than through raw aggression. If you are involved in the conflict, emphasize the fact that you are presenting your perception of the problem. Use active listening skills to ensure that you hear and understand others' positions and perceptions. Restate, paraphrase, and summarize the problem; and make sure that when you talk, you use an adult, assertive approach, rather than a submissive or aggressive tone or style.

Step Two: Gather Information. Here, you try to get to the underlying interests, needs and concerns. Ask for the other person's viewpoint and confirm that you respect his or her opinion and need his/her cooperation to solve the problem. Try to understand his/her motivations and goals and see how your actions may be affecting these.

Also try to understand the conflict in objective terms. Is it affecting work performance? Damaging delivery to the client? Disrupting team work performance? Hampering decision-making and so on? Be sure to focus on work issues and leave personalities out of the discussion: Listen with empathy. Identify issues clearly and concisely. Use "1" statements. Clarify feelings.

Step Three: Agree on the Problem. This sounds different underlying needs, interests and goals, and may cause people to perceive problems very differently. You will need to agree on the problems that you are trying to settle, before you will find a mutually acceptable solution. Sometimes different people will see different but interlocking problems. If you cannot reach a common perception of the problem, then at the very least, you need to understand what the other person sees as the problem.

Step Four: Brainstorm Possible Solutions. If everyone is going to feel satisfied with the resolutions, it will help if everyone has made a fair input in generating solutions. Brainstorm possible solutions and be open to all ideas, including the ones you did not consider before.

Step Five: Negotiate a solution. At this stage, the conflict may be resolved. Both sides may better understand the position of the other, and a mutually satisfactory solution may be clear to all. However, the parties may still have undisclosed real differences between their positions. This is the situation where a technique like win-win negotiation, can be applied to find a solution that at least satisfies everyone to some extent. At this stage, there are three guiding principles namely patience, tolerance and respect for each other must be observed.

A logical result of the right utilization of all the expertise acquired from the knowledge and use of the conflict resolution tools considered above is the benefits, advantages or merits derived from a rational, effective and durable settlement of disputes.

In many cases, conflict at the workplaces, at home or in dealing, seem to be a fact of life. We have all seen situations where different people with different goals and needs have come into conflict and we have seen the often intense personal animosity that can result. The fact that conflict exists, however, is not necessarily a bad thing, for as long as it is resolved effectively, it can lead to personal and professional growth and intimacy. In many instances, effective conflict resolution skills can make the difference between positive and negative outcomes. By resolving conflicts successfully, we eradicate many of the problems that retard or frustrate our efforts towards peace and development as well as getting benefits that we might not at first expect.

The Merits of resolving conflicts rationally and effectively include increased understanding. The discussions, dealings or interactions needed to resolve a conflict, expand people's awareness of the situation, giving them an insight into how they can achieve their own goals, without undermining those of others. Also, there is increased group cohesion. When conflict is resolved effectively, team members or protagonists can develop stronger mutual respect and a renewed faith in their ability to work together.

Furthermore, we have an improved self-knowledge. Conflict pushes individuals or groups to examine their goals in minute detail, helping them to understand the things that are most important to them, sharpening their focus and embracing their effectiveness.

On the other hand, if conflict is mishandled i.e. not handled effectively, the consequences can be damaging. In this situation, conflicting goals can quickly turn into personal dislike. Team work breaks down. Talent is wasted as people disengage from their work and amicable relationships and it is easy to end up in a vicious downward spiral of negativity and recrimination. If you are to keep your team or organization working effectively you need to stop this downward spiral as soon as possible.

Conflict wherever, can be incredibly destructive to good teamwork. Managed in the wrong way, real and legitimate differences between people can quickly spiral out of control, resulting in situations where co-operation breaks down and the team's mission is threatened. This is particularly what happens where the wrong approaches to conflict resolution are used.

To improve on these situations, it helps to take a positive approach to conflict resolution, wherein discussion is courteous and non-confrontational, and the focus is on issues rather than on individuals. If this is done, then, as long as people listen to others carefully and explore facts, issues and possible solutions properly, conflict can always be resolved effectively. Whether they are referred to as conflict resolution approaches, mechanisms, methods, skills strategies, styles, tactics, techniques, tips or tools, these are the ways and means by which conflicting parties themselves strive or are guided by conflict managers to reach an agreement on a conflict and so to diffuse it. These should be distinguished from the Alternative Dispute Resolution (ADR) processes such as negotiation, mediation, conciliation and arbitration.

Due to space constraint, the following equally important parameters for conflict resolution capacity building will only be mentioned, as discussing them will exceed the limit fixed by the journal. Conflict resolution capacity building project managers accomplish work through project teams and other stakeholders. Effective project managers acquire a balance of technical, interpersonal, and conceptual skills that help them analyze situations and interact appropriately. This expertise they transfer to their trainees and learners. Important interpersonal skills, include: leadership, team building, motivation, communication, influencing, decision making, political and cultural awareness, negotiation, trust building, conflict management and coaching. While there are additional interpersonal skills that capacity builders acquire, the appropriate use of which assist builders in effectively managing the project.[16]

Conclusion

There are just a few professionals in this domain. Realizing the deficiency in qualified staff in this field, government is presently making efforts towards developing the capacity, by the creation of academic training programs in conflict resolution at graduate and post graduate levels in State Universities such as the Department of International Law and Conflict Resolution of the Faculty of Laws and Political Science of the University of Buea. In the near future tremendous capacity in terms of numbers and quality would have been built. At that time the country would have the capacity to settle many of its disputes and thus reduce the level of disagreements, tensions, anger and hostilities which result in conflict. In so doing peace would be promoted and assured in that whenever a conflict is hatched it would be properly handled and quickly diffused.

The proper training of persons in the conflict resolution approaches, tactics, techniques, tips, strategies and styles discussed above would build capacity and if put under the management of skilled conflict resolution practitioners, will raise the chances of an effective and satisfactory resolution of conflicts. The effective and satisfactory resolution of conflicts in the country would curb the conflict spiral and increase the prospects of peace. The present deficiency in conflict resolution capacity building in Cameroon, evidenced by very few conflict resolution personnel at all levels (graduate, post graduate, skilled and highly skilled) has a negative impact on the resolution of conflicts in the country. This is evidenced by a multiplicity of unresolved conflicts in various facets of life both public and private, being glaring examples.

The inability of some state officials in Cameroon to resolve conflicts is due to the lack of conflict resolution capacities (education, training, skills and experience) which leaves them deficient in the know-how, thereby obliging them to resort to ineffective methods like threatening, bullying,

---

[16] Project Management Institute, *A Guide to the Project Management Body of Knowledge (PMBOK® Guide)*, Fifth Edition, ISBN: 978-1-935589-67-9., Inc. 14 Campus Boulevard Newtown Square, Pennsylvania 19073-3299. Appendix X3 interpersonal Skills, 2013, p. 514.

intimidation, tricks or use of force to 'resolve' or 'settle" conflicts. These crude methods hardly succeed.

Cameroon is lagging behind in conflicts resolution capacity building education and training and practice. There are just a few academic and professional institutions for the building of capacity in this field. Furthermore, the government has not yet made the use of ADR an alternative to litigation or adjudication in the courts, tribunals and other venues of disputes settlement as official means of conflicts resolution. It is hoped that with the passage of time, more conflict resolution capacities would be built and if the experts and professionals so trained work with devotion and employ their skills and experience to work, the effect of conflict resolution capacity building would be positive as it would result in an increase in conflict resolution, a decrease in the prevalence of conflict and the attainment of peace.

The aim of having not only a mere knowledge of the conflict resolution, approaches, tactics, techniques, tips, strategies and styles discussed above but also a mastery of them as well, is to be able to resolve conflicts successfully and effectively. Based on the conflict resolution approaches discussed above, a starting point for dealing with conflict is to identify the overriding conflict resolution style to be employed by yourself, your team or your organization, as the case may be.

With the passage of time, people's conflict management approaches, tactics, techniques, tips, strategies and styles tend to merge, and a "right" way to solve conflict emerges. It is good to recognize when a particular style can be used effectively, however, ensure that people understand that different techniques may suit different situations. Look at the circumstances, think about the method that may be appropriate and use the procedure below to resolve the conflict.

Recommendations

The number of conflict resolution professionals should be increased by creating, equipping and financing institutions dealing with conflicts and conflicts resolution. The government, Non-governmental Organisations (NGOs) and capable individuals should create institutions that offer courses on these subject at the advanced, graduate and post graduate levels of education. Conflicts resolution simulation or moot centres which carry out the practical aspects of the art of conflict resolution, with particular attention laid on the approaches, tactics, techniques, tips, strategies and styles should be encouraged. Only qualified persons should be employed by government to participate in the resolution of disputes. These aspects of conflicts resolution should be made compulsory for and must be made part of the curriculum for training and educating magistrates, lawyers, policemen and administrators likely to handle conflicts in the course of their daily jobs.

UB Law and Political Studies Quarterly (ULPSQ)

EDITOR'S NOTE

ULPSQ is a new quarterly peer-reviewed Journal involving discussions on contemporary issues cutting across the fields of law, international relations, peace and conflict trends, human rights and humanitarian law, comparative politics etc. It is a publication of the Faculty of Laws and Political Science of the University of Buea, Cameroon.

Contributions in the form of articles, commentaries and book reviews in the above-mentioned and related fields are welcome. Contributions should be in 12 Times New Romans font and 1 ½ line spacing. Articles should not exceed 8000 words for articles (footnotes inclusive), 3000 words for commentaries and 1500 words for book reviews. Continuous footnotes should be used and in-text references are not allowed.

All contributions submitted within stated deadlines for any issue, shall be immediately sent out for peer review and, if accepted, forwarded to the contributor for immediate corrections and adjustments, if at all.

Structures éditoriales du groupe L'Harmattan

L'Harmattan Italie
Via degli Artisti, 15
10124 Torino
harmattan.italia@gmail.com

L'Harmattan Hongrie
Kossuth l. u. 14-16.
1053 Budapest
harmattan@harmattan.hu

L'Harmattan Sénégal
10 VDN en face Mermoz
BP 45034 Dakar-Fann
senharmattan@gmail.com

L'Harmattan Cameroun
TSINGA/FECAFOOT
BP 11486 Yaoundé
inkoukam@gmail.com

L'Harmattan Burkina Faso
Achille Somé – tengnule@hotmail.fr

L'Harmattan Guinée
Almamya, rue KA 028 OKB Agency
BP 3470 Conakry
harmattanguinee@yahoo.fr

L'Harmattan RDC
185, avenue Nyangwe
Commune de Lingwala – Kinshasa
matangilamusadila@yahoo.fr

L'Harmattan Congo
67, boulevard Denis-Sassou-N'Guesso
BP 2874 Brazzaville
harmattan.congo@yahoo.fr

L'Harmattan Mali
ACI 2000 - Immeuble Mgr Jean Marie Cisse
Bureau 10
BP 145 Bamako-Mali
mali@harmattan.fr

L'Harmattan Togo
Djidjole – Lomé
Maison Amela
face EPP BATOME
ddamela@aol.com

L'Harmattan Côte d'Ivoire
Résidence Karl – Cité des Arts
Abidjan-Cocody
03 BP 1588 Abidjan
espace_harmattan.ci@hotmail.fr

Nos librairies en France

Librairie internationale
16, rue des Écoles
75005 Paris
librairie.internationale@harmattan.fr
01 40 46 79 11
www.librairieharmattan.com

Librairie des savoirs
21, rue des Écoles
75005 Paris
librairie.sh@harmattan.fr
01 46 34 13 71
www.librairieharmattansh.com

Librairie Le Lucernaire
53, rue Notre-Dame-des-Champs
75006 Paris
librairie@lucernaire.fr
01 42 22 67 13

www.ingramcontent.com/pod-product-compliance
Lightning Source LLC
Chambersburg PA
CBHW071446230926
51846CB00001B/362